Perfect Day

VIETNAM

www.marco-polo.com

Contents

For chapters: See inside front cover

Not to be missed!

Our TOP 10 hits – from the absolute No. 1 to No. 10 – help you plan your tour of the most important sights.

1 HA LONG BAY ► 175

Limestone karst formations, some as high as skyscrapers, smothered in dense vegetation, rise right out of the emerald green sea (left). The best way to explore this bay of sagas and legends is on board a junk.

2 OLD FRENCH QUARTER (SAIGON) ► 50

A stroll around the Old French Quarter in the shade of tamarind trees takes you past magnificent buildings from colonial days.

3 HOI AN ► 126

A waft of China hangs over this old port between pagodas, traditional merchants' houses, dressmakers' and souvenir shops.

4 HUE ► 129

Tracing how the emperors and kings once lived takes you to moss-covered palaces and burial sites with gardens and ponds. The imperial era is brought back to life in plays and dances.

5 SA PA ► 177

Bright green rice terraces, rounded mountain tops and colourfully clad ethnic mountain people – hiking here from one village to the next is like being in one huge landscape painting.

6 DRY HA LONG BAY ► 180

From a canoe you can marvel at the fairy-tale scenery of paddy fields gleaming in every conceivable shade of green framed by karst giants covered in tropical vegetation.

7 PHU QUOC ► 78

Vietnam's largest island is a paradise for beach-lovers with endlessly long stretches of sand and tropical jungle as a backdrop. Diving grounds bursting with brightly-coloured sea creatures wait to be explored.

8 CU CHI TUNNELS ► 53

Here, one remnant of the Vietnam War and the Viet Cong resistance movement can be experienced first hand – even if only a few minutes and just for a couple of metres underground.

9 PHAN THIET & MUI NE ► 102

This peninsula with its 1.6km (1mi)-long beach attracts holiday-makers from all points of the globe to swim, surf or kitesurf.

10 OLD QUARTER AND HO HOAN KIEM (HANOI) ► 150

Wander around the labyrinthine alleyways in the Old Quarter with their traditional craft shops, corner bars and cafés, boutiques and galleries.

THAT
VIETNAM

Experience the country's unique flair and find out what makes it tick – just like the Vietnamese themselves

TEMPLES AS OASES

Whenever your senses are the worse for wear from the sheer noise of Saigon, visiting a pagoda will soon soothe the soul – relax, here at last is a place without the rattling of mopeds and incessant hooting, a place of contemplation with Buddha where you can rest for a moment. The timeless atmosphere of this world apart, enshrouded in incense, is often just a few yards from the chaos of the main roads – in Le Van Duyet temple, for example, which lies a little further off the beaten track (126 Dinh Tien Hoang, Binh Thanh, ✚ 209 D4).

COFFEE BREAKS

Just grab a plastic stool, take a seat on a street corner and order a *ca phe sua nong*. Then watch as the delicious smelling, thick, bitter coffee drips from a dented tin filter into a glass before sweetened condensed milk is added. The whole process takes place in slow motion – and helps enormously to relax in the midst of Vietnam's frenzied everyday hectic, even if only for a few minutes.

COMMUNISM LIVE

People move slowly and reverently past the revolutionary leader's

Gymnastics and tai chi are popular pastimes at Hoan Kiem Lake in Hanoi

FEELING

sarcophagus; soldiers in pristine white uniforms scare hawkers away; nobody is allowed to talk or even whisper. Hands must be taken out of pockets, sunglasses and hats removed. 'Uncle Ho', who can be seen behind the polished glass window, looks almost as if he is wistfully turning his head to see each visitor (Ho Chi Minh Mausoleum, ➤ 155).

THE EARLY BIRD...

Everyone in Vietnam is up and about early in the morning. In the cool of the day between 5:30am and 7am people doing their morning gymnastics can be watched at Hoan Kiem Lake in Hanoi (➤ 150). Balance out your own yin and yang with a bout of shadow boxing, exercise to the rhythm of the cha-cha or play a round of badminton.

That Vietnam Feeling

HOMESTAYS

'Homestays' in Vietnam are always good for a surprise. Sometimes you spend the night in a type of dormitory under the roof, other times – in stilt houses – you sleep in the living room and meet the family personally. You can stay with the Vietnamese in their homes in cities, in the mountains (Sa Pa, ➤ 177), in the Mekong Delta (➤ 73), in national parks (Cuc Phuong, ➤ 184) and on the less touristy islands.

AT THE FORTUNE-TELLER

A glimpse into the future costs just a few *dong*. In the mountains, in particular, you can even watch the shaman telling a person's fortune. The tools of his trade include a dog-eared book in Chinese characters, two split bamboo sticks, a stone that is heated in the embers of a fire and a thread that he winds around the stone – and, there you are, his 'telephone to the spirits' is ready for use.

NIGHT MARKETS

Try a tasty treat of a special kind. Start off with a steaming bowl of soup made with noodles, beef and onions, soya bean shoots and tiny strips of banana leaf – and slurp it quietly! For the next course, just follow the columns of smoke to a barbecue stand where skewered octopus is sizzling away, as an accompaniment dunk mint and basil leaves in a dip made of salt, pepper, chilli and lemon. Save the best 'til last: *diep nuong mo hanh,* scallops decorated with shallots and finely chopped peanuts – soft and slippery and incredibly cheap on top!

TIMELESS VIETNAM

In the Graham Greene Suite in the **Metropole** (➤ 165) in Hanoi it is not difficult to imagine how, in the 1950s, the eponymous author kept to his daily writing schedule like clockwork. Or how, one war later, Joan Baez strummed *We Shall Overcome* in a bunker under the pool. And in the Mekong Delta you can retrace the steps of Marguerite Duras in **Sa Dec** (➤ 85) or of W. Somerset Maugham under the tamarinds along Saigon's tree-lined avenues, just like in the days of old.

Street food seller in Hanoi

The Magazine

Vietnam's Ethnic Groups
KALEIDOSCOPIC

In the mountain village of Ta Van, ten-year old Sung greets a tourist saying: "Where you from?" The short lady replies that she is a member of the Red Dao. The mountain tribe is just one of 54 different minorities in Vietnam, a nation embracing one of the greatest number of ethnic groups on earth!

There are 27 different mountain tribes in northern Vietnam alone, although many now live a 'Vietnamised' lifestyle – as do around 90% of Vietnam's population who consider themselves, ethnically-speaking, 'native' Vietnamese (Viet/Kinh). The Viet are descended from an amalgamation of Austronesian peoples and Mongolian ethnic groups who came from the north and settled in the Red River Delta. The people who make up the 54 tribal and minority groups, most of whom live in the mountains and in the Central Highlands and who frequently still find themselves caught in a transition phase between ancient tradition and the modern world, total around 10 million in number. Each group holds its own festivals and wears it own local costume.

TIPS ON MANNERS AND GOOD CONDUCT

If you are invited to the house of somebody from one of the mountain tribes, always take off your shoes and to not touch, photograph or point your finger at the house altar. If a bunch of bamboo twigs, chicken's feathers or leaves is hanging over the door, do not go in, as these imply a marital dispute, illness or bereavement. Always ask before taking a person's photograph.

AMERASIANS...

...are generally children born to Vietnamese women and GIs or the Western Allies. Many legally emigrated to the USA in the 1990s as part of the 'Orderly Departure Program'.

Lowland Ethnic Groups

The Chinese (Hoa) form the largest ethnic minority in Vietnam and dominate trade and the economy in cities in southern Vietnam in particular. As a result of expropriation from 1978 onwards, many families of Chinese origin fled – as so-called 'boat people' – to the country of their ancestors across the South China Sea or else took the land route.

Up to 900,000 Buddhist Khmer from Cambodia live in the Mekong Delta that has belonged to Vietnam since the 18th century. Houses on stilts, the squat towers of Khmer temples, chequered *krama* scarves and sarong-like garments are very much part of the everyday scene in this region.

Up until the 15th century, Central Vietnam was settled by the Cham people and later conquered by the Vietnamese from their territories in the north. The rule of this once powerful Austronesian people lasted some 1,400 years, to which the 250 or so temple sites, that extend into present-day Cambodia, testify. As followers of Hinduism for a long time, almost all the 100,000 Cham people today are (very moderate) Moslems.

Native Inhabitants of the Highlands and Mountains

The minorities in the southern Central (Western) Highlands (► 107) are virtually no different today from ethnic Vietnamese, their only distinguishing characteristics being their slightly darker complexion and traditions such as tooth-filing. The Jarai (or Gia Rai), who number some 250,000, form the largest indigenous tribe. Like their Malayo-Polynesian ancestors on Borneo, they build longhouses and observe certain matriarchal rules.

Over the centuries, mountain tribes from China, Thailand and Laos migrated to northern Vietnam and tilled the soil. The mountain peoples, some 5 million in number, still hold onto their sometimes archaic traditions: they build houses on stilts and chew betel (areca) nuts – blackened teeth being considered a sign of beauty. Brilliantly-coloured, embroidered traditional costumes and silver jewellery are generally only worn now by women, young and old, on market days and at festivals.

Flower Hmong selling material at Cau Cau market, north of Sa Pa

A Black Hmong in a traditional turban playing a wind instrument; a Red Dao woman sporting a huge red headdress

Many tribal people still live as semi-nomads and gatherers, cultivating vegetables, mountain rice, coffee, tea and tobacco on areas cleared by burning. Farmland, however, is becoming scarce and the soil impoverished. On farms, pigs, chickens and sometimes valuable water buffalo are kept under the house between the stilts. Clean drinking water and medical care are lacking in the most remote mountain villages to this day; signs of malnutrition are not uncommon among children who help their parents in the fields rather than going to school.

The Tay and the T(h)ai peoples, who constitute the largest groups, each comprising more than 1 million, are subdivided into Black, Red and White Thai, depending on the colour of their garments. Most work in paddy fields and live in the valleys – increasingly rarely in houses on stilts. However, they still wear their distinctive black and blue clothing to this day. Despite their own dances, written language and music they are generally regarded as 'Vietnamised'. The Dao people still hold spiritual rituals and sacrifice animals. Dao women wear red turbans decorated with pearls and coins. Their books, through which their language has been passed on, are up to a thousand years old and especially precious. The Hmong people first emigrated to Vietnam from southern China in the 19th century. Their dress is characterised by blue skirts and turban-like, partially chequered head coverings. For a long time they were considered the most hard-working opium farmers in the country; however, since 1992, the government has been trying to stem the production of opium by introducing a number of alternative measures.

Trade and Change in the Mountains

Markets are held almost every day. They are colourful and provide an occasion for local people such as the Black Dao to uphold ancient traditions. Strands of hair from deceased ancestors, for example, are woven into the centre of a superb hairdo wound around the head. Nevertheless, 'modern' civilisation has descended on the people from mountain villages near the Chinese border in full force. The earthly spirits are no longer able (or willing) to hold them back – even if future generations of Daos still ask fortune-tellers to 'read' chicken bones before getting married.

BUDDHA, CONFUCIUS & CO.

Wind chimes tinkle in the breeze in the hallowed halls. An aged monk takes off his burgundy coloured woollen cap to reveal his shaven head as he bends down, almost in slow motion. The thousands of temples and pagodas, churches and other religious sites to be found in Saigon alone, are like oases in Vietnam's boomtown.

The Vietnamese don't take the difference between religions so seriously – they can well be Buddhists and Christians at the same time. And so it comes as no real surprise that the brightly decorated houses of prayer are hopelessly overcrowded with countless people representing various religions, mythological beliefs and animism: a world in red and gold leaf, enshrouded in incense and echoing to the sound of drums, peopled by legendary folk heroes, deities and demons, Buddhas draped in fairy lights and guardian spirits, 'princes of darkness' and martial custodians, dragons, phoenixes and other mythical creatures.

Confucianism and Taoism
Confucius (c. 551–479BC) attends to the needs of the majority of Vietnamese, looking after the strictly hierarchical social structure in the

Buddhist monks dressed in orange – a colour that, in their religion, stands for the highest level of enlightenment on earth – pray for a deceased person's soul

The Magazine

here and now. He dictates the code of behaviour in the family and in society, whether during the Imperial or the Communist eras: the young assume a subordinate role to their elders, women to men, subjects to their rulers. The five most important virtues of an 'honourable' person are benevolence or love, integrity, diligence, honesty and propriety.

Laozi (6th century BC), who would ride around on a water buffalo, is the founder of Taoism; his most important representatives on earth are the Jade Emperor and his helpers who, as the supreme ruler of all, decides on the life and death, victory and defeat of his subjects. The esoteric-mystical doctrine is based on harmony, symbolised by the yin and yang symbol, representing the fundamental male and female principles in nature.

Buddhism

In Vietnam, the depiction of (generally-speaking) five different Buddhas from three generations or rather in three manifestations can be confusing.

Sakyamuni (*Thich Ca* in Vietnamese), the 'Buddha of the Present', stands for the historical figure of Buddha, also known as Siddharta Gautama (probably 563–483BC); he is usually depicted meditating on a lotus throne or as a child pointing his finger heavenwards. Amitabha (A Di Da) is the 'Buddha of the Past', and of 'immeasurable light' who, in Vietnam, is normally shown standing, his hand raised to give a blessing. The third is Maitreya (Di Lac; Chinese: Mile Fo), the fat, mischievously laughing 'Buddha of the Future'. These are accompanied

Joss sticks are to carry a person's request to the gods from wherever they are

stands for frugality, the papaya for pleasure, the prickly green sugar-apple for the fulfilment of a wish, the plum for longevity, the pink-coloured pitahaya or dragon fruit stands for power and strength and the 'dragon eye' – the longan – for relaxation.

■ Many western visitors are surprised to see swastikas in (Buddhist) temples. The swastika is an ancient Indian symbol and is believed by the Vietnamese to bring good luck and a long life. The Nazis misappropriated it and actually depicted it back-to-front.

■ Joss sticks and candles lit in remembrance of the dead burn in huge numbers on the 1st and 15th of every month in Taoist temples in Cholon, Saigon's old Chinatown (▶ 66).

by Bodhisattvas – enlightened beings who, in Mahayana Buddhism, remain on earth to point other believers in the right direction along the 'Noble Eightfold Path' to enlightenment – such as Quan Am, the goddess of mercy, who is also depicted in a variety of different ways (generally standing and dressed in white, seated with '1,000 arms' or as Thi Kinh with a child in her arms). A worshipper's karma is however the decisive factor as to whether, following the reincarnation process, a person is given the ultimate redemption from all suffering and enters Nirvana.

Ancestor Cult, Fortune-Telling, Superstition

An altar dedicated to a family's ancestors can be found in virtually every Vietnamese home. To ensure the spiritual soul does not mutate into a begging poltergeist, the bereaved provide their dead with rice, vegetables and soup on feast days and anniversaries. Little gifts made of cardboard are offered up and burnt in pagodas: complete dolls' houses, cars, deceptively authentic looking paper money, hats and shoes – anything in fact that could possibly be of use in the world beyond. The dead return the favour by giving relatives some wise advice of varying degrees for decisions important during life. These are transmitted by a fortune-teller. Others turn to superstitions that are not related to gods or spirits. *Xin keo* (little wooden dice) are thrown in the air – up to three times. Should they fall in the right position, they can provide the right answer to the question posed to the spirit.

Any amount of money can be given to an ancestor for the world beyond

ASIA'S GALAPAGOS

Vietnam is an eldorado for wildlife biologists thanks to the variety of species that live here. Some even call it 'Southern Asia's Galapagos' where tigers, bears, gibbons, elephants and a potpourri of colourful birds have held their own.

Where bombs and napalm once laid whole swathes of countryside to waste, the local fauna – comprising some 280 different mammals alone – has won back its territory over the past few decades. Zoologists have rediscovered several species considered long extinct such as, in 1987, the **Delacour's langur**, the **grey-shanked douc langur** and a colony of 450 **white-cheeked gibbons**.

Threatened species of animal in Vietnam (from left to right): the Indochinese tiger, elephants and Delacour's langur

Exotic Zoological Species

The list of zoological rarities also includes the antelope-like saola (or Vu Quang bicorn) and the giant muntjac, a species of small deer, two of the six species of large mammal discovered in the 20th century. Both were traced to the 'lost world' in the wilderness of Vu Quang National Park in the northern province of Ha Tinh.

There are 30 national parks in Vietnam in total and more than 130 nature reserves. Particularly important UNESCO biosphere reserves that enjoy special protection include Cat Ba (► 182), Ha Long Bay (► 174), Phong Nha Ke Bang National Park (► 136), the Red River Delta near Hanoi and the Can Gio mangrove forest near Saigon. A primate research project is being run by European wildlife specialists in Cuc Phuong National Park (► 184) in the north and most of the estimated 100 last wild elephants roam the dense forests and grasslands in the south of Vietnam. Even just a few decades ago the Indochinese tiger was still a sought-after trophy for big-game hunters. There are now only a maximum of 50 animals of this species in existence.

In the bird world, scientists have listed some 800 different species, eleven of which are endemic (such as Yersin's laughing thrush). Ornithologists delight in the multitude of cranes, cormorants, pheasants, peacocks, hornbills and snake eagles.

Animal Welfare and Superstition

Superstition is firmly anchored in the Chinese way of life – and unfortunately in Vietnam as a consequence too. Men eat tigers' genitals to 'increase their potency' and turtles' eggs for longevity. Tigers' bones ground to a powder are used in ointments to relieve rheumatism, rhinoceros horns 'help' to prevent nosebleeds, fevers, insomnia and even epilepsy. Not forgetting all the 'sumptuous' delicacies such as the boiled brain of a monkey, snake meat, civet cats, etc. Animal protection is a never-ending, up-hill struggle. Unfortunately the profits are tantalising. Just like the Javan rhinoceros that

was finally eradicated in Vietnam in 2010, the few remaining elephants are under extreme threat as the highest prices in the world for ivory are paid in Vietnam – US$1,500 a kilo. Although it has been illegal to sell ivory since 1994, this rule does not apply to ivory of an older date – and it is virtually impossible to prove its age or origin. A rhino horn can even bring in several US$10,000; tiger bones more than US$6,500.

DOMESTICATED ELEPHANTS

In Vietnam, pachyderms have been domesticated for centuries. Today, there total some 500 in number. They were used as a means of transport by Viet Cong soldiers along the Ho Chi Minh trail. Elephants are bred in the Central Highlands near **Buon Ma Thuot** (► 112). In spring, a festival lasting several days is organised by the locals where traditional costumes and dances can be seen as well as elephant races. The seemingly sedate animals can reach speeds of up to 40km/h (25mph) without any trouble!

The Vietnam War
DAVID & GOLIATH

The war in Vietnam may have ended the country's division but it was to take many more years before the people of North and South Vietnam actually grew together again. For the USA, being defeated by jungle warriors was a traumatic experience in both political and social terms.

When the French left Vietnam to its own devices after its defeat in the Indochina War their legacy was a country scarred by war. Following the resolution made at the Geneva Conference to end the Indochina War in 1954, the country was temporarily divided – the North was to be ruled by the Communists under the leadership of Ho Chi Minh in Hanoi, the pro-Western South by the anti-Communist Catholic, Ngo Dinh Diem, in Saigon. The latter ultimately turned into a dictator and took blatantly relentless action against Buddhists and political dissidents until he was assassinated in 1963 during a coup d'état with the help of the CIA, sanctioned by the US President John F. Kennedy.

  The first combat operations in the Vietnam War, the bloodiest conflict in the Cold War, took place two years later, although the USA never officially declared war on North Vietnam. 'Operation Rolling Thunder' was the name of the campaign started when the first US soldiers landed on the Vietnamese coast near Da Nang in March 1965. Their number was to raise over the next four years from 25,000 to more than 500,000.

'Jungle Warriors', 'Charlie' and the Viet Cong
Communist troops who had infiltrated South Vietnam were to be chased out through the use of heavy weapons, tanks and shelling and North Vietnam,

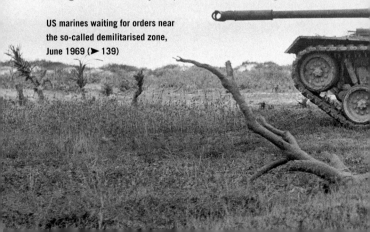

US marines waiting for orders near the so-called demilitarised zone, June 1969 (▶ 139)

supported by the Soviet Union and China, was to be conquered. But the National Liberation Front for South Vietnam, known as the Viet Cong – opposed to the US presence – were incredibly disciplined fighters who employed guerilla tactics on a terrain familiar to them, partly with the help of local peasants. Due to the repression and the number of civilian war victims, many South Vietnamese defected to the Communists. A large percentage of the rural population was ultimately moved to so-called 'strategic hamlets' and to the towns in an attempt to cut the Viet Cong off from their supplies.

Through the use of land mines, booby traps, surprise attacks and acts of sabotage, 'Charlie' – the name given to South Vietnamese guerilla soldiers by US troops – was responsible for large losses on the American side. The Cu Chi tunnels (► 53), now open to tourists, made the Viet Cong virtually invisible. As a result Communist fighters successfully managed to approach the South Vietnam capital, Saigon, without being stopped, by using this extensive network of tunnels. During the day, it seemed as if the US forces had the upper hand. At night, however, the Viet Cong fought back and inflicted a painful defeat on the world power. An overall military victory by the Communist partisans was, however, an impossibility simply due to the sheer number of American, South Vietnamese and Allied soldiers. More than 600,000 allied troops were fighting against Ho Chi Minh's some 200,000 or so men. In order to end the stalemate situation, the US military even considered the use of nuclear weapons.

'Free-Fire Zones': Napalm and Agent Orange

General Westmoreland, the commander of the US forces, ultimately ordered the use of the dioxin-based chemical 'Agent Orange'. Large swathes of countryside were declared free-fire zones for B-52 bombers. The principle target for defoliation campaigns with napalm bombs and explosives was

The Magazine

the Ho Chi Minh trail (➤ 140), a broad network of tracks and paths some 16,000km (10,000mi) long, sections of which were on border territory in parts of the south of Laos and in Cambodia. Without interruption, North Vietnamese fighters transported military equipment along these mountainous trails to the south, before returning to the north to start their mission anew.

Turning Point at Tet

The turning point in the war coincided with Tet, the Vietnamese New Year celebrations, on 31 January 1968. Despite the ceasefire on this major public holiday, those fighting for Ho Chi Minh and the Viet Cong attacked American and South Vietnamese military units across the country. Although the success of this military action was minimal and losses among their own troops were high (with an estimated 30,000–50,000 dead), it had a devastating impact on the US government. TV footage showed a number of Viet Cong soldiers even in the grounds of the US embassy in Saigon and disproved the exaggerated claims the Americans had been making for years that the war was nearly over. The images were a shock to the American people and, in the course of that year, the mood in the USA finally turned. More and more war veterans and GIs who had returned as disabled persons joined the anti-war movement. In America and western Europe millions of people took to the streets to demand an end to the Vietnam War.

That same year the US president Lyndon B. Johnson announced official peace talks that began in May in Paris. The truce, one of the prerequisites for negotiations being started, only lasted for a brief period. Hostile action was soon resumed; this ultimately officially expanded into Laos and Cambodia whose people had already been effected for years by secret airstrikes along the Ho Chi Minh trail. Under President Richard Nixon, the 'Vietnamization' of the conflict was to be enforced from July 1969 onwards, resulting in the

Nick Ut's pictures of the girl with burns running after a napalm attack appeared all over the world and became a symbol of the suffering endured by the Vietnamese people

THE HORROR OF WAR IN FIGURES

- **Victims:** Estimates of the number of dead vary between 1.7 and 3.5 million, including victims in Laos and Cambodia. Some 58,000 US soldiers were killed. 10 million people fled the war, either temporarily or permanently. Hundreds of thousands were maimed.
- **Bombs:** 7.5 million tons were dropped from the air with the same quantity again being fired by ground troops (more than three-times as much as in World War II).
- **Nature and the environment:** 80 million tons of the defoliants Agent Orange, Agent White and Agent Blue were used; 10,000mi² of jungle, forest and farmland were destroyed, laid to waste and contaminated, as were almost half the towns and villages together with their factories, schools, hospitals and infrastructure.
- **Cost of the war for the USA:** approx. US$150 billion.

gradual withdrawal of the US army. On 27 January 1973 representatives of the conflicting sides signed the Paris Peace Accord to establish an end to the war and the pull-out of American troops. However, the government in North Vietnam pushed ahead with its conquest of the south after US troops had been withdrawn and, in early 1975, launched an all-out attack. On 30 April 1975 North Vietnamese troops ultimately entered Saigon and captured the presidential palace without being met by opposition of any scale by the South Vietnamese army which had been greatly weakened by desertion. The Republic of South Vietnam capitulated unconditionally and the country was united. What remained were wounds that were only to heal slowly in time.

As the war drew on, a peace movement emerged in the USA and demonstrations took place like this one in Los Angeles in June 1967

LIKE A PHOENIX FROM THE ASHES

With a talent for improvising and a pragmatic attitude the Vietnamese not only survived a war against Goliath but also the years of hunger that followed – and made spoons and tools from scrap metal gleaned from bombshells, flower vases from 40-mm calibre cartridges and fishponds out of bomb craters.

Their diligence has given the Vietnamese the reputation of being 'Asian Germans'. A lot of hard work really does lie behind turning a country scorched by napalm into a leading rice exporting nation (the second most important). And not only that: after two decades with a growth rate almost in double figures Vietnam has grown to become the largest producer of black pepper and the second largest coffee exporting country. In addition, Vietnam provides the world with cashew nuts, tea, shellfish, rubber, textiles and shoes. Even in the mid 1990s the World Bank listed Vietnam as the eleventh poorest country on earth. Seen in this light, it is really not too much of an exaggeration when it is referred to as an Asian economic miracle. The poverty rate has been halved, at least in towns and cities. The gap between urban and country communities, however, continues to grow. Monthly incomes range from US$30 to US$1,000. The average annual Vietnamese wage has risen from US$200 in 1993 to around US$1,300 today.

Turbo-Capitalism and the Tourist Boom

The Vietnamese are in the midst of a rapid transition from being an agricultural nation to a service-orientated society. Vietnam is striving to

MISGUIDED HELP

However insistently children may beg, don't give them any money. Donate to charitable companies and NGOs dedicated in helping the disabled and street children such as 'Save the Children International' (vietnam.savethechildren. net) or 'ChildrenVietnam' (www.childrenofvietnam.org), among others.

The contribution made by women is immense – especially in traditional farming, such as the cultivation of rice and, more recently, in industrial production too

achieve the status of an industrial nation by 2020. Through adopting a 'turbo-capitalist' approach the Vietnamese are being catapulted from the Middle Ages into the Modern Era and, in doing so, are even overtaking other industrialised countries. It is not surprising that a survey among young Vietnamese carried out several years ago as to the person they most admired was not the father of their nation, Ho Chi Minh, who had been highly revered for decades, but Bill Gates instead!

One catalyser for this swift ascent is Vietnam's virtually unlimited potential as a tourist destination, not least of all thanks to its 3,200km (2,000mi)-long coastline. With some 8 million visitors a year tourism is already one of the most important sources of foreign currency. Experts think Vietnam is capable of becoming one of the most rapidly growing destinations worldwide – with mass tourism expected from the whole of Asia. As a result the Vietnamese are thinking big rather than taking half-measures. The tourist boom has already seen the construction of luxury hotels, especially near beaches between Da Nang and Hoi An.

Down Side

The negative side of such a booming economy can, however, already be seen where little consideration has been given to either people or the environment. The country is battling problems with sewerage and refuse, rampant corruption, migration into cities and a continuously widening gap between rich and poor and between the urban and rural population. The change in society is a reflection of the gradual dissolution of family structures that, for some 1,000 years, were governed by Confucian principles. The younger generation of today is more interested in smartphones and mopeds.

Action!

Since the 1970s the Vietnam War has been the subject of a number of Hollywood films – some are kitschy, others realistic and a few are even spiced with humour.

Among the most famous and haunting US war films is Michael Cimino's epic, *The Deer Hunter* (1978), starring Robert De Niro, and Francis Ford Coppola's double Oscar winning *Apocalypse Now* (1979), with Marlon Brando as the mad ex-colonel in a jungle in Cambodia. Oliver Stone, himself an infantryman who served in Vietnam, directed *Platoon* in 1986. The film, awarded four Oscars, is highly controversial as it is thought to downplay the My Lai Massacre (➤ 138); many survivors however initially described the film as a whole as 'realistic'.

The senselessness of the war is bluntly revealed in the film *Hamburger Hill* (1987). The name comes from a fiercely fought over but otherwise insignificant hill near the Ho Chi Minh trail (➤ 140). Stanley Kubrick's *Full Metal Jacket* about an American training camp in Vietnam also appeared in 1987, as did the war-comedy film *Good Morning Vietnam* with Robin Williams in the leading role as the radio DJ, Adrian Kronauer, always with a quip on his lips. In 1993 Oliver Stone directed his third Vietnam film, this time from a Vietnamese perspective: *Heaven & Earth* with Tommy Lee Jones, based on the autobiographical novels *When Heaven and Earth Changed Places* and *Child of War, Woman of Peace* by the Vietnamese Le Ly Hayslip, who marries a US soldier, moves to the USA with him and, far away from home, yearns for her native Vietnam.

An extended version of Francis Ford Coppola's masterpiece appeared in 2002 under the title *Apocalypse Now Redux* (below); Michael Caine in the leading role in the film *The Quiet American* (right)

On the Trail of Greene and Duras

Anyone interested in exploring the stomping grounds of colonial authors will find things increasingly difficult. While a lot of the colonial buildings in Saigon described by Graham Greene still exist, the cafés he frequented, Brodard (now a Sony shop) and Givral, have long since had to make way for profit-makers and modern-day Vietnam with its skyscrapers stretching ever higher into the 21st-century heavens. Only the venerable Continental Hotel in what was formerly the promenade, the Rue Catinat (now: Dong Khoi), where Greene stayed in room 214, defies the modern era and is still reminiscent of the setting of *The Quiet American*. Greene's best-known novel, made into a film in 2002, is about a war correspondent, Thomas Fowler, who is drawn into the confusion of the Indochina War.

Colonial Vietnam lives on in a completely different film genre: *The Lover*, a story about a young Vietnamese girl and a Chinese man, is set on the Mekong and in Sa Dec (▶85). Marguerite Duras' novel was made into a film by Jean-Jacques Annaud in 1991/92. Shot at the same time, Ha Long Bay, the Red River Delta and Hanoi are the setting of the film *Indochine* starring Catherine Deneuve – a love triangle with a plantation owner, her adopted child and the man they both fall in love with.

LIVING in a SWARM

Saigon without mopeds would be like London without cars. 4 million motorised two-wheelers allegedly buzz around this mega Asian city. One incessant spluttering madness which visitors should risk experiencing too – but preferably with a guide who is used to the rush-hour!

Evenings in Saigon start with a cacophony of horns. Up until this time of day the heat weighs heavily like a wet cloth over everything. But now a slight breeze can be felt through the visor when a myriad of mopeds, all sounding their horns at once, race off at every traffic light and plunge into the nocturnal swarm. As a tourist you don't even need to rent a bike: among all the madness there are thousands of mopeds used as taxis **(xe om)** – these have a lot going for them and not just during the rush hour.

Spluttering Madness

After sunset the Saigonese congregate at one of the countless street food eateries and bars under the stars. But before that comes the obligatory drive around the block. Since the 1990s, and especially on Fridays and Saturdays, the *chay vong vong* breaks loose – a 'see-and-be-seen' spectacle on two wheels with no particular destination in mind, complete with zigzagging, incessant hooting and a brash 'get out of the way, here I come' attitude. Every year it gets more and more congested – and slower. The Saigonese can manage a cosy chat with friends at 30km/h (20mph), a cigarette in the corner of their mouths, a mobile pressed to one ear. Some even turn this into a family outing for four with children and the whole caboodle, showing

Opposite: Socialising in a swarm – mopeds on brightly lit Le Loi in Saigon

off the latest helmets in weird colours and shapes – a ladybird with antennae for the youngsters and a military-style version for adults, or ones decorated with lips, hearts and 'Hello Kitty' images. Many wear creatively designed face masks too as a protection against dust and exhaust fumes.

They swarm and avoid obstacles like a shoal of sardines, tightly packed side by side. If someone riding in front just moves a hand's breadth to the right, then all veer off at exactly the same angle in one smoothly flowing mass, as if they were all tied together by an invisible piece of string. A four-stroke choreographic miracle. Hundreds of Hondas move off together heading straight for the jam at the crossroads ahead – and somehow an opening appears as if by magic. Nobody would ever dream of insisting on who really has priority. And anyone who is really in a hurry and is caught in a traffic jam during the daytime simply drives on the pavement instead.

Join the Swarm and Hoot for Fun

Even when the Vietnamese go shopping, they seldom get off their mopeds. In the most densely packed of all districts around the night market, for example, customers on mopeds weave in and out of the narrow alleyways like little battleships, squeezing between wooden poles supporting baskets full of fruit and vegetables, hens and chirping chicks. Plastic buckets of fish and crabs are stacked on top of one another. 'Lucky birds' twitter from cages, market women try to tout their wares above the cacophony of moped engines. Returning to the main thoroughfare and down the shopping mile Ngyuen Trai, with its bright neon advertisements and clothes stands in the middle of the street, the endless caravan on two wheels moves on through the night.

A family outing with a difference – there's always room on a moped

SAIGON ON A SCOOTER

The company XO offers unusual tours of the city with moped-taxi guides taking tourists as pillion passengers. Leave the air-conditioned serenity of your car or sightseeing bus behind you and dive headfirst into the chaos of this bustling metropolis. Several stops will give you the chance to have a bite to eat – on plastic stools, of course, as it should be at any proper soup stand. Classical sightseeing or shopping tours on a moped are also available. The guides are always women (tel: 09 33 08 37 27; www.xotours.vn, tour incl. insurance VND930,000– VND1.6m).

Insider Tip

The Tet Festival
'Happy New Year'

For one whole week, during Tet Nguyen Dan – the Vietnamese New Year festivities in January or February – nothing is quite the same in Vietnam. The most important holiday of the year is a mixture of Buddhist, Taoist and Confucian customs, of animistic beliefs and ancestral worship.

Celebrations start one week before New Year. On the 23rd day of the 12th lunar month a ceremony is held in every household in which offerings such as fruit, flowers, food and gifts made of paper are placed on the home altar. The God of the Kitchen and the Stove, Tao Quan, rendered benevolent and good-humoured as a result, leaves the house to return to heaven to give his annual report on the situation on earth to the ruler, the Jade Emperor. He returns on New Year's Eve. During the week of festivities in which the gods are absent, the Vietnamese have to protect their homes themselves from any evil spirits.

Houses are covered with fairy lights, red banners are hung in the streets with the words *Chuc Mung Nam Moi* (Happy New Year) and living rooms are decorated in red and gold, as well as with peach and apricot petals and little orange trees. Chinese characters painted on red tissue paper and hung inside the house or on the front door also wish everyone a Happy New Year.

New Year greetings cards – red and gold are the predominant colours for Tet

THE LUNAR CALENDAR

Traditional festivals in Vietnam are timed according to the cycles of the moon. The lunar year has twelve months – with an extra month added in a leap year. The beginning of each new year varies between mid January and mid February (2017: 28 Jan, 2018: 15 Feb, 2019: 4 Feb). Each year is in the sign of one of twelve animals of the zodiac. From 2016 onwards the sequence is as follows: monkey, cockerel, dog, pig, rat, ox, tiger, cat/rabbit, dragon, snake, horse, goat. Based on the Chinese lunar calendar that is some 4,600 years old, astrologists can also work out days which will bring good and bad luck.

Delicious Sticky Rice Cakes

Tet is also the time when Vietnamese buy new clothes and send greetings cards, pay off their debts and give little presents to close family members. One component that cannot go missing is called *banh chung* in the north and *banh day* or *banh tet* in the south. *Banh chung* are square, sticky rice cakes filled with pork and mung beans and wrapped in *la dong* leaves. In the south they are round, symbolising the earth, and banana leaves are used instead.

The temples at this time of year are full of people, especially at midnight at the turn of the lunar year. Many people pay worship their ancestors and welcome the good spirits back to earth with a selection of food as well as joss sticks.

When the Owl Hoots

Superstition plays an all-important role at this time. The first noise heard in the New Year tells the course the year will take. A cock crowing for example means lots of work and a poor harvest; a dog barking will bring trust and confidence. The hoot of an owl is a very bad omen as it will bring an epidemic and misfortune to the whole community. It is also bad luck if a glass is broken at this time or if anyone washes clothes, swears or says anything improper. But who really wants to arouse evil spirits?

Traditional sticky rice cakes are a must at any Tet celebration

Delicious Dishes
from the WOK

Don't worry – Vietnam's cuisine may be exotic but no tourist need fear that they will unwittingly be served roast dog, raw monkey brain or geckos on a skewer. The Vietnamese wouldn't waste such delicacies on a *tay*, a clueless 'long-nose'! And, compared to the explosively hot dishes found in Thai and Indian curries, the food here is very mild with fresh herbs dominating the Vietnamese menu.

The Vietnamese equivalent of 'bon appétit', *moi ong xoi com,* actually means 'enjoy the rice'. Any number of interesting facts and countless legends tell of the importance of rice. Rice comes in all sorts of variations, e.g. as pure white rice *(com)*, as rice soup *(com pho)*, rice noodles (thick *banh* or thin *bun*), transparent rice paper to wrap spring rolls in (*cha gio* or *nem* in the north), rice pancakes *(banh xeo),* as biscuits, cakes and puddings. It was probably more than 1,000 years ago that this type of grain was used for brewing beer and making wine. And steamed sticky rice is processed into a distilled liquor called *ruou de, ruou gao* or *can* (50 percent alcohol by volume).

Hot Dishes in the Cooler North
Due to Vietnam's geographical extremities, regional dishes evolved differently. In the cooler north, stews, deep-fried specialities, pan dishes

MOONCAKES AND DRAGON EYES
When it comes to sweet things, you'll be spoilt for choice. Try *bot loc* or *troi nuoc*, for example, a jelly-like dessert with sesame seeds or a pudding with 'sweet dragon eyes' (*che long nhan* with longan berries). Or perhaps the slightly cheesy dessert (*sau rieng*) made from the (in)famous durian – a powerfully smelling fruit. Not forgetting of course a variety of other delicacies such as yoghurts, caramel pudding and coconut desserts, banana fritters and pineapple flambéed with rice wine. Golden-yellow *banh nuong* and *banh deo*, small round mooncakes made of fried sticky rice, rice flour and sugar water – flavoured with coconut milk, sesame seeds, almonds, cashews or peanuts – appear at the full-moon festival.

and rice pudding are common. The best-known export from the north is the spicy noodle soup *pho* that is also eaten for breakfast. It has since become a national dish and has even made its way onto T-shirts with the world-famous Apple trademark and the proud announcement 'iPho – made in Vietnam'! A hot bouillon is poured over the rice or wheat flour noodles which is served with wafer-thin slices of beef or chicken and a few soya bean shoots. *Pho*'s delicious aroma comes from the spices used: pepper, coriander, ground chili and lime juice as well as herbs that are always available everywhere.

The hot-pot *lau* is not to be missed either. Rather like a Vietnamese-style fondue, ingredients such as fish, seafood, beef and glass noodles are added to a boiling stock in a clay pot and cooked at the table in front of guests. It is served with onions, garlic, tomatoes, cucumber, mushrooms, beans, soyabean and bamboo shoots, aubergines and carrots. *Bun cha* is a well-known grilled meat dish: balls of minced meat or slices of filet are cooked on a charcoal barbecue and served with long, thin rice noodles, raw vegetables and any amount of herbs. The sauce however is all important. And the best in the country are to be found in Hanoi.

Central Region: Eat like an Emperor

200 years ago the Emperor of Hue was not going to miss out on whatever was *en vogue* in Europe –

Classical Vietnamese food: *pho* with thick rice noodles, deep-fried spring rolls and stuffed pancakes, *banh khoai* (from top to bottom)

WAITING AND DRINKING COFFEE

If you fancy a cup of traditional coffee you have to have a little patience. The *ca phe nong* drips very slowly through a (generally rather battered) tin filter into a glass in which condensed milk has already been added *(ca phe sua nong)*. And if you prefer sweet iced coffee, just order a *ca phe sua da*.

such as potatoes, asparagus and cauliflower. Everything was garnished in the most elaborate way for his Highness, well spiced and presented in a mouth-watering way. The pork sausages typical of Hue were not lacking either. Hue's gastronomic hit, however, is *banh khoai*: crisp pancakes filled with crab, pork and soyabean shoots with a peanut and sesame dip. When eating *da nang* on the other hand, you could well believe you are in Japan. The Vietnamese sushi *goi ca* comprises a raw filet of fish marinaded in a delicious sauce and covered with breadcrumbs. In the little fishing port of Hoi An, *cao lau* is the hot favourite – a noodle soup with strips of pork, a whiff of mint, roast onions and crisp rice paper.

The Spicy South

More exoticism and spice can be found in the pots and pans of the south: stir quickly, sauté deftly but not for too long, add a generous number of spices and place on the grill – preferably with coriander, sweet basil, Vietnamese parsley, lemon grass, chili, pepper, star anise, ginger, saffron and tamarind paste. Curries are very much part of every housewife's standard repertoire just as shrimp paste *man tom* and fish sauce *nuoc mam* (▶ 79) are a must in every kitchen. Small, spicy spring rolls, served as a starter, are a speciality of the south – the deep-fried *cha gio nam* and the transparent 'lucky rolls' *goi cuon* and *banh cuon*, that are served fresh and not deep-fried – and require a certain amount of skill in the making. Fine slithers of pork, shrimps, cucumber, slices of star fruit and the usual herbs are rolled in a sheet of wafer-thin rice paper; the tight roll is then dunked in an accompanying dip.

Finding Your Feet

First Two Hours

Most tourists from Europe and America land at one of the two international airports in either Saigon (Ho Chi Minh City) or Hanoi (Noi Ba), or arrive via Bangkok or Singapore. Other airports such as Da Nang, Can Tho, Phu Quoc, Cam Ranh (near Nha Trang) and near Hai Phong (opened in 2015) play a negligible role in international air transport. Many backpackers arrive overland.

Passports & Visas

- **Visa applications** are generally dealt with by tour operators via a travel agent. Price: £32 (€45) (one-time entry, valid for up to 15 days). Individual travellers without a tour operator must apply for a visa from an embassy directly: £46 (€65) (one-time entry, valid for up to 15 days), £53 (€75) (for up to 30 days), £55–£80 (€88–€110) (for up to 90 days).
- **Passports** must be valid for at least 6 months at the time of application and at least one month longer than the period for which the visa is valid.
- **Application forms** must be submitted at least 14 days before your journey and include a stamped addresses envelope with a passport photo and crossed cheque; applications made in person are faster (further information under: www.vietnamembassy.org or http://visa.mofa.gov.vn).
- **Children** must have their own passports and visas.
- Extending or changing the validity of a visa in Vietnam is possible via a travel agent; excessive fees however are often charged.

By Air
Saigon Tan Son Nhat International Airport (Ho Chi Minh City)

- **Tan Binh district**, 6km (3.75mi) north of Saigon; www.hochiminhcity airport.com
- **Facilities:** Exchange bureaux (poor exchange rates), hire car companies, cafés, restaurants and shops as well as free WiFi everywhere.
- **Tourist information:** Saigon Airport Service Center; tel: 08 38 48 67 11 and 08 38 44 66 65
- **Taxis** from the airport to the city centre (1st district), approx. 30 mins, cost VND150,000–VND200,000 depending on the time of day. Ask to the left of window at the taxi companies Vinasun or May Linh (►37).
- Vietnam Airline **shuttle buses** (c. VND25,000) run every 30 mins. from 7am–6pm. Alternatives: **bus** no. 152 to Ben Thanh Market and to Pham Ngu Lao, no. 147 to Cho Lon/Chinatown; both leave to the right of the exit (VND7,000, 6am–6pm, every 15 mins.).

Hanoi Noi Ba Airport

- **45km (28mi) north** of Hanoi; tel: 04 38 84 35 63 and 04 38 86 50 02; www.hanoiairportonline.com
- **Inland flights** depart from Domestic Terminal 1 (shuttle bus).
- **Facilities:** Exchange bureaux (poor exchange rates) are located inside the terminal building, hotel booking service, travel agents, hire car companies, restaurants, booths and shops, free WiFi covering most areas.
- No exchange bureaux are open at the airport in Hanoi after 10pm; there are however cashpoints/ATMs – alternatively bring US dollars to pay for taxi to hotel.

Insider Tip

- **Taxis** (►37) from Hanoi airport cost VND350,000–VND500,000 (US$15– US$22) for the 60 min. journey.

- Vietnam Airline **shuttle buses** (around VND25,000) run every 30 mins. from 7am–6pm. Alternatives: **shared minibus taxis** (only leave when full; VND38,000–VND76,000) or **bus** no. 7 (West Lake, 5–22, every 15 mins., around VND7,000).

By Land

- The situation has recently improved considerably; most **border crossings to and from China, Laos and Cambodia** are now open to European tourists (except in restricted military areas).
- The Mekong border crossings Moc Bai–Ba Vet and Prek Chak–Xa Xia bei Ha Tien are the most frequently used (visa obligatory). You can best reach your destination by taking a trip organised by a tour operator or a shared taxi or moped taxi.

Getting Around

Most tourists spend two to three weeks exploring this huge country on organised tours using buses and inland flights. You can however travel around Vietnam relatively easily under your own steam as a backpacker or independently, but you will need to plan more time for this. Tickets for all means of transport can be bought for a small fee in hotels – preferably several days in advance. Railway, bus and boat tickets bought from non-official booking offices may well be fake. The Foreign Office helps to keep those travelling well informed: www.gov.uk/foreign-travel-advice/vietnam.

From Town to Town

Long-Distance Buses

- Journeys on long-distance, publicly-operated buses are generally **time-consuming** and **not entirely without danger** compared to trains. You should avoid travelling at night due to the increased likelihood of accidents. All buses run to timetables and leave from central bus stations to all points of the compass. *Insider Tip*
- **Reliable bus companies** are May Linh Express in Saigon (tel: 08 39 29 29 29; www.mailinh.vn, in Vietnamese) as well as Hoang Long in Hanoi (tel: 04 39 28 28 28; www.hoanglongasia.com).
- There are some more comfortable buses with **reclining seats** or **loungers** and Internet that also travel to neighbouring countries. The seats however are designed for the average Vietnamese and the air-conditioning in the buses is freezing cold.
- 'Open tour' tourist buses operate at reasonable prices on fixed routes and offer the possibility of breaking your journey at certain towns and seaside resorts. Prices vary from season to season.

Trains

- The **Reunification Express** runs five times a day from the north of Vietnam to the south and vice-versa. The journey takes 32–38 hours.
- A bed in an **air-conditioned sleeper** in both 1st and 2nd class (with two/four bed compartments – **soft sleeper**) must be booked in advance.
- **Prices:** Saigon–Hanoi, e.g., from VND1.2m.; during the trip between the two cities 3 meals are included in the price.

Finding Your Feet

Insider Tip

- **Advance booking** means at least 3 days before departure.
- **Sanitary facilities** and **service** are not comparable to European standards.
- The **Victoria Hotels' express train** runs from Hanoi to Sa Pa (terminus: Lao Cai; only for hotel guests; www.victoriahotels-asia.com).

Inland Flights

- **Vietnam Airlines** has a fleet of modern Airbus planes and is generally punctual, except during the monsoon. It operates between a number of different cities and flies to both Phu Quoc and Con Dao islands (www.vietnamairlines.com).
- **Prices:** Saigon–Hanoi, for example, around £100 (€140).
- The **budget airlines** for inland flights, Jet Star Pacific Airways (www.jetstar.com) and Viet Jet Air (www.vietjetair.com), have the reputation of employing less well trained staff.
- Early booking is essential especially before **public holidays** and the Tet festival in particular.

Ferries & Boats

- Hydrofoils and ferries operate between the mainland and the islands and between Saigon and the **Vung Tau** peninsula (➤ 114); Vung Tau ferries are in a poor state of repair and the number of accidents has increased in recent years.
- Sampans converted into passenger boats ply the **Mekong Delta** in the south (e.g. Cai Be Princess; www.caibeprincessmekong.com; Mekong Eyes; www.mekongeyes.com). The hotel boat operated by the Victorial Hotel from Chau Doc crosses the border to **Cambodia** (➤ 90; www.victoriahotels.asia). Blue Cruiser speedboats are a cheaper alternative (www.bluecruiser.com).
- In **Hue** (➤ 129), in the centre of the country, dragon boats take visitors along the Perfume River to see the imperial tombs.
- Some 400 tourist barges and motorised junks weave their way around **Ha Long Bay** (➤ 174) every day.
- Be warned: most boats do not meet European safety standards and often lack lifejackets, for example. Avoid old ferries and night boats at all costs.

Hire Cars

- More than 12,000 people die on Vietnam's roads every year. For tourists travelling under their own steam it is advisable to **hire a car with a driver**.
- **Prices:** VND1.2m/day, for example, incl. driver and fuel.
- If you choose to **drive yourself**, an international (or Vietnamese) driving licence is essential (➤ 37).
- The leading international **hire car company** in Vietnam is Avis (www.avis.com.vn; www.avis.com); one alternative is VN Rent-a-Car (www.vnrentacar.com, e.g. US$265 for four days).

Mopeds and Moped Taxis (xe om)

- Riding pillion on trips operated by one of the nationwide moped agencies is becoming increasingly popular.
- Vietnam is however one of the countries with the highest mortality and accident rate on roads; often no insurance coverage is given.
- The **fare** must be agreed upon beforehand: in Saigon and Hanoi this is usually around VND10,000/km. It is best to get an appropriate guide price from the your hotel reception.

■ **Helmets** must be worn. If you are planning a number of tours, take a good helmet with you.
■ To **ride a moped yourself** you will need an international driving licence (➤ below).

The Most Important Traffic Rules
■ Drive on the right.
■ Speed limits: in built-up areas max. 40km/h (25mph), on ordinary roads: max. 60km/h (40mph).
■ Foreigners are allowed to drive a motorised vehicle themselves but must have an **international driving licence** for the respective category of vehicle. A national driving licence must be translated into Vietnamese (a number of agencies can 'obtain' the necessary documentation for tourists; however, according to the Foreign Office, there is no insurance coverage and the 'rich' foreigner is always the guilty party). A fine or even a prison sentence (in the case of an accident) is the consequence.
■ When vehicles overtaking or coming in the opposite direction (esp. lorries and buses) sound their horns move over to the side of the road immediately!
■ Never drive at night under any circumstances!
■ Only park on monitored car-parks (for a small fee).
■ **Drink-drive limit:** Bicycle/moped: 0.5 ‰, car 0.0 ‰

Urban Transport
Taxis
■ There are any number of taxis with taximeters in the cities but, unfortunately, there are also lots of **fraudsters** and even **'fake taxis'** on the roads (instead of 'Vinasun' or 'Vinataxi' they call themselves 'Vinsun' or Vinasun', for instance).
■ The **basic fare** should be VND12,000–VND14,000 with each additional kilometre costing around VND15,000.
■ Make sure that the **taximeter** is turned on, at all costs. If the taximeter clocks up the miles obviously too fast and irregularly, make the driver stop immediately, give him an appropriate sum and get out. For your information: '622…' on the display of a taximeter means VND62,200 and not VND622,000.
■ Order a reputable taxi at your hotel reception: **Vinasun** (Saigon; tel: 08 38 27 27 27), **May Linh** (Saigon; tel: 08 38 38 38 38), **Hanoi Taxi** (tel: 04 38 53 53 53).

Cyclos (xich lo)
■ Tricycle rickshaws, with the rider sitting slightly above and behind the passengers, may be fine for tours of a town but they have an increasingly bad reputation (for fraud, thefts and muggings). And, in addition, they have been banned from lots of places as they hold up the traffic.
■ You can however join a safe 'caravan' of rickshaws operated for tourists or book a reliable cyclo driver at a good hotel or, of course, have the name of the place you want to go to written down in Vietnamese together with the approximate price.
■ Negotiate the **price of a journey** before setting off, preferably based on minutes or hours: VND50,000–VND100,000/hour., short distances VND20,000 (depending on negotiating skill, season and region). Most drivers in Saigon's 1st district and in the Old City in Hanoi demand a

minimum of VND200,000 per hour from tourists as a matter of course or even for one journey.

- Write down the price negotiated and ensure that it is clear whether it is in dongs or dollars. Count out the notes and, if possible, have the exact amount with you; if not, check your change.
- When **out and about** you should approach the driver yourself, not vice-versa. Fraudsters and charlatans often wait directly outside hotels and tourist sites – it is often better to walk a little first.
- **Safety:** Don't take a cyclo at night. Carry handbags and cameras diagonally over your shoulder and hang on to them. Don't take smartphones, expensive sunglasses or jewellery with you.

City Buses

- Modern air-conditioned city buses run every day in **Hanoi** and **Saigon**. You can, for example, take a bus from Ben Thanh market right to the other side of the city; no. 127 goes past a number of tourist sites (daily 5:30am–8pm, every 10 mins.: VND4,000).
- A folding map of the Saigon bus network is available from the tourist information office and at Ben Thanh bus station.
- You should have the exact fare of a few thousand dongs with you and pay the driver directly.
- Beware of pickpockets!

Accommodation

Vietnam has a wide range of places to stay on offer, from 'homestays' in private houses to historical buildings from colonial days, in mini hotels so typical of the country to beach houses, on junks during a two-day trip around Ha Long Bay (▶ 174) or a converted sampan in the Mekong Delta (▶ 73). You'll certainly find something best suited to your needs!

Hotels

- Prices in tourist centres and beach resorts can double at certain times such as during the **high season** in winter, at weekends and during the Tet festival (end of Jan/early Feb).
- Hotels in the mid to superior range are best booked via a tour operator as this will help save having to pay **supplementary tax and service charges** of around 15% that are frequently levied.

Mini Hotels & Guesthouses (£)

- Most backpackers and people travelling on their own stay in cheaper mini hotels; these usually provide bedlinen, towels and soap and have hot water in the showers, air-conditioning, satellite TV and Internet access (some even provide laptops).
- You should take your time and inspect and compare several hotels. They are often grouped together along certain roads or in one district. There are often genuine bargains to be had, depending on the season and demand, such as in Saigon's Pham Ngu Lao and Hanoi's Old City.
- Rooms without a window (or to a light well) are generally quieter than rooms with a balcony facing the street. Even if rooms are not always swept every day, they are mostly very clean.

Resort Hotels (££/£££)

- These mid-of-the-range hotels are usually on a beach and have their own restaurant and a pool.
- Staff frequently do not speak much English.

Luxury Hotels (£££)

- Anyone who places value on international standards should choose a luxury hotel. The staff in such hotels speak sufficient English or French.
- **Top category (4-star)** hotels have now opened in tourist regions in rural areas as well, such as in Dry Ha Long Bay and on remote islands such as Con Dao.
- A unique French flair can be enjoyed in restored **hotels from the colonial era** where Graham Greene and William Somerset Maugham stayed and found inspiration for their novels (e.g. Sofitel Legend Metropole in Hanoi, ► 165, Continental in Saigon, ►51).
- You will have to invest at least VND2.4m a night for a double room, suite, bungalow or pool-side villa. At the upper end of the market the sky's the limit since major international hotel chains such as Six Senses (Nha Trang, ► 110, Con Dao, ►92) have become established in Vietnam.
- Such hotels generally have several restaurants and bars, spa and gym facilities, a landscaped pool area, a business centre and a range of water sports, among others things.
- By the way: day passes for the whole family are available at a lot of 👥 **hotel pool compleexes** (around VND120,000).

Price
of a double room per night:
£ under VND1m.   ££ VND1–VND2.4m.   £££ over VND2.4m.

Homestays

- 'Homestays' in the house of a guest family are becoming increasingly popular. These range from 'community homestays' where you are together with the family to more luxurious variations with a pool and staff. In mountain villages around Sa Pa (► 177), in the Mekong Delta and on a few of the less touristy, smaller islands, tourists can unroll their sleeping bags in the space under the roof or in rooms of their own. In Saigon and Hanoi more and more young people are renting out their second homes or rooms to tourists.
- 'Homestays' are generally organised by **local tour operators** as part of a trekking tour or a boat trip on the Mekong. Otherwise book directly via www.homestay.com.

Food and Drink

From soup kitchens without any menus and typical tourist eateries with ridiculously cheap fast food from all over the world to gourmet restaurants – there is something for every taste and budget in the major cities and beach resorts.

Finding Your Feet

Eating Habits & Dishes

- The Vietnamese eat big meals three time a day, generally at the same times and preferably in large social groups with the family or business partners. Meat, fish and seafood, egg dishes, vegetables, salads and soups – everything is served at the same time. The meal is opened with the words **xin moi** (please tuck in!) and everyone helps themselves to little morsels with their chopsticks, placing them in their bowl of rice.

- For **breakfast** most tourists plump for baguette with cheese, chicken or pork; the Vietnamese on the other hand often eat *the* classic dish their country has to offer, even first thing in the morning: **noodle soup** in all its variations, such as famous *pho* (pronounced *far*) with chicken or beef, spices, herbs and lime juice. It can be found in the many street kitchens and is served with chopsticks and a spoon. For tourists it costs about VND30,000–VND60,000.

- Incredibly cheap fried rice dishes can also be found everywhere as can omelettes and **banh bao**, dumplings with vegetables, minced meat or shrimps, and *banh mi* fresh baguette sandwiches.

- **Spring rolls** are an all-time favourite – deep-fried or cooked in rice paper (*nem* or *cha gio* in the south).

- Quite a number of eateries have chosen to specialise: for example in Vietnamese grilled food or, in Hanoi, in popular *bun cha* noodle dishes, grilled filets of meat, belly of pork or meatballs served with long thin rice noodles in a spicy stock with fish sauce (from around VND60,000).

- In most restaurants various different types of meat (beef: *thit bo,* pork: *thit heo,* chicken: *thit ga*) and/or freshly caught fish (*ca*) or seafood (prawns: *tom,* crab: *cua*) are eaten with **rice** (*com*) – the Vietnamese 'bread' – as an accompaniment.

- **Vegetarians** have a wide choice of vegetables (**rau**), tofu and rice dishes.

- With a **hot-pot** (*lau*) all the ingredients are cooked over a flame at the table in a metal pot.

- Lychees (*vai*), mangos (*xoai*), papayas (*dudu*), dragon fruit (*thanh long*), banana fritters (*chuoi*) or pineapple flambéed with rice wine are eaten **after a meal** as are coconut desserts, little sweet cakes and crème caramel. Or you pluck up the courage to try the slightly cheesy dessert made from the (in)famous stinking durian (*sau rieng*).

Eating Out
A Practical Guide

- Many dishes often come with a plate of **raw vegetables** – anyone with a weak stomach shouldn't touch them.

- The fish sauce **nuoc mam** is often available at the table for customers to spice their own dishes. Take a small bowl and make a dip adding fresh chili, garlic, sugar, pepper and lime juice.

- When you have finished, never leave your **chopsticks sticking in the rice** as this is a bad omen!

- Moist napkins sealed in plastic bags that are provided on the table, as well as peanuts and crisps are not included in the price and have to be paid for. Tea, however, is often free of charge.

- In better restaurants you may want to give a **tip** but this is in fact already included in the price (**service charge**). No tips are expected in street kitchens.

Food and Drink

Health & Hygiene

■ For reasons of hygiene it is advisable only to eat **thoroughly cooked dishes** from street stands when you are out and about. Avoid ice cream, unpeeled fruit, raw salads and raw vegetables.

■ If you do buy food from street hawkers you should ensure that the food has been protected from flies; fresh little *banh bao* dumplings are a better way of staving off hunger.

■ Anything you can peel or open yourself (fruit, peanuts, hard-boiled eggs) are safe to eat. Only drink coconut milk with a straw.

■ Always wipe **chopsticks and spoons** as well as the rim of canned drinks properly before use (the Vietnamese even do this themselves).

■ Only eat **ice cream** in luxury hotels; best of all, avoid it altogether in northern Vietnam (Hanoi, Ninh Binh, etc.) due to the risk of cholera.

■ Always drink **lots of water** but only out of bottles with an intact seal; this also applies to when you clean your teeth.

(Tourist) Restaurants

■ Sushi, pizzas, pasta (from VND60,000), tapas and a number of other European dishes can be found in touristy places. Many restaurants near beaches and city hotels provide holiday-makers with familiar, international and sometimes top-quality food – at correspondingly high (often European) prices.

■ **Gourmet restaurants** can now be found in Saigon and Hanoi.

■ Tourist restaurants are open daily from around 10am–10pm.

Street and Soup Kitchens

■ Take a seat on one of the tiny, brightly-coloured stools at one of the countless simple street restaurants. Either there is just one dish such as the noodle soup *pho* or else you can choose by pointing your finger at one (or better still, at several) vegetable and other dishes on display behind glass. For £3–£5 (€4–€7) you can eat your fill.

■ **Don't expect too much** as regards hygiene or service and always wipe the cutlery with a serviette. Slurping, spitting and burping are all part of the experience!

Drink

■ **Water** (*nuoc suoi, soda,* 1 litre bottle, VND5,000–VND10,000) should be drunk from sealed bottles only. Other non-alcoholic beverages available include fruit juice, fresh sugar cane juice (*nuoc mia*) and coconut milk (*nuoc dua*) as well as slightly more expensive soft drinks.

■ **Beer** is popular throughout Vietnam (*bia*, e.g. 333, from VND30,000). Imported beer such as Tiger or Heineken is more expensive. A very light (3–4%) beer on the other hand costs just VND5,000 in simple *bia hoi* corner bars where you perch on a child-sized stool.

■ **Cocktails** are comparatively cheap (from VND40,000).

■ Vietnamese **coffee** (*ca phe nong*) is an export hit that is popular in Europe too (➤ 32).

■ **Tea** (*che, tra*) is available everywhere and is often free.

Shopping

The range of crafts and souvenirs in Vietnam is irresistible and sheer endless: from classics such as chopsticks or conical hats to pretty silk blouses and silk Chinese lanterns, baskets, lacquerware and wood carvings that are particularly popular at New Year, ceramics and woven items.

- Food (fruit, vegetables, meat and living animals) can be found at **(night) markets** (*cho*), alongside everyday items such as flowers, costume jewellery, textiles, crafts and brightly-coloured, cheap bits and bobs.
- The range of things available in **department stores** varies from ridiculously cheap, fake items, T-shirts and jackets, rucksacks and luggage to leather goods – everything that the average tourist loves or might need.
- Glittery and **palatial high-rise shopping complexes** offer everything from Armani to Valentino. The prices are generally what you would expect to pay in Europe but – due to import tax – they are sometimes even higher. Good-value 'food courts' can often be found here too.
- **Service areas** with huge shopping hangars, only open to tourists, line the main roads near Hanoi and Saigon. Tourists are ferreted through them *en masse* while stopping to use the facilities. Craft centres stock everything imaginable – but you'll have to haggle over the price.

Vietnamese Specialities

- The slightly see-through **conical hats** are made of stitched palm leaves and decorated with silk thread. Sometimes these sun shades that have been worn for thousands of years have pictures of landscapes or sayings on them.
- **Propaganda posters** of 'Uncle Ho', Ayurveda **flip-flops** with a healthy bamboo cushion and cinnamon bands from Hoi An (► 126) or tailor-made *ao dai* **tunics and trousers** are all the rage!
- **Sand pictures** (*tranh cat*) are beautiful little works of art that can be found in Nha Trang (► 110), Phan Thiet City (Phi Long Sandpainting, Alley 4444, Thu Khoa Huan, Than Hai-Bez) and Saigon (Kim Sat; www.tranhcatkimsa.com.vn; Sand painting My art; www.tranhcatmyart.com; Y Lan; www.tranhcatylan.com.vn), in particular.
- **Lacquerware** and **mother-of-pearl** are popular throughout the country whether used as decorative applications on chopsticks or on pieces of furniture.
- Silkworms have been cultivated in Vietnam for some 1,000 years and silk is cheap. Throughout the country – and especially in Hoi An – tailors and dressmakers make dresses and suits within a couple of days. Tip: don't order anything just a couple of days before you leave as small changes often have to be made after trying on the finished garment.

Social Aid Schemes

- Craft items often come from ethnic mountain groups or workshops for the handicapped. The proceeds from the sale of woven goods, silverware and other souvenirs is poured back into projects that provide help for minority groups and disadvantaged people.

Trademark Piracy & Illegal Reproductions

- Vietnam is infamous for its fake brand-name articles and pirate copies. Clothes allegedly by major international fashion labels and sport brands,

cosmetics, perfume, medication (Viagra), computer programmes, mobile phones and even scooters can be found at ridiculously cheap prices.
- In certain places dealers have specialised in the sale of fake master-pieces – a 'Picasso' for example for a mere US$50! In Saigon and the Old City in Hanoi there are even whole 'painting streets' (Saigon: Tran Phu and Bui Vien).

Importing & Exporting
- Whether genuine or not, an export licence is required for **antiques** or else the goods will be confiscated. A lot of shops provide the necessary documentation and have the items sent by air to your home address.
- **Opium pipes** may cause problems as their sale is theoretically not permitted.
- Returning to Europe: Black corals, seashells, ivory and other animal-sourced products such as pelts, skins/leather, feathers, crocodile and snake skin, tortoiseshell, claws and teeth come under the **Washington Convention** for the protection of endangered species, as do Far Eastern 'medicines' such as snake wine and, of course, live animals. Such items will be taken from you by the time you reach customs in Europe, if not long before – and you will face high fines. This also applies to fake brand-name products that exceed items for personal use (i.e. 1 item!).

Payment & Haggling
- Haggling is part and parcel of shopping at a market in Vietnam; you should expect a 30–50% reduction; at Ben Thanh market in Saigon you can even cut the price by up to 70%. As a rule of thumb, you start haggling at half the price given.
- Have a good think beforehand as to how much you are prepared to pay. It works wonders if you can keep up a friendly smile and appear relaxed – and simply move on to the next stand. If a trader has **accepted your offer**, you are obliged to buy the item, especially in the case of cheap things.
- In air-conditioned **retail outlets** for high-quality brands the prices displayed are set prices. There is however no harm in asking for a discount if buying several items.
- **Payment is usually made in cash** in notes to the exact value; exceptions are brand-name stores where you can usually pay with a credit card.

Insider Tip

Opening Times
- **Markets** are open every day from around 6am–6pm; they are at their busiest early in the morning. **Night markets** operate between 5pm/6pm and 10pm/11pm.
- **Shops** and **department stores** are open daily from 8am–6pm, in tourist centres until 8pm/9pm; however they often close for a lunch break.
- **Shopping centres** are open from 9am until 10:30pm.

Entertainment

Magazines & Websites
- The **free magazines** *What's on in Saigon/Hanoi* and *Time out Vietnam* with their countless tips appear either weekly or monthly.
- Other useful sources are the **magazines** *The Guide*, *Word* (www.wordhcmc.com) and *Asia Life* (www.asialifemagazine.com/vietnam).

Finding Your Feet

■ Evening events are also listed in the daily papers *Saigon Times Daily* and *Vietnam News*, both published **in English**; these are available free of charge in some hotels.

Festivals

■ Vietnam has a lot of religious and traditional **festivals and holidays** as well as animist and propaganda-related ones.
■ For all Vietnamese, the most important festival is Tet Ngyuen Dan (➤ 28).
■ Most holidays are based on the **lunar calendar**.

Music & Theatre

■ The **water puppet theatre** in the Museum of Vietnamese History in Saigon is unique and should not be missed (➤ 65)!
■ A wide variety of different events are held in the old **opera houses** and **municipal theatres** in Saigon and Hanoi, ranging from tourist shows to circuses, classical concerts and fashion shows.
■ **Traditional, classical operas** such as those performed during the Thuong Dien Festival, are really something more for connoisseurs. With their dissonant, atonal sounds these take a bit of getting used to for most Westerners (➤ 96).
■ **Court music (*nha nhac*)** can be enjoyed during Hue Festival (➤ 144) or in the Citadel, also in Hue (➤ 144); **chamber music (*ca tru*)** is performed in Hanoi and other places (➤ 168).

Night Life

■ Night life is limited to major cities (Saigon, Hanoi) and tourist resorts (Nha Trang, Phan Thiet).
■ Otherwise the Vietnamese go to their much-loved **karaoke bars** (that may or may not be shady establishments as well) or to loud discos and on deafening pleasure steamers.

Sport

■ The paths through the Mekong Delta in the shade of fruit trees and palms are well suited for **cycling**.
■ **Hiking** in the magnificent mountain scenery of the north and in the Highlands is possible.
■ **Extreme sports** such as climbing, deep-water soloing and caving are new trends in Vietnam – the cliff and rock climbing in Ha Long Bay and in the Marble Mountains near Da Nang is excellent; Phong Nha Cave with its huge caverns provides a real adventure playground.
■ Ha Long Bay (➤ 174) and Dry Ha Long Bay (➤ 180) can be explored in a **rowing boat** or a **kayak**.
■ A wide variety of **watersports** is on offer at all beach resorts.
■ **Golf** can be played near Hanoi and Saigon, in the mountains and in the Highlands (Da Lat), near the beach at Phan Thiet, on Phu Quoc and near Da Nang.

Activities

■ Relax with a bit of **tai chi chuan** or simply join in the mass gymnastics in one of the parks – you only have to get up early (➤ 148)!
■ **Cookery courses** which include a visit to the market are offered by a lot of hotels throughout the country and in many bars and restaurants.
■ The Highlands are the best place to go for **elephant rides** (➤ 113).

Ho Chi Minh City & Environs

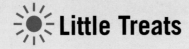 **Little Treats**

A journey through time

Settle down and be carried back to the 'good old days' by immersing yourself in *The Quiet American* in its original setting in the **Continental** (▶ 51).

Modern Saigon…

…can be experienced from the **'sky bars'** (▶ 72) where you have a bird's eye view of the metropolis below.

Spending spree

Explore the brightly coloured stalls of Saigon's **markets** (▶ 63 & 72) – and haggle for all one's worth!

Getting Your Bearings

Visiting Ho Chi Minh City (Saigon) is like a journey through time to different eras that have left their mark in world history. It has that typically Asian 'boomtown' flair with incessant hooting and teeming masses of people, coupled with enticing delights such as the countless temple oases and pagodas. Retracing the steps of Graham Greene and Marguerite Duras will take you to the French district where colonial villas – weathered by monsoons or recently renovated – are still to be found.

The French colonial past is omnipresent in the form of splendid buildings and traces of the Vietnam War only crop up in local museums. Meanwhile the skyline of this metropolis of some seven million seems to be growing at the blink of an eye. But even when the Saigonese use rocket-like lifts to ascend heavenwards, any attempt to move around on the ground seems to end up on a Far Eastern variation of the scooter. Millions of motorised two-wheelers carve a path through the throng like little battleships. And anyone who manages to make it in one piece from the old French centre to the former Chinese district of Cholon in a taxi, as a pillion passenger on a moped or in a 'cyclo' tricycle (*xich lo*) heads for a pagoda and disappears headlong into a red and golden world of incense and smoke – for the uninitiated a chaotic mixture of folk heroes, gods and demons.

Just the name of the city needs some clarification: even when the Communists changed the name of Vietnam's biggest metropolis to Ho Chi Minh City, nobody who lives here ever stopped calling the old city area around the port by the name that had been used for centuries: Saigon.

Ga Sai

Cach Mang

21
Chua Giac Lam & Chua Ho Dat

Thang Ta

Museum of Vietnamese Traditional Medicine
20

3 Thang 2

Dien Bien Phu

Ly Thai To

Ch

22 Tay Ninh

Dau Tieng

0   10 km
0   5 mi

Go Dau
22 Cu Chi Tunnels   Thu Dau Mot
Cu Chi   Bien Hoa (1A)

Duc Hoa

(1A)
HO CHI MINH CITY (SAIGON)
Chua Giac Lam & **21**
Chua Ho Dat

Nha Be

(1A)
Can Giuoc

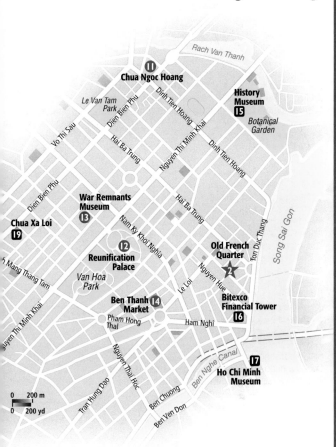

TOP 10

Don't Miss

At Your Leisure

Ho Chi Minh City & Environs

Two Perfect Days

French colonial buildings, the skyline of a western metropolis, testimonies to recent history and, in the midst of all this, ancient and traditional pagodas and markets – experience the many different facets of a modern-day Vietnam reaching for the stars.

Day One

Morning

To get a general overview go up to the 49th or 50th floor of the futuristic **16 Bitexco Financial Tower** (▶ 65). A stroll along the main street, Dong Khoi (below), will tempt you to explore the ★ **Old French Quarter** (▶ 50), with its lovely buildings dating from colonial days, that extends to either side of this street in the 1st district. The splendid French architecture of yore is reflected in the Old Opera House that should not be missed, the Central Post Office and Notre Dame Cathedral, as well as the venerable old hotels and the City Hall at the northern end of Nguyen Hue Boulevard.

11 Chua Ngoc Hoang

15 History Museum

21 Chua Giac Lam & Chua Ho Dat

War Remnants Museum

Old French Quarter

19 Chua Xa Loi

12 Reunification Palace

20 Museum of Vietnamese Traditional Medicine

16 Bitexco Financial Tower

14 Ben Thanh Market

17 Ho Chi Minh Museum

Chinatown 18

Midday

To escape the merciless midday heat why not visit one of the museums? You are really spoilt for choice in this city and will need to plan more than just a few hours to explore the three museums listed here. The bombastic **12 Independence Palace** (also known as **Reunification Palace**) (▶ 59) on

Nam Ky Khoi Nghia, with its huge rooms and escape tunnels in the cellar, is impressive. Anyone interested in the Vietnam War should not miss the **13 War Remnants Museum** (▶ 61). And if you prefer the marvel at countless figures of Buddha, ceramics and a water puppet theatre, just take a taxi or a **cyclo** to the **15 Museum of Vietnamese History** (▶ 65) a few blocks to the north.

Afternoon
From the History Museum it is just a stone's throw (1km/0.8mi) to Saigon's most important pagoda. At the ⑪ **Chua Ngoc Hoang** (➤ 57) the Jade Emperor sits among smouldering incense and gigantic joss sticks and oversees the fate of his minions.

Evening
After all that sightseeing, the boulevards in the 1st district are an open invitation to shop 'til you drop. You will find everything from chopsticks to lacquerware, silk garments, antiques and dusty Buddhas in all shapes and sizes. Or else you elbow your way through the crowds at ⑭ **Ben Thanh Market** (➤ 63), built in 1914. In the evening this is transformed into a delightful night market with umpteen street kitchens.

Day Two

Morning
It's well worth getting up early to take a day trip to the much-visited ⑧ **Cu Chi Tunnels** (➤ 53), some 60km (37mi) to the west of Saigon. Your best bet is to choose one of the many organised coach trips or charter a hire car and chauffeur.

㉒ Tay Ninh

Cu Chi Tunnels

★ ⑧ **HO CHI MINH CITY (SAIGON)**

㉑

Chua Giac Lam & Chua Ho Dat

Midday and Afternoon
The second destination for today, the extremely colourful and much-photographed Cao Dai Temple in ㉒ **Tay Ninh** is also within easy reach (some 35km/22mi further to the west, ➤ 68). Watch the priests in their brilliantly coloured robes from above, in the gallery, during prayers held at noon.

Evening
In the evening leave your flip-flops and shorts in your hotel, step out into Saigon's night life and visit one of the 'sky bars' where nothing is done by half! **Chill SaiGon Skybar & Restaurant** (above, ➤ 72) on the 23rd floor in the AB Tower is a good place to start.

⭐ Old French Quarter

Take a step back to the days when Vietnam was still a French colony – gentlemen in white summer suits riding down elegant boulevards in rickshaws, such as the rue Catinat (now Dong Khoi), past men in 'pyjama suits' bent double over board games and women selling noodle soup carried on yokes. Today, a never-ending stream of mopeds battles its way up and down the roads in the area and along the promenade on the banks of the Saigon River. Our tip: just let yourself be carried along with the crowds!

Start your tour at the northern end of Nguyen Hue Boulevard where you will find one of Saigon's landmarks, the **Hôtel de Ville** (City Hall), constructed in 1901–08. The yellow and white building with a red tiled roof, columns, decorative plasterwork and balconies is dominated by a central bell tower. Today, the People's Committee sits in the ornate neo-Baroque structure. A statue of Ho Chi Minh with a child on his lap watches over the square planted with bonsai trees in front of the City Hall. Every evening 'Uncle Ho' is the ever-patient backdrop for souvenir photos for hundreds of Vietnamese tourists and residents alike.

Hotel Legends

Immediately on the left is the legendary **Rex Hotel** with its popular roof garden and prominent crown on the fifth floor. During the Vietnam War press conferences were held every day in the hotel theatre by the US army – the 'five o'clock follies' – as described by Graham Greene in **The Quiet American**.

Equally famous as the setting of a novel from the early 1950s is the **Hotel Continental** that, long before the Indochina War, was a meeting place for western journalists and writers such as Somerset Maugham who stayed here in the 1920s. The figures in Greene's novel watched Vietnamese-French life pass by the bar on the veranda – graceful women in long *ao dais* with slits up the sides. And this was where the British journalist Thomas Fowler first met the 'quiet American', the secret agent, who was to fall in love with his Vietnamese bride.

A jewel from the colonial era – the Central Post Office in Saigon with its elaborately decorated façade

Colonial Glory

At the heart of all the hustle and bustle, on Lam Son Square, is the prominent **Old Opera House** that was built in 1899. The South Vietnamese National Assembly operated from here up until 1975. From 1976 onwards the building became a municipal theatre under the aegis of the Communists. Today, operas, ballets, pop concerts, folkloric performances and fashion shows are held here (▶72).

At the northwestern end of Dong Khoi is another delightful colonial building, the neo-Romanesque **Notre Dame Cathedral** with its two square towers (1877–83). Throughout the year it forms a backdrop for photo sessions for bridal couples in white dresses and dark suits.

To the right, the yellow painted **Central Post Office** (1886–91) with green shutters cannot be missed. The high central hall, spanned by a barrel-vaulted roof with glazed panels that is often (erroneously) attributed to Gustave Eiffel, is impressive. Ho Chi Minh smiles wisely down on today's visitors from a huge portrait. The beautiful old wooden telephone cabins on the left-hand side with their world clocks are especially noteworthy; they now house cash dispensers.

If you follow Dong Khoi in a southeastly direction towards the river you pass one exclusive store after another. Luxury brands from all over the world, from Armani to Versace, are quickly forcing out the old established shops and affordable tailors – even historical bars such as the almost 100-year-old Café Brodard that closed in 2012 and Givral, once frequented by Graham Greene. Today Sony sells mobile phones from this premises instead.

Up in the Clouds

One last stop on this journey back through time is the roof garden at the top of the **Hotel Majestic**, first opened in 1925, at the southeastern end of Dong Khoi right on the Bach Dang/Ton Duc riverside promenade. The view extends some way over the countryside on the other – swampy – side of the Saigon River that has, surprisingly, hardly been built on. Graham Greene was inspired by this place as he sat sipping his evening cocktail to the sound of shell fire.

TAKING A BREAK

You can watch the goings-on from above at **Highlands Coffee** (££; 135 Nguyen Hue, on the right next to the Royal Hotel and opposite the Rex Hotel; daily 9am–11pm) – a roof café belonging to the popular Vietnamese coffee-house chain, either over a chilled beer or a typically Vietnamese iced coffee. Snacks are also served and WiFi is available.

Two square towers flank the neo-Romanesque brick cathedral of Notre Dame

Rex Hotel
✚ 209 E2
✉ 141 Nguyen, Hue corner of Le Loi
☎ 08 38 29 21 85; www.rexhotelvietnam.com

Hotel Continental
✚ 209 E2
✉ 132–143 Dong Khoi
☎ 08 38 29 92 01;
www.continentalsaigon.com

Opera House ➤ 72

Notre Dame Cathedral
✚ 209 E3 ✉ Dong Khoi
🕐 Daily 7am until 8pm ✋ Free

Central Post Office
✚ 209 E3
✉ Dong Khoi, with bureau de change
🕐 Daily 7am–8pm

Hotel Majestic
✚ 209 F2 ✉ 1 Dong Khoi, 1st district
☎ 08 38 29 55 17; www.majesticsaigon.com

INSIDER INFO

An estimated 5 or 6 – even 7 – million mopeds, scooters and bicycles squeeze their way through Saigon's streets, narrow alleys and markets. Crossing a road without the help of a traffic light is hazardous but virtually unavoidable. Nobody would ever even think of stopping at a crossroads. As a pedestrian trying **to cross a road**, never stand still but, keeping your eyes on the continuous stream of traffic, head for the safety of the far side. The mopeds will go around you! Or you trail on the heels of the Vietnamese as they cross the road.

Insider Tip

⭐8 Cu Chi Tunnels

No visit to Vietnam would be complete without seeing the (in)famous Viet Cong tunnels. School classes, former partisans and US veterans – even guests on a state visit – come here to have a look. The first tunnel builders were members of the resistance in 1934 fighting against the French. They would probably never have imagined in their wildest dreams that, decades later, their descendents would be guiding tourists through the network of tunnels.

The area around Cu Chi was one of the regions in Vietnam most heavily bombarded by pesticides and napalm. Today, the two tunnel systems **Ben Duoc** and **Ben Dinh**, some 35 and 60km (37mi) northwest of Saigon, are memorial sites but, at the same time, tourist fairgrounds overrun with souvenir stalls and shooting ranges, tanks and helicopters.

The sites include field kitchens and military sick areas, trap doors, captured tanks and overgrown bomb craters. The **tourist routes** leads through 'mine fields' with blank explosives. As a demonstration, slim-built Vietnamese guides 'disappear' through well-camouflaged **tunnel entrances** which measure a mere 20 × 40cm (8 × 16in). A 50m (164ft) section of the tunnel has been enlarged for tourists from the West; it is dimly lit and fitted with emergency exits.

The Early Days

The first trenches and subterranean rooms dug as weapon stores in the 1930s and '40s by anti-colonial resistance fighters were only gradually linked up by tunnels. By the end of the 1960s a **250km (155mi)-long, invisible network of passageways** had been created. The tunnels were originally only wide enough for two (Vietnamese!) people to squeeze past one another. Partisans lived on three levels up to 10 metres under the ground; towards the end of the Vietnam War there were some 16,000 people living in the tunnel network.

Even the tunnel for tourists is a tight fit – anyone with claustrophobia should steer clear of it

The Viet Cong's Underground Realm

In the 1930s and '40s subterranean chambers and trenches were used by guerillas in their fight against the French as hiding places and weapon stores. Gradually the passageways were linked to one another and the network expanded in the war against the Americans.

Extent: By the end of the Vietnam War the invisible, 250km (155mi)-long network of tunnels stretched from the border of Cambodia and Vietnam along the Ho Chi Minh Trail as far as Cholon, the Chinese district of Saigon.

❶ An underground city: The partisans lived in three tightly packed tiers up to 10m (33ft) below the ground. Children were even born in this tunnel realm and only saw the light of day years later. The shafts opened up into a subterranean labyrinth of dormitories and common rooms, sick bays with operation tables, kitchens, prayer rooms with shrines, workshops, storage areas and bomb shelters. The food eaten by the tunnel inhabitants was simple – generally manioc (arrowroot) with salt, pepper and crushed peanuts. All underground chambers were connected by tunnels some 80cm/2.5ft wide. (For tourists from the West one section has been enlarged to a height of 1.20m/4ft and a width of 80cm/2.5ft).

❷ Entrances: Tiny hinged doors, covered above ground by leaves and grass, led to the outside world. All of these were protected by primitive but effective booby traps. Some tunnels led to rivers that made escape easier in the case of pursuit or shelling.

❸ Perfect camouflage: Ventilation was via inconspicuous bamboo poles. Smoke from underground cooking areas was diverted several miles. Pepper and chili were planted around ventilation shafts to confuse search dogs. In time, the dogs were no longer able to differentiate between Vietnamese and Americans as the Viet Cong began to use American soap and aftershave and wore their prisoners' clothes.

❹ Lethal traps: Attempts to flush the Viet Cong out of the tunnels were met with a variety of tricks, e.g. traps doors above ditches in which bamboo shoots had been placed, pointing upwards, their spikes sometimes dipped in poison. Tunnels and entrances that looked real lured intruders to booby traps. Bombs and mines were also hidden under pieces of turf.

Hidden entrances, just 20 × 40cm (8 × 16in) in size, were all over the jungle. The covers were camouflaged with grass and leaves. A guide reveals one of the ways in.

Ho Chi Minh City & Environs

Shots from nowhere

The headquarters of the US army's 25th Infantry Division was set up near the tunnel in Cu Chi. At first the Americans could not explain the mysterious night-time assaults on the heavily protected military camp – until they discovered the tunnel. Everyone around Cu Chi was then forced to evacuate the area and it was declared a **'free-fire zone'**. Millions of gallons of poisonous substances and countless bombs rained down over the region that was ultimately virtually completely defoliated through the use of napalm.

The once deathly trap doors have now been made 'suitable' for tourists

Some 50,000 US soldiers searched the area for entrances to the tunnel system. Attempts to drive the Viet Cong out of the tunnels were countered with tricks and gruesome resistance tactics. They installed **trap doors** over ditches fitted with bamboo sticks with poisoned spikes pointing upwards. Scattered chili pepper kept American search dogs at bay.

Slightly-built soldiers from the allied forces of Thailand and the Philippines were used by US troops as 'tunnel rats'. When surprised by the Viet Cong they could be pulled out again by a rope tied to their feet. On the Vietnamese side alone, 12,000 resistance fighters were killed in the tunnels.

TAKING A BREAK

At the entrance and on the site simple snack bars provide visitors with classical Vietnamese food and drinks. There are several places to eat near Ben Duoc down on the river. During the day, the **Cassava Root Restaurant** (£/££), right on the N22 near Ben Dinh, is open.

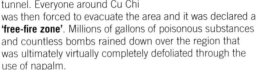

➕ 213 E4
✉ on the N22 after Tay Ninh 🕐 Daily 7:30am–5:30pm
🚌 Bus 13 from Saigon Park 24/9 near Pham Ngu Lao, change at terminus to bus 79 to Ben Duoc or bus 94 from Cholon to the station Cu Chi and beyond by moped taxi
🎫 VND90,000

INSIDER INFO

- **Half-day tours**, mostly to Ben Dinh, are available through every local travel agent for VND80,000–VND200,000; day tour variations which take in Cao Dai temple are a little more expensive. A hire car and chauffeur to Ben Duoc will set you back around VND1.1m.

- Wild animals accidentally caught or kept and then set loose by private individuals are prepared for being returned to the wild at the **Wildlife Rescue Center** near Cu Chi. Visitors should inform the centre of their arrival beforehand (Ap Cho Cu II, An Nhon Tay, Cu Chi; tel: 09 84 28 11 90; www.wildlifeatrisk.org, a 'donation' of around VND200,000 is expected).

Insider Tip

⓫ Chua Ngoc Hoang
(Jade Emperor Pagoda)

The Jade Emperor, Ngoc Hoang, is one of the most venerated figures in Taoist philosophy. From a hierarchical point of view, he is above all gods, saints and king and rules over all worlds. This temple, a masterpiece of Chinese architecture, is dedicated to him.

From the outside it is hard to imagine what a plethora of deities and other figures await the visitor inside

Visitors first enter the **outer courtyard** of the Jade Emperor Pagoda (or Temple) that was constructed in 1906. The pools are full of little turtles that can be bought from stalls at the entrance and then returned to 'freedom'. The animals that reach a ripe old age are seen as a symbol of longevity on earth. Two monumental figures of the Jade Emperor's generals guard the entrance to the altar area – to the left, Bach Ho on a tiger; to the right, Thanh Long in a victory pose on a dragon.

In the Realm of the Jade Empire

The temple combines a multiplicity of gods, guards, heroes and Buddhist Bodhisattvas. The **room at the back** however is unmistakably ruled over by the Jade Emperor in his magnificent glittering robes, seated before an altar piled high with offerings such as fruit and sacks of rice for the monks. In addition there are three huge safes where people can deposit their donations. Most worshippers who come here light an incense stick, pray standing or kneeling, bow slightly three times and hold an intimate dialogue in a mumbled tone in the midst of the religious bustle and smoke with the man made of painted papier-mâché.

A further six life-sized figures standing in two rows provide the Emperor with some company. The two middle ones, the gods of the heavens – Nam Tao and Bac Dau – decide over the fate of the living and the dead, over victory or defeat. Phat Mau Chuan De, the 18-armed goddess with three faces, is worshipped as the mother of the Buddhas of the Five Points of the Compass.

The **left-hand room** represents Hell and visitors experience something of the fate of the dead. However, gods also dwell here and reward good deeds and punish bad ones. The King of Hell, Than Hoang, watches over the scene from a raised altar. It is advisable to circle the altar in a clockwise direction together with the worshippers present. In a corner on the left is the god of prosperity, Than Tai, dressed in a white robe with a white hood, seated in front of another collection box. And while wood carvings on the wall depict scenes of torture in Hell, the faithful can draw hope from the figure of the goddess of all-embracing mercy, Thi Kinh, on the opposite wall who confers a blessing on everyone.

TAKING A BREAK

The **Cuc Gach Café** (£; 79 Phan Ke Binh, Da Kao, 1st district; daily 7am–8pm) is tucked away in a villa with antique furnishings. Typical Vietnamese fare, including vegetarian dishes, generally speedy service but slightly over-priced drinks.

🕂 209 D/E4
✉ 73 May Thi Luu, 1st district   ☎ 08 38 20 31 02
🕐 Daily 6am–6pm   🚌 18 from Ben Thanh bus station   🎟 Free

The Jade Emperor (left), flanked by his guards and pupils, is judge over good and bad deeds

INSIDER INFO

- The **pagoda festival** takes place on the 9th and 10th days of the New Year after the Tet festival (Jan, Feb).
- In non-Buddhist Taoist temples and pagodas in Vietnam you do not have to take off your shoes but it is expected that visitors **dress respectfully** (i.e. no hot pants, shoulderless (tank) tops, etc.). Do not stand on the **high thresholds** but step over them!

Insider Tip

⑫ Reunification Palace

The building was at the heart of the decisive battle for Saigon. On the morning of 30 April, 1975, the world could see on television how a North Vietnamese T-54 tank broke open the iron gates and Communist soldiers occupied the building. The flag of the Democratic Republic of Vietnam was flown from the roof.

The 'Reunification Palace' (Dinh Thong Nha) was built in 1966 on the site of the Palais Norodom of 1868. The palace of the much-feared dictator Ngo Dinh Diem (ruled 1955–63) had been heavily bombed four years earlier and was ultimately demolished. The modern replacement has a total of 100 rooms on four floors with a helipad on the roof. Up until 1975 the building served as the presidential palace; after the Communist victory reunification negotiations were

the modern, restrained façade of the palace

held here in the winter of 1975. The red flag with a yellow star now flutters over the building and the victorious army's disused tanks are parked outside.

Tour

Extending over 4,500m² (48,500ft²), the interior is in the functionalist '60s style with vast **assembly halls and conference rooms**. The **banqueting rooms** are exaggeratedly ostentatious. One of the most pleasing rooms is the ambassadorial audience chamber. The former **presidential reception and living areas** are on the first floor. In addition, there is a ballroom (4th floor), a small private cinema (3rd floor) and numerous opulently furnished rooms with red carpets and billowing curtains, chandeliers, leather armchairs and antique pieces. In the **stairway**, elements on the façade to provide shade to the full-length windows are particularly noteworthy. These were designed in the style of Le Corbusier from whom the architect Ngo Viet Thu obviously drew inspiration.

In the two-storey basement, an underground **escape tunnel** and a **command centre** of sorts can be viewed. The latter includes a bed for the president in the case of emergency and two telephones on a bedside cabinet. Photos and documents tracing the history of the Palais Norodom and the battle on 30 April 1975 can be seen in the adjoining **museum**.

Functionalism is the dominant style of the huge assembly halls with endless rows of chairs

TAKING A BREAK

Insider Tip
On the roof (4th floor, lift) there is a bar, serving snacks and drinks, with a wonderful view. A more substantial lunch can be found to the north in Pasteur Street that runs parallel, for example at **Nha Hang Ngon** (formerly Quan An Ngon).

✚ 209 D2/3
✉ 135 Nam Ky Khoi Nghia, 1st district
☎ 08 08 50 37 39; www.ditich.dinhdoclap.gov.vn
🕐 Daily 7:30am–11am, 1pm–4pm
💵 VND30,000

INSIDER INFO

- The palace is sometimes closed for international congresses, on the Victory Day anniversary (29/30 April) and during state visits.
- A 35-min. introductory film in English is screened on the ground floor and in the basement.

Insider Tip
- **Bus no. 127** runs daily from 5:30am until 8pm roughly every 10 mins. following a 10km (6.2mi)-long route past a number of attractions (e.g. Ben Thanh market, the Reunification Palace, the zoo and several museums; buy tickets from the conductor: VND4,000).

⑬ War Remnants Museum

Until the 1990s the War Remnants Museum was still known as the 'Museum of American War Crimes', among other names. This was finally changed so as not to insult US veterans who were visiting in increasing numbers. The pictures speak for themselves and are not for people of a nervous disposition. And – hardly surprisingly – there's no shortage of propaganda here either.

Several fighter jets used during the Vietnam War are on display in front of the museum building

The museum (Vietnamese: Bao Tang Chung Tich Chien Tranh) that first opened in 1975 includes Vietnamese tanks, US Air Force fighter jets and anti-aircraft guns displayed outside, in front of or on which the majority of Asian visitors like to pose for photographs. Notices that say 'no not climb on the exhibits' are deliberately ignored!

The Plain Truth
Inside the bunker-like three-storey building, on the other hand, there is little to make anyone laugh. Figures and facts to do with the war are recorded on the many often gruesome photographs. On the first floor there is a display entitled **'Historical Truths'** – obviously seen from a Vietnamese perspective and correspondingly one-sided, as criticised by a lot of western visitors. But how can a massacre be presented 'objectively'? For example, on 16 March 1968 in My Lai (► 138), a total of 504 villagers, including women, small children and the elderly, were murdered by US marines. The photographs of this atrocity, like virtually all others in the

The horror of the Vietnam War is made tangible in the War Remnants Museum

museum, however, were taken by American photographers such as Larry Burrows.

The longer-term **effects of the war** – in Vietnam as well as the struggle by injured American veterans seeking recognition in the USA as 'Agent Orange' victims – are also presented. Malformed foetuses, the result of chemical warfare, are preserved in rows of jam jars. Just a few years ago these were on public display in a Saigon hospital. An array of different weapons is also presented. The last room is dedicated to Vietnamese war heroes and generously peppered with propaganda. Near the exit is the exhibition on the **prison island Con Dao** (► 92) which includes models of the notorious 'tiger cage' cells (2.70×1.50×3m/9×5×10ft) and an original guillotine from the French colonial era. The last execution it was used for took place in 1960.

The **souvenir shops** come as an abrupt contrast. Visitors can buy 'genuine' US army lighters, watches and cartridge cases and all sorts of craft items.

TAKING A BREAK

A very quietly situated vegetarian café bar has opened near the museum serving beautifully presented food: **Hum** (££; 32 Vo Van Tan, 3rd district; www.hum-vegetarian.vn; daily 10am–1pm) – an oasis with a lovely inner courtyard.

➕ 209 D3 ✉ 28 Vo Van Tran, 3rd district
☎ 08 39 30 55 87; http://warremnantsmuseum.com ⏰ Daily 7:30am–noon, 1:30pm–5pm, last admission 4:30pm 🚌 14 and 28 💵 VND15,000

INSIDER INFO

Insider Tip

- As many of the photos are deeply disturbing, children should not be taken into the exhibition rooms. There is a 🧸 **children's playroom** on the second floor supervised by Vietnamese women.
- A film in English is shown in a **media room** on the ground floor at 9am, 10am, 11am, 2pm, 3pm and 4pm (the sound however is poor).

⑭ Ben Thanh Market

The striking market building at the heart of the city cannot be missed. With its prominent tower it has become one of Ho Chi Minh's landmarks since it opened in 1914. Apart from being a popular place for taking photos of the mountains of fruit and vegetables and the thrashing, creeping and crawling on the fish and meat stands, it is the souvenirs and notorious fake brand-name articles that are more often or not the object of desire.

It's all push and shove in the narrow aisles at the tourist market (Cho Ben Thanh). One sign that stands out in particular reads 'Genuine Fake Watches' – cheap imitations with gaudy numbers and hands, a far call from the original, yours for a snip at US$5. The real jewels are generally hidden from view, only shown by the stall-holder to 'connoisseurs': the 'Rolex Daytona Quartz' is much heavier in the hand and is priced at a full US$250 – but it's still a fake, just like 90% of the brand items at Ben Thanh Market.

Beg, Steal or Borrow...

Vietnam is, after all, one of the main centres for trading in **pirated goods** in Asia. Watches, bags, CDs and DVDs, paintings by Picasso for US$50 – everything is copied without any inhibitions, even 'Honda' scooters. The products on offer at Ben Thanh market are no exception. Sports shoes supposedly from US companies are particularly popular – except that they fall apart at the seams after being worn just a few times, as are surprisingly realistic looking luxury 'Swiss-made' chronometers which pack up after three days. Traders also push undrinkable 'Johnnie Walker', deceptively similar 'Tampro' packaged in blue and even medication such as 'Viagra'. More often than not, however, you can see what is a **fake** at a fleeting glance – like when a top-of-the-range blouse has loose threads, or trendy sneakers smell strongly of plastic.

The square in front of Ben Thanh market is always full of activity

Insider Tip

...or perhaps it is genuine?

Vietnam is one of the world's leading textile manufacturers for up-market brands, whether for Diesel jeans or chic Burberry fashions. So it really is possible that a low-priced pair of Nike shoes is actually the real thing. They could be seconds or have 'fallen off the back of a lorry' between the factory and the port.

Classic souvenirs, from lacquerware to conical hats and from T-shirts to coffee and tea can be found nearer the west entrance where material is also sold by the metre. But, even here, all that glitters is not necessarily silk! But a stroll through the market is great fun, despite everything else!

A hawker selling street food outside the market building; an inviting display of glittering fakes

TAKING A BREAK

Pho 2000 (£), the legendary soup kitchen that was even visited by Bill Clinton is immediately to the left of the main entrance (▶ 71). In the evening the sizzling sound from umpteen food stands and open kitchens around the market is a tempting invitation to sample authentic and cheap Vietnamese food.

➕ 209 E2
✉ Le Loi and Le Lai, 1st district; www.ben-thanh-market.com
🕐 Daily 6am–6pm 🖐 Free

INSIDER INFO

- **Cash dispensers** are located at the main entrance.
- Be careful of **pickpockets** – rucksacks, bags and valuables in particular should be left in your hotel. If there is a problem contact the tourist police here.
- **Haggling** is worthwhile: the final price should be some 30–50%, even up to 70% less than the initial asking price.
- The price quoted for things **sold by weight** such as tea and coffee is normally for 100g.
- European **customs** don't consider product piracy a laughing matter. Anyone who is caught returning to Europe with fake brand-name items and pirated copies risks being fined and being taken to court by the company that holds the rights.

At Your Leisure

🔟 National Museum of Vietnamese History

The History Museum (Bao Tang Lich Su) is a beautiful colonial building with ornamental plasterwork, crowned by a pagoda-like cupola. The 16 rooms house the country's most important treasures and the museum is very much worth a visit for anyone interested in gaining a deeper insight into Vietnam's (art) history.

Highlights in the collection include the Bronze Age **Dong Son drum** (Room 2) and the imposing, almost 4m (13ft)-high copy of **Quan Am**, the 'lady Buddha with a thousand arms' (Room 7) – the gold-plated original from But Thap pagoda dates from 1656. The almost 2000-year-old bronze **Dong Duong Buddha** from the early Champa period (3rd century), an elegant statue some 1.2m (4ft) (Room 12) is especially noteworthy, as are the colourful traditional costumes and everyday objects of the ethnic minorities (Room 15).

Mythological animals such as dragons and a phoenix, as well as lions and a fox, are the principal

characters in performances in the small 🎭 **water puppet theatre** on the ground floor (Room 11). Three actors standing waist-deep in water behind the scenes operate the figures that are fixed to long bamboo rods.

🚩 209 F4 ✉ 2 Nguyen Binh Khiem, 1st district ☎ 08 29 81 46, 08 29 02 68 🕐 Tue–Sun 8am–11:30am, 1:30pm–5pm 💵 VND15,000

🔟 Bitexco Financial Tower

The futuristic building cannot be missed and is a testimony to modern Ho Chi Minh City. Vietnam's first real skyscraper, located in the 1st

The hypermodern Bitexco Financial Tower dominates Saigon's skyline wherever you are

OASIS OF PEACE

In the extensive grounds of the 🎪 **zoo and botanical gardens** (Thao Cam Vien, 2B Nguyen Binh Khiem corner of Le Loi and Nguyen Thi Minh Khai, www.saigonzoo.net, daily 7am–6pm, admission: VND50,000) next to the History Museum, visitors can admire the orchid collection and visit the two white tigers and komodo dragons. However, do not expect the animal enclosures to be exemplary. There are also several fairground stalls, snack stands and merry-go-rounds for children.

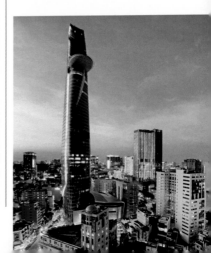

Incense sticks are lit in Chua Ba to honour the deceased

district, was completed in 2010. From 200m (660ft) up, you have a wonderful view over the chaos below: 68 floors with a **sky deck** (49th floor), restaurants, bars, a shopping centre and a helipad at a height of 265m (870ft). Tip: by taking the lift from the shopping centre to the café on the 50th floor you save having to pay an admission fee – as if a glass of beer or a cappuccino were not expensive enough.

➕ 209 F2 ✉ Between Ngo Duc Ke and Hai Trieu
☎ 08 39 15 61 56 (hotline);
www.bitexcofinancialtower.com
🕐 9:30am–9:30pm 💰 Skydeck VND200,000

🔢 Ho Chi Minh Museum

The Ho Chi Minh Museum (Bao Tang Ho Chi Minh; not to be confused with the Ho Chi Minh City Museum!) is located at the end of Bach Dang, the road along the Saigon River. A bridge leads over the Ben Nghe Canal to the museum on the other side that is housed in the imposing

arcaded **Dragon House** (Ben Nha Rong) that was once the head-quarters of the French port authority. It was from here that the young Nguyen Tat Thanh boarded the steamship 'Admiral Latouche Tréville' on 5 June 1911 at the start of his journey round the world working as a galley hand. Some 30 years later he returned to his native country and rose to become its president: Ho Chi Minh (1890–1969, in power: 1945–69), who is still highly revered by all. A number of photographs, documents and newspaper articles, personal items such as sandals, a wicker suitcase, a walking stick and 'Uncle Ho's' typewriter are displayed in five rooms in the museum.

On the second floor an array of gaudily colourful propaganda posters can be seen. An old Peugeot from 1964, once owned by Ho Chi Minh, and an original three-wheeled rickshaw are parked outside.

➕ 209 F1 ✉ 1 Nguyen Tat Thanh, 4th district
☎ 08 39 40 20 60, 08 39 40 10 94
🕐 Tue–Sun 7:30am–11:30am, 1:30pm–5pm
💰 VND15,000

🔢 Chinatown

The first Chinese to settle in Cholon, the oldest district in Saigon in the southwestern part of the French Quarter (Walk ► 190), fled from southern China some 300 years ago. This is where most of Saigon's more than 180 pagodas and temples are to be found. Many line Nguyen Trai. The donation of money and offerings provides a good income, first and foremost in

22

★**8** **HO CHI MINH CITY (SAIGON)**
21

Chua Ba (also known as Thien Hau Pagoda). The temple is dedicated to the goddess of the sea and is considered the most beautiful example of southern Chinese temple architecture from the early 19th century. Thien Hau is shown in a wall painting near the entrance and is worshipped as the patron saint of sailors and fishermen. The main shrine boasts three statues of Thien Hau in embroidered gowns, painted in gold. The central figure is carried through the streets during the procession on the 23rd day of the 3rd lunar month. Couples who are hoping for a child pray to the goddess of fertility, Kim Hue, at the shrine on the left. A small bed with a curtain can be found on the altar pedestal.

➕ 208 B1

Chua Ba
✉ 710 Nguyen Trai 🕐 Daily 6am–5:30pm
🚌 1 (from Ben Thanh market bus station)
🎫 Free

🔟 Chua Xa Loi (Xa Loi Pagoda)

This Buddhist temple built in 1956 with its imposing seven-storeyed tower and the swastika talisman on the roof, was at the centre of the resistance against the dictator Ngo Dinh Diem in the early 1960s. 400 monks and nuns sought protection here from government reprisals under the Diem regime. Several set fire to themselves in protest, including the monk Thich Quang Duc (▶ 111) whose memorial can now be seen not far from the pagoda. This act of desperation caught people's attention worldwide and weakened the president's reputation. The pagoda was stormed by soldiers in August 1963 and the monks and nuns arrested.

Inside, a 5m (16.5ft)-high, gold-plated Sakyamuni Buddha can be seen on a lotus seat. 14 murals illustrate the most important events in the life of the 'Enlightened One'. A small shrine at the back commemorates Thich Quang Duc.

➕ 208 C3
✉ 89 Ba Huyen Thanh Quan, 3rd district
☎ 08 39 30 01 16 🕐 6am–11am, 2pm–9pm
🎫 Free

🔟 Museum of Vietnamese Traditional Medicine

Some 3000 exhibits related to traditional medicine that has been practiced in Vietnam for at least 2000 years are displayed by a pharmaceutical company in 18 little rooms in a lovely old building. These include mortars and antique scales, tea services and vessels for herbs and old documents and books. And of course you can buy teas and potions for headaches and coughs in the adjoining shop.

➕ 208 A2 ✉ 41 Hoang Du Khuong, 10th district
☎ 08 38 64 24 30; www.fitomuseum.com.vn
🕐 Daily 8:30am–5:30pm 🎫 VND50,000

🔟 Chua Giac Lam & Chua Ho Dat (Giac Lam & Giac Vien pagodas)

Chua Giac Lam, that lies slightly off the beaten track, was built in 1744. It is the oldest and most beautiful

The modern Xa Loi Pagoda picks up on certain traditional architectural elements

A moment of silence – monks at the main altar in Giac Lam Pagoda

Buddhist temple in Saigon and is known for its **118 statues of Buddha**, some of which are extremely old. The main altar to the left of the entrance, framed in wood with exquisite carvings and pillars, boasts an impressive collection of wooden Buddhas, enlightened beings (Bodhisattvas) and guards. Amitabha (Buddha of the Past) is at the centre surrounded by his favourite pupils, Ananda and Kasyapa; a Sakyamuni Buddha in bronze (Buddha of the Present) can be seen in the middle row along with the portly, laughing Di Lac Buddha (Buddha of the Future). Next to Di Lac is a bronze figure of the Jade Emperor. Right at the back of the entrance area is a small, hidden altar with the oldest figure in the temple – a wooden Sakyamuni Buddha some 300 years old.

Chua Ho Dat is very similar to Giac Lam pagoda and lies in the same street (2km/1.25mi) to the southwest). This dreamy wooden structure also has a garden with the abbots' magnificent burial stupas.

Chua Giac Lam

✚ to the west 208 A3

✉ 163 Lac Long Quan, Tan Binh district

☎ 08 38 65 39 33 🕐 wv7am–noon, 2pm–6pm

🚌 27 from Cong Vien 23/9-Park, Pham Ngu Lao 🎟 Free

Chua Ho Dat

✚ to the west 208 A3 ✉ Lac Long Quan, next to Dam Sen Water Park 🕐 7am–6pm

🟦22 Tay Ninh

The Cao Dai religious movement, founded in 1926, has its head-quarters in the provincial capital Tay Ninh with a kitschy, brightly-coloured main temple from 1933–55. The movement's teachings are a rather jumbled mixture drawn from Buddhism, Confucianism, Taoism, Christianity and Islam, with certain occult practices still being carried out to this day. Figures vary, but there are now up to 6 million adherents in Vietnam alone. Only those who respect the principles of humanity, love and justice will find redemption and happiness in Nirvana. Deeply religious Caodaists are generally vegetarians and most priests observe celibacy. The movement's syncretism is reflected in the paintings inside the temple that depict not only Buddha but also the trinity of Hindu gods – Brahma, Shiva and Vishnu – as well as Jesus. The huge, all-seeing eye symbolises that of god and, for Caodaists, is a sign of righteousness.

✚ 213 E5 ✉ 99km (62mi) northwest of Saigon 🕐 1-hour services at 6am, noon, 6pm and midnight 🎟 Free

Lucky mythological creatures – like the dragon that stands for wisdom – decorate the columns of the Cao Dai temple

Where to...
Stay

Blue River £
Unbeatably cheap and centrally located accommodation for backpackers and those travelling on a tight budget. Young, friendly staff. This little guesthouse is in a quiet side street near busy Pham Ngu Lao with hundreds of restaurants and bars just round the corner. The modern rooms with laminate floors are simply furnished but have flat TVs, minibars, safes and decent albeit small shower rooms. Own small bar, mopeds for hire, airport transfer service and travel agency offering a variety of tours.

✚ 208 C1
✉ 283/2C Pham Ngu Lao, 1st district
☎ 08 38 37 64 83; www.blueriverhotel.com

Cat Huy £
Consistently good for many years, helpful and friendly: this B&B in a lively area popular with backpackers and hidden in a 6-storey mini-hotel (no lift!), has 10 large and cosy rooms, some surprisingly quiet, with flatscreen TVs, WiFi, mini-bar, good shower rooms; some have balconies, others don't even have a window. You can sample the Vietnamese cuisine to your heart's content at the market right outside the front door.

Insider Tip

✚ 208 C1
✉ 353/28 Pham Ngu Lao, 1st district
☎ 08 39 20 87 16; www.cathuyhotel.com

Duxton ££–£££
Centrally located 4-star hotel popular with business people and tourists alike. The four 2-storey luxury apartments offer every conceivable comfort to make you feel at home, as do the other 200 rooms that are furnished in an unfussy style. A delicious breakfast buffet is served in the mornings and cakes and sweet delicacies with afternoon tea. Not forgetting of course the WiFi, mini-pool, spa and gym.

✚ 209 E2
✉ 63 Nguyen Hue, 1st district
☎ 08 38 22 29 99;
www.saigon.duxtonhotels.com

EMM ££–£££
Fashionable, stylish hotel – a new chain with conspicuously helpful staff. This hotel has just 12 very different rooms, suites and one apartment that are all comparatively cheap and located right in the centre of the city. The pretty, cosy lounge bar on the 11th floor, where you can also have your breakfast with a view over Saigon, is inviting, as is the gym. It is advisable not to book using the hotel website; rooms are to be had at half the price via web portals such as booking.com. WiFi available.

Insider Tip

✚ 209 D4 ✉ 157 Pasteur Street, 3rd district
☎ 08 39 36 21 00; www.emmhotels.com

Grand Hotel £££
Perfect location on Dong Khoi. The journey back in time begins as soon as you enter the wonderful lobby in the old wing of the original two-storey hotel from 1930. There are 230 elegant rooms furnished with lots of wood in this part of the hotel and in the new building. The pool is in the large and beautiful

inner courtyard of the old building. The new section with 20 floors offers far-reaching views over the river and city. The café-bar on the roof is perfect for that evening drink. Good packages available online.

➕ 209 F2 ✉ 8 Dong Khoi, 1st district
☎ 08 39 15 55 55; www.grandhotel.vn

Kingston £–££

Strategically well placed for shopping fans – near Ben Thanh market. 3-star hotel with an impressive marble lobby that promises more than the 100 pleasant and spacious rooms live up to. All have high-speed WiFi; rooms without windows are quieter by the way. Best to steer clear of the spa.

Insider Tip

➕ 209 D2
✉ 52–54 Thu Khoa Huan, 1st district
☎ 08 38 24 55 88; www.kingstonhotel.com.vn

Majestic £££

A classic from days of old where the atmosphere of colonial times still lingers on. Opened in 1925 this hotel on the Saigon River has an impressively ostentatious lobby with chandeliers and lots of marble. Some of the 175 elegant rooms in the colonial style have balconies overlooking the river (rather loud) or Dong Khoi (a little quieter). The quietest rooms face the courtyard with a view of the small pool. Breakfast on the terrace is outstanding; live music is performed in the evenings in the roof bar on the 8th floor.

➕ 209 F2 ✉ 1 Dong Khoi, 1st district
☎ 08 38 29 55 17; www.majesticsaigon.com.vn

Ma Maison ££

Natasha Long's family-run guest-house turns out to be a boutique hotel in a typical if somewhat out-of-the-way residential district, 30 mins. on foot from the tourist area. This oasis with a French feeling has 12 small but cosy rooms in a villa from the 1940s

(no lift), including creaky boards and floor mosaics, WiFi and a garden.

➕ 208 A3/4
✉ 656/52 Cach Mang Thang Tam, 3rd district
☎ 08 38 46 02 63; www.mamaison.vn

Ms. Yang 1+2 £

Staying at Ms. Yang's is a 20 minute walk to the centre but, like 'couch-surfing', means being with two delightful sisters who provide visitors with lots of tips for trips off the beaten track. The four simply furnished rooms have balconies, air-conditioning, WiFi and their own shower rooms. Even Nutella is served at breakfast as is traditional noodle soup. Book well in advance!

➕ 208 C2 ✉ 306/7 Nguyen Thi Minh Khai, Ward 5, 3rd district ☎ 012 03 40 73 48, msyanghomestay@gmail.com

Town House 50/ Town House 23 £

This chain heralds a new generation of backpacker hostels on the Saigon market. The tucked-away, non-smoking guesthouses have 12 modern rooms with WiFi, lovely bathrooms and a hearty breakfast with lots of exotic fruit. The ultra-chic designer hotel (Town House 23) also has a dormitory.

➕ 208 C2 ✉ 50E Bui Thi Xuan and 23 Dang Thi Nhu, 1st district ☎ 09 03 74 09 24.

Villa Song Saigon £££

How about staying in a villa, perhaps as a unique and intimate honeymoon hideaway? This oasis comprises just 23 rooms in a colonial building outside Saigon but right on the river. A complementary shuttle boat service takes you to the city centre in just ten minutes. Pool in the garden, an excellent private restaurant for dinner and a small spa all suggest that such exclusivity comes at a price.

➕ northeast 209 F5 ✉ 197/2 Nguyen Van Huong, Thao Dien (2nd district)
☎ 08 37 44 60 90; www.villasong.com

Where to...
Eat and Drink?

Price
of a double room per night:
£ under VND1m.   **££** VND1–VND2.4m.   **£££** over VND2.4m.

Bun Bo Hue Dong Ba £

This soup kitchen only sells one dish: *bun bo hue*. Huge portions of steaming noodle soup with strips of beef and onion are brought to the table – a classic form of Vietnamese 'fast-food'.
🚏 209 D2 ✉ 110 Nguyen Du (near Ben Thanh market) ☎ 08 62 73 75 89, 09 89 39 39 67; www.bunbohuedongba.com ⏰ 8am–10pm

Com Minh Duc £

Metal tables, plastic bowls and a station-like atmosphere – in this authentic street kitchen that is always very popular you can choose a tasty dish at the window from the pots on display or from the menu. Brisk service and very cheap.
🚏 208 C2 ✉ Nos. 35 and 100 Ton That Tung (northwest of Pham Ngu Lao), 1st district ☎ 08 38 39 22 40 ⏰ Daily 8am–10pm

Eastgate £

This Vietnamese bakery chain is well-known for excellent coffee from its own roastery, **bahn mi** sandwiches, filled croissants and pastries, delicious baked items and little cakes. It also serves soup, snacks and cold beer.
🚏 209 F3 ✉ 8A Le Thanh Ton ☎ 08 66 54 44 45; www.eastgate.vn ⏰ Daily 6:30am–9:30pm

Hoa Tuc ££–£££

This trendy restaurant is in the pretty courtyard of an old opium factory and serves contemporary – but pricey – Vietnamese food. The set lunch however is good value. The manager runs cookery course focussing on street food.
🚏 209 E3 ✉ 74/7 Hai Ba Trung ☎ 08 38 25 84 85; www.hoatuc.com ⏰ Daily 11am–11pm

Pho 2000 £

Ever since Bill Clinton wolfed down his noodle soup here, the prices have shot through the ceiling. This simple canteen-like soup kitchen has since modestly called itself 'Pho for the President'!
🚏 209 E1/2 ✉ Phan Chu Trinh, at Ben Thanh market ☎ 08 38 22 27 88 ⏰ Daily 8am–10pm

Saffron ££–£££

Here you can eat Mediterranean food for a change. Good service but prices like in Europe.
🚏 209 F2/3 ✉ 51 Hai Ba Trung, 1st district ☎ 08 38 24 83 58; www.saffronvietnam.com ⏰ Daily 11:30am–11pm

👪 The Nest £

Tiny eatery and ice cream parlour. While little children play in the sand-pit or paddling pool, the grown-ups enjoy their lunch break. Simple rice dishes and chips but also vegan food, teas, fruit juices and shakes.
🚏 208 C4 ✉ 21/3 Ly Chinh Thang, 3rd district ☎ 09 07 00 02 13; thenestofficial.blogspot.com ⏰ Daily 7:30am–11pm

Wrap & Roll £

Great for finger food fans! This popular snack bar chain offers umpteen variations of (roll-your-own) spring roll and dips and many other things too. Hot-pots in the evening.
🚏 208 C1/2 ✉ 97B Nguyen Trai and 62B Hai Ba Trung, 1st district ☎ 08 38 37 12 31; www.wrap-roll.com ⏰ Daily 10am–9pm

Where to…
Shop

MARKETS

Phan Van Khoe is primarily for food – including all sorts of everything that creeps and crawls.

    Cho An Dong (An Duong Vuong, 5th district, Chinatown), housed in a bunker-like building, is Saigon's biggest market; it's not as touristy and therefore a little cheaper than Ben Thanh (▶63).

    Cho Nguyen Dinh Chieu (1 Le Tu Tai, 3rd district) is a cheap open-air market in the north selling a complete mixture of things from clothing to gold and tea.

CRAFTS & GALLERIES

There are many galleries near the art museum and on Nguyen Van Troi. Antiques-fans will love the wonderfully old-fashioned shops in **Le Cong Kieu**. (Antiques are not allowed to be taken out of the country without an export certificate).

    Don't miss the **'painting streets'** (Tran Phu, Bui Vien) where (faked) masterpieces are going for a song!

SOUVENIRS

Most souvenir shops are on Dong Khoi (expensive), Hai Ba Trung and Le Loi (leather goods) and in the little streets around the backpacker area Pham Ngu Lao.

    Mekong Creations (68 Le Loi, 1st district; tel: 08 22 10 31 10; www.mekong-creations.org; daily 9am–7pm) sells pretty souvenirs made of papier-mâché, bamboo, wicker and water hyacinth, e.g. hats, textiles, bags and quilts made by disadvantaged women.

Where to…
Go Out

Magazines such as *What's on Vietnam*, *Time Out Vietnam*, *Asia Live HCMC* and *Metro*, that are available free in hotels and bars, list what is going on in the evening.

THEATRE

The symphony orchestra performs in the **Old Opera House**/Municipal Theatre (7 Lam Son Square; tel: 08 38 23 74 19; www.hbso.org.vn); the **AO Show** staged there – an entertaining mixture of circus and folklore – is very touristy but nevertheless worth seeing.

    The 🎭 **Rong Vang Golden Dragon Water Puppet Theatre** (55B Nguyen Thi Minh Khai, 1st district, reservations: 08 39 30 21 96; www.golden dragontheatre.com; shows daily 5pm, 6:30pm and 7:45pm) upholds legends and ancient traditions with mythological creatures playing the leading roles in these colourful performances. Only space for 200 spectators – get there early!

SKY BARS

The **Chill Saigon Skybar and Restaurant** is on the 23rd floor of the AB Tower (76 Le Lai, 1st district; tel: 08 38 27 23 72; www.chillsaigon. com; daily 5pm–1am). The 360° panorama makes up for the hefty prices. You can also chill out on the 23rd floor of the Sheraton Tower at **Level 23** (88 Dong Khoi; tel: 08 38 27 28 28; www.level23saigon.com).

FESTIVALS

The Chinese New Year festival **Tet Nguyen Dan** transforms parts of Saigon into a sea of flowers in January/February.

Mekong Delta

 **Little Treats**

Sundowner on the beach

Watching the sunset from one of the beaches on **Phu Quoc** over the Gulf of Thailand is an unforgettable experience (➤78).

Fish salad with a twist

A superb herring salad with glass noodles is served at snack bars on the fishing beach **Bai Kem** on **Phu Quoc** (➤78).

Short trips to Cambodia

The Buddhist country next door is so completely different and yet so near – and a quick trip over the border at **Chau Doc** (➤89) is well worthwhile.

Getting Your Bearings

**The Mekong Delta is about the size of Switzerland – but as flat as
a pancake. A vast network of branching waterways extends over a
length of 5,000km (3,100mi), seething with slumbering amphibian
life! Where this Asian river giant spreads out its eight arms over
its last 200km (125mi) and is divided by a shipping channel
and a network of thousands of smaller canals, everything
conceivable glides and chugs through its delta. Even the
markets here float...**

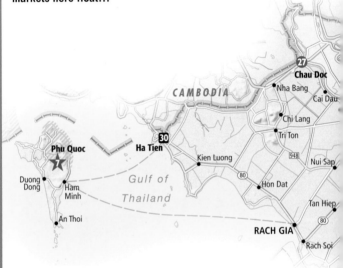

Green in every imaginable shade dominates the endless
labyrinth of waterways that branch off Song Cuu Long,
the 'Nine Dragon River', as it is known in Vietnam. It flows
through the 'nation's rice store', never-ending paddy fields
that are harvested three times a year, and bamboo and
palm forests. The delta only makes up 10% of Vietnam's
overall area but supplies half the nation's rice crop. The
fertile alluvial soil around the provincial capital Can Tho
is not only where rice farmers live but also fishermen,
prawn and fruit farmers. The home of fish breeders is
Chau Doc, near the Cambodian border, when tons of
thrasing fish flourish in 'cellars' under houseboats.

Drift along the canals past villages, orchards and mangrove swamps and explore the floating markets, take a
cycle ride along idyllic tree-lined avenues or simply enjoy
beach life to your heart's content on islands like Phu Quoc
and Con Dao – a trip through the Mekong Delta is certainly
never boring.

**The Mekong
Delta is
Vietnam's
rice store
with 3 million
rice farmers
looking after
the plant
and its need
for masses
of water**

74

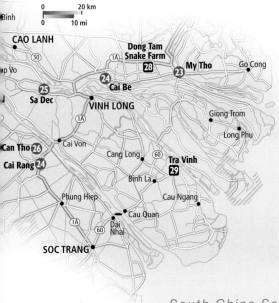

Mekong Delta

Three Perfect Days

Most organised tours depart from Saigon on a two-day trip through the delta. The following is an alternative suggestion for a very varied, three-day tour in a hire car with a chauffeur which takes in the waterways, a pilgrim mountain, floating markets and the colonial heritage before relaxing on a beach on one of the two islands in the south.

Day One

Morning
Make an early start, leaving Saigon for ㉓ **My Tho** (►81). This trading centre is on a peninsula with the Tien Giang River on three sides and criss-crossed by a number of canals that are spanned by fragile-looking 'monkey bridges' made of intertwined bamboo. To get a real feeling for the delta's amphibian flair take a boat to the river island **Ben Tre** (►82). There are any number of eateries for a lunch break serving the local speciality – elephant ear fish with jasmine tea.

Afternoon
The imposing 1,553m (5,095ft)-long My Thuan Bridge over the Tien Giang can be seen from afar. On the other side is ㉕ **Sa Dec** (►85) where you can stroll along the road down the river to where Marguerite Duras' novel **The Lover** is set and where it was filmed.

Evening
Settle into your hotel in ㉖ **Can Tho** (►86) and take a stroll in the evening along the lively riverside promenade Ninh Khieu.

Day Two

Morning
The early bird catches the worm – the women at ㉔ **Cai Rang** floating market (right, ►83) are already paddling down the Tien Giang at 5am to sell their wares. And by 8am there are more tourist barges than boats selling rice and vegetables on the river.

Afternoon
Head up the N91 for about 150km (95mi) to the northwest to the Cambodian border at ㉗ **Chau Doc** (►90), from where there is a wonderful panoramic view across the paddy fields from the pilgrim mountain Nui

Sam (right) where you can watch one of the most beautiful sunsets Vietnam has to offer.

Evening
Stay the night in a hotel in Chau Doc. The choice may not be large but one of the most beautiful hotels in the colonial style anywhere in the country can be found here on Hau Giang River – the **Victoria** (▶ 93).

Day Three

Morning
After having a quick look around this quiet little town and its floating fish farms you may be interested in visiting **Ba Chuc** (▶ 90), a memorial to Vietnamese victims of the Khmer Rouge in Cambodia, 55km (35mi) away.

Afternoon
Time for the beach, e.g. at ⭐**Phu Quoc** (▶ 78) – that can be reached either by boat or air from the little town of Rach Gia on the Mekong or by taking a speedboat from **30 Ha Tien** (▶ 92). (Give the old night ferries that are no longer seaworthy a wide berth!).

If you intend heading back to Saigon, plan at least 6 hours for the 300km (186mi) return journey as traffic jams are the order of the day.

⭐ Phu Quoc

Phu Quoc, the country's largest island, is destined to become Vietnam's Phuket – with 2–3 million visitors a year! The calm before the storm can still be enjoyed on a total of 40km (25mi) of beach with coconut palms and the jungle as a backdrop.

Phu Quoc lies in the far south near the Cambodian border in the Gulf of Thailand. Covering an area of 586km² (226mi²), two-thirds of the 'Island of 99 Mountains' is a protected national park and forms part of a UNESCO biosphere reserve. Apart from this, Phu Quoc has considerable additional potential as a tourist destination. The island, that just 10 years ago was an insider tip, now has an international airport, luxury accommodation and hotel complexes as well as a 27-hole golf course. 'Do things in a big way' is the motto in this 'special economic zone'. By 2020 a pier for luxury liners, two more golf courses and a casino are planned.

Beaches

A mass of building plots the length of the most beautiful beaches in the west and south have now been staked-out. The most popular main beach, **Bai Truong** –'Long Beach' – is a golden yellow strip of sand with lots of palm trees and lined with countless bungalow complexes, hotels of several storeys and beach bars. It extends more than 20km (12.5mi) as far as the little fishing harbour An Thoi at the southern tip of the island, interrupted every now and again with rocky areas and fishing villages. A range of leisure activities – from kiting and tennis to billiards and 'jungle yoga' – provide a welcome break from all that relaxing on the beach. Further inland, the sprawling **Long Beach Village** has everything to offer that you could possibly wish on holiday.

Beautiful **Bai Sao** (Star Beach) right in the south near An Thoi, nestling between densely forested hills, has a Caribbean air about it with fine snow-white sand and palm trees. This once deserted beach is now well visited by day-trippers. **Bai Kem**, on the south tip, was used by the military up until 2014 but is now open to anglers and tourists. It's not really the best place for sunbathing as the atmosphere is spoilt by the early-morning fish market, the huts and all the rubbish.

Lovely curved **Bai Ong Lang** on the west coast towards the north is still a peaceful and remote stretch of beach between rocky outcrops. **Bai Vung Bau**, a little further north, is a good snorkelling area. Neighbouring **Bai Dai**, an elongated but narrow beach with casuarina trees belongs to the Vinpearl golf course. On beautiful Bai Ganh Dau, some 500m long, near the village of the same name at the northwestern-most point, and on **Cua Can Peninsula** in the north, there are a number of beach bars that cater for sunbathers' needs. Small, unspoilt **Bai Thom** is tucked away in the extreme northeast. Nearby **Phu Hai Crocodile Farm**, home to some 2,500 animals, is open to the public. *Insider Tip*

Island Sightseeing

Put a little spice in your life and visit the pepper island Phu Quoc – where the beautiful beaches are nothing to be sneezed at!

The few sights in the island town of **Duong Dong** (pop. 60,000) are clustered around the harbour – a local museum, fish sauce factories, three pepper plantations, a lighthouse and little Dinh Cau Pagoda dedicated to Thien Hau, the sea goddess, that looks as if it is balanced on a rock.

A short walk to the southeast of Duong Dong leads to a number of little waterfalls such as popular **Suoi Tranh**. The **national park** in the north of the island includes hills that rise to 600m (2,000ft), bushland, majestic giant trees and grasslands as well as mangroves along the coast.

VIETNAMESE 'MAGGI' SAUCE

Around 10 million litres of the fish sauce *nuoc mam* are produced every year on Phu Quoc from the little, protein-rich fish called *ca om*. These salted sardines are kept in barrels for about a year where they ferment and are then bottled. Lemon juice, vinegar, fresh chili, sugar, pepper, garlic and coriander are added, as required. A taste for this strongly aromatic spice is something foreigners seldom acquire; for the Vietnamese it is just like adding a little salt.

Mekong Delta

Some 1,000 different types of plant, including 23 genera of orchid alone, more than 100 species of bird and 28 kinds of mammal, such as langurs, macaques and civet cats, make up the varied flora and fauna. Although the majority of this wilderness is still a re-stricted military area there are several trails through the park, some up to 5km (3mi) long. Good places to start from are near the villages Ganh Dau, Rach Vem and Rach Tram and on the main road between Duong Dong and Bai Thom.

Heading towards Bai Sao in the south will take you past the **Phu Quoc Coconut Tree Prison Museum** – a rather bizarre set-up. Life-sized figures of soldiers, guards and prisoners, representing the 40,000 or so Viet Cong fighters who were held here, have been placed among watchtowers, huts and barbed wire.

Phu Quoc's beaches now have the infrastructure to match, with bars and much more

TAKING A BREAK

Seafood, as fresh as it comes, can be bought at **Dinh Cau night market** in Duong Dong (Vo Thi Sau Street, £) every day from 5pm onwards. Tasty treats are served at little metal tables.

---

212 A3
Hydrofoils from Rach Gia and Ha Tien
International Airport Phu Quoc: regular flights from Saigon to Tho & Rach Gia

Phu Quoc Island Information Center
26 Nguyen Trai, near the harbour in Duong Dong
077 3 99 41 81; www.phuquocislandguide.co

Phu Hai Crocodile Farm
212 A3 Da Chong, near Bai Thom and the pier
Daily 8am–4pm VND20,000

Phu Quoc Coconut Tree Prison Museum (Cay Dua Prison):
212 A3 c. 5km (3mi) north of An Thoi
Daily 8am–11am, 1:30pm–5pm, Museum Sat, closed Sun Free

INSIDER INFO

Phu Quoc is considered one of the best places for **diving** in Vietnam (best conditions Nov–April, lots of rain May–Oct). The underwater canyons and coral reefs are alive with seahorses, reef sharks, stingrays, barracudas, starry pufferfish, sea snakes and scorpionfish. Popular places to visit include the turtle island, Hon Doi Moi, in the northwest in shallower water and the An Thoi archipelago of 26 little islands in the south. Tours are organised by **Vietnam Explorer PADI Dive Center** (36 Tran Hung Dao, Duong Dong; tel: 077 3 84 63 72; www.vnexplorer.jimdo.com), among others.

㉓ My Tho

My Tho is the tourist heart of the Mekong Delta. The only thing most day-trippers from Saigon see of this up-and-coming commercial centre on the banks of the Tien Giang is the pier. From here, they board one of the countless boats lining the promenade to explore everyday life in the delta and its countless islands.

Once the day-trippers have left in the afternoon things become quiet again. This is the time for a stroll in the shade down the riverside promenade past the old villas or for a visit to the lively **market** on Bao Dinh Canal. **Vinh Trang Pagoda** (Chua Vinh Trang), some 3km (2mi) to the east, on the other side of the canal, is well worth visiting. This building, around 200 years old, is surrounded by carefully pruned trees and lotus ponds. Among its many statues are three huge Buddhas or Bodhisattvas: a reclining Buddha on the threshold to Nirvana, a 'Happy Buddha' – as most tour guides describe well-fed, satisfied and permanently smiling Di Lac (Mile Fo) – and a large upright statue of Quan Am, the goddess of mercy.

Insider Tip

Other Sights in the Area

Rattling boats leave the pier on the promenade for trips down the river and to the **river islands in the area**. Chunky, half-rounded barges and sampans with a watchful eye painted on the bow criss-cross the water, fully laden with coconuts, rambutans, grapefruits and rice. At some stage passengers have to change to smaller boats rowed by women standing at the back, rather like gondoliers. You glide along narrow channels past luxuriant tropic vegetation with plantations of banana and orange trees, bonsais and coconut palms. Here and there markets and little temples suddenly appear among the undergrowth.

Fairy tale-like Vinh Trang Pagoda with its playful ornamental decoration

'IT BECAME NECESSARY TO DESTROY THE TOWN TO SAVE IT'
This – possibly invented – statement, allegedly made by a US major and quoted by the AP correspondent Peter Arnett about the bombing of Ben Tre in 1968, makes the absurdity of the Vietnam War that much clearer. The thick jungle in the area around My Tho was thought to be one of the Viet Cong's strongholds – and therefore became a principle target for the US 'defoliation program' using napalm and Agent Orange. A memorial has been erected on the 'Island of 1000 Widows' to commemorate those who died.

Insider Tip

One place to visit that is not far away is the 'dragon island' **Tan Lon** – a lovely place for a walk in the shade of the palm and fruit trees. Most day-trippers however head for the idyllic neighbouring province of **Ben Tre**, 12km (7.5mi) south of My Tho.

A must for many is a trip to the river islands **An Binh** and **Thoi Son** which are a buzz of activity due to the puffed rice, coconut sweets and incense stick factories, bonsai and lychee farms and the brickworks. A visit to a craft village is always an opportunity to nibble a coconut or sample rice spirits or tea to the traditional jingle-jangle of a group of musicians. You can – and are expected – to buy souvenirs on such outings like conical hats, snake liquor or ginger marmalade.

Tourists glide past mangroves and palm fronds in sampans

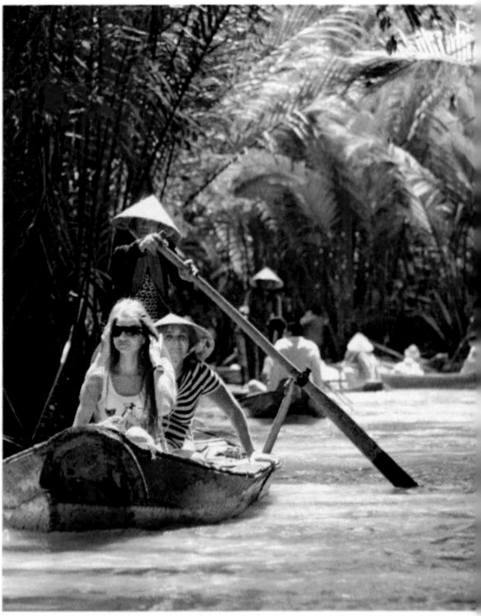

TAKING A BREAK

Masses of street kitchens with 1001 pots of delicious food can be found at the **night market** (£) at Le Thi Hong Gam on the river from 5pm until 10pm.

213 E3

Vinh Trang Pagoda
Nguyen Trung Truc
073 3 87 34 27
Daily 7:30am–noon, 2pm–5pm
Free

INSIDER INFO

- **Boats** can be hired for VND70,000–VND100,000 an hour for two people; a whole day costs around VND600,000.
- Things can be pretty chaotic at weekends and on public holidays. The epicentre is Rach Mieu bridge in My Tho – the further away one goes the quieter it becomes! Perfect for a visit to **Go Cong Dong**, for example, where scallop farms can be found along the river.

㉔ Cai Rang & Cai Be

The floating markets in the Mekong Delta form the region's economic backbone. Two of the most interesting are to be found in the towns Cai Rang and Cai Be, some 70km (45mi) apart. You can easily spend hours just watching the colourful comings and goings – whereby early risers are undoubtedly at an advantage!

The canals are lined with seemingly endless paddy fields or plantations bursting with exotic fruit such as longans, bananas, oranges, mangosteens, mangos, durians, papayas, melons and pineapples. Even before the sun rises there is a mass of activity on the **myriad of market boats**. You can see what is being sold if you look at the top of the long bamboo poles where a coconut or pineapple, cucumber or taro swings around up in the air.

The fruit the market women sell in Cai Rang comes straight from the plantations in the area

Cai Rang

The 🍴 **floating market at Cai Rang** near Can Tho is the largest of its kind in south Vietnam and, at the same time, a huge magnet for tourists in the region. Fruit and vegetables, noodle soup and all sorts of household goods are proffered for sale from countless little craft, houseboats and hopelessly overladen barges. It is best to hire a boat from Ninh Kieu pier in Can Tho as early in the morning as possible and, bearing the 30-minute journey in mind, get there well before all the other tourist boats. By 8am it is full and video and mobile phone cameras sway to the rhythm of tour guides' megaphone commentaries blasting out from both port and starboard!

Insider Tip

Cai Be

The smaller 🍴 **floating market in Cai Be** near Vinh Long is also a good way to get a glimpse of what shopping on water is like. You should be here as early as possible too.

Baskets piled
high with exotic
fruit at the
floating market
in Cai Be

And perhaps you can persuade the guide or boatsman afterwards to make a detour to the fruit plantations and rice noodle factories (► Insider Info).

TAKING A BREAK

Due to the early start, breakfast on-board your boat is just the thing needed. And there's no shortage of fresh coffee and fruit. The market women are pleased to be able to earn something from the tourists rather than just being extras filmed through a zoom.

Floating market in Cai Rang
✚ 213 D3
✉ Da Sau bridge, 7km (4.5mi) southwest of Can Tho
🕐 Daily 5am–1pm

Floating market in Cai Be
✚ 213 E3
✉ Vinh Long 🕐 Daily 5am–5pm

INSIDER INFO

- **A boat** for two people can be chartered for VND70,000–VND100,000 an hour; a whole day costs around VND600,000 (depending on the season, the demand and how good you are at haggling).
- Cai Be can also be reached from Saigon by car; the journey takes about 2½ hrs.
- If you can't get enough of life on the water you can visit the quieter and more authentic markets in **Phong Dien** (a further 10km/6.2mi southwest of Cai Rang or 20km/12.5mi southwest of Can Tho; daily 5am–5pm) and **Phung Hiep** (25km/15.5mi southeast of Can Tho on the N1; daily 5am–5pm).
- Quick-witted market traders know how to get the **best prices** for their wares. Guides and boatsmen can generally say what the typical price should be. A pineapple, for example, at the time of writing this guidebook, cost around VND10,000.
- At **Sau Hoai's Rice Noodle Factory** (Lo Hu Tieu Sau Hoai, 476/14 Vong Cung, An Binh, Ninh Kieu, 8km (5mi) outside Can Tho; tel: 0918 21 42 34, 0922 15 55 51, Mon–Sat 6am–10am) Hoai's son explains the different stages in the manufacturing process from tapioca to the finished noodle or little noodle cakes. You can also have breakfast here with, of course, as is customary, a big bowl of noodle soup…

Insider
Tip

Insider
Tip

㉕ Sa Dec

Stroll around Sa Dec and explore the original sites in Marguerite Duras' novel *The Lover*. The French in particular are drawn to the places mentioned in this autobiographical story. The film of the same name, directed by Jean Jacques Annaud, was also made in this little town.

Duras, whose mother was a French teacher, was born in Vietnam and lived in Sa Dec between 1928 and 1932. She fell in love with a man from a rich Chinese business family, thirteen years her senior. It was not until 1971 that the former 'lover', Huynh Thuy Le – by then an elderly man – phoned Duras while on a visit to Paris and confessed his life-long love of her. The Chinese man died in 1972. His house, built in 1895, is on the river and was used as a government office by the anti-drug authority for many years. The imposing and elegant **villa** was opened as a museum in 2007. Architecturally it is a combination of far-eastern and western (French) stylistic elements; the predominantly Chinese interior decoration is in reds and gold with shrines and antiques.

A tiled roof in the style of a north Vietnamese padoda and a delightful plasterwork façade mark the striking exterior of Huynh Thuy Le's villa

The rest of Sa Dec is equally worth exploring. Visit one of the last remaining Chinese single-storey **rows of shops** and the **bustling markets**. The many flower markets in the town that the colonial settlers once called the 'garden of Cochinchina' are a huge tourist attraction.

Insider Tip

TAKING A BREAK

Thuy (£; 439 Huong Vuong; daily 8am–8pm), serving Vietnamese and a few western dishes, is a popular place. Hot-pots **(lau)** eaten sitting on plastic chairs or loungers are served along the river bank in the evening.

➕ 213 D3

Museum in Huynh Thuy Le's Villa
✉ 225 A Nguyen Hue
🕐 Daily 10am–5pm 💲 VND30,000

INSIDER INFO

Duras fans may want to spend a night in the museum villa; the two simple **guest rooms** ooze character and charm (£; book through the Dong Thap Tourist Company in Cao Lanh; Dong Thap; tel: 067 3 87 30 25).

㉖ Can Tho

The university city of Can Tho, the largest in the Mekong Delta, is a good starting point for excursions in the surrounding area. From here, you can visit the floating markets in the delta or explore the mangroves and wetlands. As the countryside is flat, it is a perfect base for a relaxed cycle tour over several days. The city itself however also has a number of sights worth seeing.

The **Municipal Museum** in Can Tho boasts a surprisingly large collection with more than 5,000 exhibits – with finds dating from the ancient Oc Eo culture to natural history and the region's flora and fauna, agricultural implements and objects connected with traditional medicine and folklore. Weapons from both Vietnam wars are also on display. A presentation by the Can Tho Institute focuses on research in rice growing and aquaculture in the delta region.

Munirangsyaram Temple (also known as Munirensay Temple) is on the same road nearer the city centre. Entered through an imposing Angkor Wat-style gateway, this Buddhist temple, built in 1946, is where the local Khmer community meet. A marvellous 1.5m (5ft)-high Sakyamuni Buddha statue under the sacred Bodhi fig tree can be seen on the upper floor in the main building.

A small, brightly-painted **Ong pagoda** from 1894, situated near the promenade along the river bank, is a fascinating sight. Smoke billowing from huge incense spirals envelop the many Chinese Confucian statues.

Can Tho is the main hub in the delta from where a network of waterways takes visitors to floating markets and through dense mangrove forests

Life in the Big City

In the evening, the riverside promenade is teeming with life. The masses of bars and cafés in Ninh Khieu Park, lit up by

'Uncle Ho' keeps a watchful eye over the lively crowds of people along the riverside in Can Tho

garlands of fairy lights, do a brisk trade while a huge, silver-coloured statue of Ho Chi Minh watches over what is going on down by the river. The ear-splitting restaurant and party boats with brightly flashing lights ply their way up and down the nearby waterways from 6pm onwards.

Day trips

Early morning **boat trips up tributaries of the Mekong River**, with a visit to one of the floating markets (►83), are among the top tourist attractions. Hobby ornithologists will enjoy day trips by boat or moped taxi to one of several bird sanctuaries, e.g. the 32-acre **Bang Lang** stork reserve, 50km (30mi) northwest of Can Tho, that is home to some 500,000 white storks. Another stork sanctuary can be found in the province of Tra Vinh further to the east ►91).

The **Bat Temple** of Chua Doi near Soc Trang is not only interesting for its pictures from the life of Buddha but also for its colony of bats that lives in the trees around the temple. In the late afternoon they wake up and set off on their nocturnal search for food. Some bats have a wing span of up 1.50m (5ft).

TAKING A BREAK

Hai Ba Trung, the riverside promenade, is lined with one eatery after another. You will find a huge selection of seafood and Vietnamese dishes, ranging from spring rolls to hot-pots, in the **indoor market** right on the river, e.g. in **Sao Hom** (££, 50 Hai Ba Trung; tel: 0710 3 81 56 16; daily 6am–11pm) which also has an extensive list of ice creams.

✚ 213 D3

Can Tho Tourist
✉ 50 Hai Ba Trung (on the river)
☎ 0710 3 82 18 52; www.canthotourist.info; www.cantho.gov.vn

Municipal Museum
✉ 1 Hoa Binh ☎ 0710 3 82 09 55
🕐 Fri–Mon 8am–11am, Sat–Sun also 6:30pm–9pm, Tue–Thu 2pm–5pm 🎟 Free

Munirangsyaram Temple
✉ 36 Hoa Binh ☎ 0710 3 81 60 22
🕐 Daily 8am–11:30am and 2pm–5pm 🎟 Free

Mekong Delta

Ong Pagoda
✉ 32 Hai Ba Trung, Ninh Kieu
🕐 Daily 7am–6pm 🎫 Free

Bang Lang (Vuon Co)
✉ Thot Not (45km/28mi northwest of Can Tho)
🕐 Daily 6am–6pm 🎫 VND8,000

Bat Temple
✉ Soc Trang (65km/40mi southeast of Can Tho)
🕐 Daily 8am–6pm 🎫 Free

INSIDER INFO

- Anyone who wants to get to know the country and its people that much better may like the idea of a **two or three-day cycling tour** through the Mekong Delta, starting and finishing in Can Tho. A route some 80km (50mi) long follows concrete paths and avenues partly shaded by coconut palms, through bamboo and banana plantations and past grapefruit and orange trees. Bridges big and small cross the countless canals and waterways. And you will always have a chance to chat to the local fruit farmers and vilagers. In **Tra On** a floating market waits to be explored. Take a ferry or a private boat (don't forget to haggle!) to cross the Tien Giang, a branch of the Mekong, into the neighbouring province of **Tra Vinh** (▶ 91) which is less touristy. Enjoy a break at one of the many Khmer Buddhist temples. Eat your fill of little coconut sweets made in the family-run 'coconut candy' factories in **Mo Cay** or exotic fruit from the plantations in **Ben Tre** (▶ 82). This tour can be booked, e.g. through **Sinhbalo Adventure Travel** (283/20 Pham Ngu Lao, Saigon; tel: 08 3 8 37 67 66; www.sinhbalo.com; www.cyclingvietnam.net), with pre-arranged 'homestay' accommodation.

- The cruise operator **Mekong Eyes** (9/150 KDC no. 9, 30 Thang 4, Can Tho; tel: 0710 3 78 35 86, mobile hotline 093 3 36 07 86; www.mekongeyes.com) is a German-operated company in Can Tho that offers tours of the delta on a fleet of converted **rice barges** (▶ below) which have up to 30 pretty double cabins for trips lasting several days.

㉗ Chau Doc

A mixture of different peoples lives in the city of Chau Doc in the Mekong Delta – Vietnamese, Cambodian Buddhist Khmer, Muslim Chams and Chinese. It is known for its fish farming in particular and thousands of fish are nurtured as 'sub-tenants' in water tanks under houses.

Fishing nets in the canals off the Mekong are attached to spindly rods like octopus tentacles

Since time immemorial, the people here and the river have lived in symbiosis side by side. The **fish farming tanks** next to and in the water produce more than 100,000 tons of fish and prawns every year. Most breeders live in houses that float on empty oil barrels. Catfish bred for export press against the nets and wire mesh below the waterline.

Different Religions Coexisting Peacefully

The city on the west bank of Hau Giang (also called Bassac), a tributary of the Mekong, is marked by its numerous Khmer temples, Champa mosques and churches. Ferries provide a link to the other side of the river where the stilt homes of the Chams, a Muslim minority, are to be found. In **Chau Giang** craftspeople can be watched producing finely woven wrap-around skirts. Outside prayer times you can enjoy a lovely view of the city from the top of the minaret in the **Mubarak mosque**.

Insider Tip

One of the most important places of pilgrimage in the country, which boasts a number of temples, is also in the vicinity. **Nui Sam** lies at an altitude of 230m (755ft) and is well known for the **Via Ba Pagoda**, built in 1820, that draws up to 2.5 million visitors during the Via Ba festival in April/May. Protected behind glass, numerous valuable offerings brought by pilgrims can be admired in a separate room. These include mother-of-pearl vases as tall as a man, pearl necklaces and gold ingots.

Mekong Delta

Ba Chuc, a Khmer pagoda to the southwest near the Cambodian border and now a memorial site, is testimony to the fact that things have not always been so peaceful in this region. The skulls and bones of 3,157 civilians who were murdered in April 1978 in a massacre perpetrated by the Khmer Rouge on Vietnamese territory, are housed in a huge, futuristic building.

Not Only for Hobby Ornithologists

Another popular place to visit is **Tra Su Cajuput** bird sanctuary. The **xuong ba la**, steered by women paddlers who stand at the stern, glide across a green carpet of water-fern along peaceful canals in which the roots of mangrove trees rise out of the water like splayed stalks. Little egrets and black herons, storks, ducks and many other waterbirds can be glimpsed in the water or the treetops.

All sorts of devotional objects can be bought in Nui Sam (below); elaborately decorated Khmer temples can be admired around Chau Doc, such as in Tri Tou (bottom)

TAKING A BREAK

There are food stands and tiny eateries around the **indoor market** on Bach Dang. Simply point to what you want, sit down on one of the plastic stools and enjoy your meal.

✚ 209 F3

Mekong Chau Doc Travel
✉ 14 Nguyen Huu Canh
☎ 091 8 66 92 36 (Mrs. San);
www.mekongchaudoctravel.com

Via Ba Pagoda (Ba Chua Xu)
✉ 5km (3mi) south of Chau Doc
🕐 Daily 8am–6pm 🎟 Free

Tra Su Cajuput
✉ Van Giao, Tinh Bien (25km/15mi south of Chau Doc), An Giang ☎ 076 87 74 23
🕐 Daily 6am–5pm
🎟 VND75,000 for a 1-hr. boat trip

Ba Chuc
✉ 55km (35mi) southwest of Chau Doc
🕐 Daily 8am–4pm 🎟 Free

INSIDER INFO

Insider Tip

Speedboats operate between Chau Doc and **Cambodia**, e.g. the **Victoria Hotels'** boat (www.victoriahotels.asia). Public boat services such as **Blue Cruiser** (www.bluecruiser.com) and **Hang Chau Express Boat** (www.hangchautourist.vn) in the capital Phnom Penh are cheaper. A visa for Cambodia can be acquired on arrival (US$30 + US$4 of 'other fees', 2 passport photos are needed!).

At Your Leisure

28 🍴 Dong Tam Snake Farm

40 different species of snake are bred on the farm for their skins, including 100 or so king cobras, the heaviest weighing a proud 12kg. But the business-like Vietnamese are not merely looking to make a big profit here. The farm primarily **produces serum** for the 1000 Vietnamese a year who are bitten by snakes and treated at the local emergency centre. By the way, anyone who buys a snake product, here or anywhere else in the delta, can expect to have problems at customs (➤ 204). Snake meat can be sampled in the adjoining eatery.

✚ 213 E3
✉ 10km (6.5mi) west of My Tho, Binh Duc
🕐 Daily 7am–6pm 🎫 VND20,000

29 Tra Vinh

Nowhere else are there as many temples – 141 in all. The town also attracts visitors because of its stork popu-lation; more than 100 storks live on the site of the **Hang pagoda** alone, some 6km (3.75mi) south of the centre. They can best be watched in the morning. The more than 100-year-old **Sam Rong Ek Temple**, a little outside the town, is a beautiful example of Cambodian Buddhist temple architecture. Garudas, mythological bird-like creatures, support a stepped tiled roof. Inside, there are several colourful, almost life-like statues of Buddha. **Ong Pagoda** on the lake Ba Om is dedicated to the heroic, red-faced general Quan Cong who peers down somewhat grimly from a wall painting. The red and golden interior with carved wooden shrines, Chinese calligraphy and huge incense spirals is impressive.

Sam Rong Ek Temple (Chua Samrong Ek)
✚ 213 E3
✉ 4km (2.5mi) south of the centre of Tra Vinh
🕐 Daily 8am–5pm 🎫 Free

Ong Pagoda (Chua Ong)
✚ 213 E3
✉ Dien Bien Phu
🕐 Daily 8am–5pm 🎫 Free

Touristy but interesting – a visit to the snake farm

Guarding the tomb of the Mac Cuu dynasty

The endlessly long sandy An Hai Beach on Con Son

30 Ha Tien

This pleasant little coastal town is some 80km (50mi) southwest of Chau Doc. More and more tourists now pass through it on their way overland to Cambodia via the border crossing just 10km (6.25mi) to the northwest, or to the island of **Phu Quoc** (➤ 78), an hour away, reached by modern catamaran hydrofoils and ferries. It is however worth spending a little longer in this lovely area that the Vietnamese call the 'Ha Long Bay of the South'. Long sandy beaches can be found on the **Hong Chong** peninsula – the only ones on the mainland in the Mekong Delta, several caves steeped in history in the typical karst landscape and a number of tombs of local dynasties from the early 19th century, such as the **Mac Cuu** family on Nui Lang. ✚ 212 B3

Mac Cuu Tombs (Lang Mac Cuu)
✉ Mac Tu Hoang, 3km (2mi) northwest of the centre 🕐 7am–6pm 🎟 Free

into a trendy holiday destination having shaken off its inglorious past as a prison island. From 1862 onwards, the French – and later the South Vietnamese and the Americans – held around 12,000 political prisoners here, some in cells known as 'tiger cages'. Ton Duc Thang, Ho Chi Minh's deputy and later president of Vietnam, was imprisoned here for seventeen years.

As a **national park** the archipelago is a protected area and is especially popular with divers. There are more than 1300 species of marine animals and fish that live among the intact coral reefs. Hawksbill sea turtles and green sea turtles, among others, lay their eggs on the beaches here in May/June and September. Dolphins, whales and the dugong that is threatened with extinction swim in these waters too. ✚ 213 E1
✈ Daily from Saigon (45 mins.)

31 Con Dao

The Con Dao archipelago in the South China Sea, covering 76km² (29mi²), is made up of sixteen islands. The mountainous main island, **Con Son**, is gradually turning

31

Where to...
Stay

Price
of a double room per night:
£ under VND1m. **££** VND1–VND2.4m. **£££** over VND2.4m.

BEN TRE

Oasis £
This family-run, quietly situated hotel on the riverbank opposite Ben Tre is a perfect base. Nine, simply-furnished rooms with air-conditioning and bathrooms are arranged around a small pool in an inner courtyard with hammocks. The owners, a New Zealand/Vietnamese husband and wife team, look after their guests and are happy to help organise trips, whether by arranging guided tours and giving tips for excursions or hiring bikes or mopeds.

➕ 213 E3
✉ 151C My An C, My Thanh An, Ben Tre
☎ 075 3 83 88 00, 075 2 46 77 99; http://bentrehoteloasis.com

CAN THO

Kim Tho ££
This 12-storey, 3-star hotel at the end of the river promenade provides a welcome platter of fruit in its 51 well-furnished rooms, each with a modern bathroom. WiFi and a very good buffet breakfast. The roof bar offers the best views.

➕ 213 D3 ✉ 1A Ngo Gia Tu
☎ 0710 3 81 75 17; www.kimtho.com

Nam Mon £
This modern 'boutique-style' hotel, run by Bryan and his wife Truc, is 3km (2mi) from the riverside promenade and is popular with young guests. Pleasant rooms with air-conditioning, WiFi and TV, large shower rooms and a junior suite.

Lovely roof terrace, helpful tour organisation, bikes available for hire.

➕ 213 D3
✉ C 233/4 Nguyen Van Linh, Hung Loi
☎ 0710 6 25 08 66; www.nammonhotel.com

CHAU DOC

Trung Nguyen £
This popular hotel has 15 rooms on four floors (some with balconies and WiFi). Being right next to the market you have to contend with noise from 4am onwards – the higher up the building the quieter! The staff are especially friendly and helpful and provide reliable help arranging tours and transfers.

➕ 212 C4 ✉ 86 Bach Dang
☎ 076 3 56 15 61

Victoria Chau Doc £££
A luxury hotel, the best in Chau Doc. Elegant rooms and suites with fascinating views of what is going on along the river and of the pool. A hotel speedboat takes guests on excursions to Cambodia.

➕ 212 C4 ✉ 1 Le Loi
☎ 076 3 86 50 10; www.victoriahotels.asia

CON DAO

Six Senses Con Dao £££
This beautiful complex is considered the ultimate trend-setter with regards to luxury and pampering. Guests in the beach-side villas with a pool can even enjoy the services of their own butler.

➕ 213 E1 ✉ Bai Dat Doc, Con Son
☎ 064 3 83 12 22;
www.sixsenses.com/sixsensescondao

Mekong Delta

MY THO

Island Lodge ££

This French-run hotel is hidden away on Thoi Son, an island in the Mekong. 12 rustically but tastefully furnished rooms with rattan and bamboo furniture with the benefit of modern bathrooms, views of the river from the verandas of some rooms and espresso machines. A number of pavilions are scattered around the garden; fusion cuisine is served in the restaurant. Large pool right next to the river. This all makes it not difficult to want to stay at least three days – the minimum period of stay required.

✚ 213 E3
✉ 390 Ap Thoi Binh, Xa Thoi Son, My Tho
☎ 073 6 51 90 00; www.theislandlodge.com.vn

PHU QUOC

Chen Sea £££

Prices on Phu Quoc have shot up over the past few years. As one of a Thai chain of luxury hotels this may not exactly be a bargain but it is a chic, quietly situated beach hotel complex with 36 'villas', some two storeys, offering large rooms and parquet floors. Guests can look forward to huge bathrooms (some with showers in the open air), private pools and a jacuzzi overlooking the sea. Other plus points include a large pool in the palm garden, cookery and salsa courses, massages, meditation and tai chi.

✚ 212 A3 ✉ Bai Xep, Bai Ong Lang ☎ 077 3 99 58 95; www.centarahotelsresorts.com

Coco Palm Beach ££

This bungalow complex on the most beautiful stretch of Ong Lang Beach opened in 2012. 13 small, brick-built structures with plain interiors are scattered around the Vietnamese owners' lovely landscaped grounds. Nice, little, natural-stone bathrooms open to the sky. The breakfast, served outside, could be a little more generous.

✚ 212 A3 ✉ Bai Ong Lang
☎ 077 3 98 79 79; www.cocopalmphuquoc.com

Paris Beach £–£££

Quietly situated bungalow complex in the medium (overpriced) category, rather off the beaten track in Bai Truong. Vastly varying prices – and lots of cats and dogs. The rooms are simply furnished but do have mosquito nets and verandas overlooking the garden or sea. The big plus point is the pool (with a children's area); the beach becomes very narrow when there is a heavy swell.

✚ 212 A3 ✉ Cau Ba Phong, Cua Lap ☎ 077 3 99 45 48; www.phuquocparisbeach.com

Peppercorn Beach £££

One of just three resorts on remote, (virtually) private Ganh Dao Beach. Guests enjoy a family-like atmosphere with Linh and her family staying in lovely, very comfortable, if slightly overpriced bungalow suites right on the beach. Book early! Good own restaurant and bar.

✚ 212 A3 ✉ To 8, Ap Chuong Vich, Bai Ganh Dao ☎ 077 3 98 95 67; www.peppercornbeachresortvn.com

Thai Tan Tien £–££

Long Beach is just 50m or so from the simple cabins, down a small boardwalk. Terraces with hammocks, rustic beach eatery. The photos on the website however are a little misleading.

✚ 212 A3 ✉ Tran Hung Dao
☎ 077 3 84 77 82; www.thaitantienresort.com

TRA VINH

🏠 Suonsia Homestay £

45km (28mi) southwest of Tra Vinh. Six simple rooms with bamboo beds and shower rooms rented out by the family. Bikes can be hired; cookery courses and traditional food available in an open-air eatery nearby. Children under 12 free. WiFi. *Insider Tip*

✚ 213 E3 ✉ 222 Street 2, Ba Mi, Cau Ke
☎ 09 39 29 92 78, 054 33 16 52;
www.suonsiahomestay.com

Where to...
Eat and Drink?

Price
for a main course without drinks:
£ under VND120,000   **££** VND120,000–VND240,000   **£££** over VND240,000

BEN TRE

Noi Ben Tre £
A wide range of local fare, ranging from chicken to frog dishes, is served on this multi-decked boat... just as well that the menu is in English too!

✚ 213 E3   ✉ Hung Vuong   ☎ 075 3 82 24 92
🕐 Daily 10am–9pm

CAN THO

Buoi Thi Quan £–££
A rather unusual little restaurant that is popular among young Vietnamese. Hot-pots and barbecued fare served in a relaxed atmosphere.

✚ 213 D3   ✉ Dinh Tien Hoang
☎ 09 32 84 56 58   🕐 Daily 10am–9pm

Mekong Inn £–££
Simple eatery for those passing by with a typical range of dishes from fried rice or noodle soup to hot-pots, pizza and vegetarian food. And don't forget the banana pancakes for breakfast or as a dessert.

✚ 213 D3   ✉ 38 Hai Ba Trung
☎ 071 08 82 16 46   🕐 Daily 6am–10pm

CHAU DOC

Con Tien Floating Restaurant £–££
This two-storey Hang Chau tourist restaurant is moored on the river. It serves delicious seafood and offers a variety of set menus of several courses. Good value for money.

✚ 212 C4   ✉ Tran Hung Dao
☎ 076 56 27 71   🕐 Daily 10am–9pm

HA TIEN

Oasis Bar £
The first 'western bar' in Ha Tien is a meeting place for backpackers. The British owner, Andy, dishes up not only typically English and European fare, hearty breakfasts and cold beer, but is also happy to give people interesting tips.

✚ 212 B3   ✉ 42 Tuan Phu Dat   ☎ 077 3 70
15 53; www.oasisbarhatien.com   🕐 9am–9pm

MY THO

Trung Luong £
The speciality of this large garden eatery – fried elephant ear fish – has even been enjoyed by leading European politicians. Boats from here down the Bao Dinh River to the islands or the town centre.

✚ 213 E3   ✉ Nguyen Trung Truc
☎ 073 3 85 54 41   🕐 Daily 10am–8pm

PHU QUOC

Palm Tree £
Lots of fresh fish, seafood and barbecued fare, as well as Viennese schnitzels, burgers, pizzas and cocktails are served in this large and friendly family-run restaurant.

✚ 212 A3   ✉ Tran Hung Dao, Bai Truong
☎ 097 8 99 80 27   🕐 Daily 10am–10pm

Sakura £–££
Mrs. Kiem serves typical Vietnamese dishes, lots of seafood and curries in her restaurant a little off the beaten track

✚ 212 A3   ✉ approach road to Bai Ong Long
☎ 0773 98 51 37   🕐 Daily 11am until 10pm

Mekong Delta

Bang Lang Tim £
A garden oasis: this small, modern café serves predominantly Vietnamese food; music in the evening.
🔲 213 D3 ✉ Nguyen Cu Trinh
☎ 067 3 77 28 10 ⏰ Daily 7am–10pm

Where to...
Shop

Insider Tip

The markets in the Mekong Delta are always worth a detour, whether just to browse or to sample the street food. These include the **night markets** in **Can Tho** (on the river, Cho Dem, Hai Ba Trung; daily from 6pm) and **Tay Do** (33–35 Ngo Duc Ke; daily 5pm–10pm) or the street markets on **Phu Quoc** in Duong Dong and An Thoi.

Lots of 'green' yet pretty souvenirs ranging from handbags made of recycled rice sacks to little notebooks can be found as **Viet Artisans** (110/9 An Thanh, An Binh, Long Ho, Vinh Long Province; tel: 09 15 18 39 11; http://vietartisans.org; 9am–5pm). There are some souvenir shops on the beach road Tran Hung Dao, Long Beach Village in Duong Dong; all sorts of organic products against mosquito bites and sunburn, as well as cosmetics are available, e.g., at **Green Boutique** (no. 92; www.thegreen-boutique.com).

Phu Quoc is known for its cultured pearls. The pearl farm **Ngo Chien Pearl** (Ap Duong Bao, Xa Duong; tel: 077 3 98 89 99; daily 10am–4pm) has an exhibition and a shop selling pearl jewellery which attracts crowds of Asian and those on cruises in particular.

And why not buy pepper where it grows – especially hot and aromatic red pepper that puts the fire in any culinary dish. **Pepper plantations** can be found near Duong Dong and Cua Can (Mon–Fri 8am–4pm) on Phu Quoc

Insider Tip

Where to...
Go Out

In the south and the Mekong Delta you will have to look hard for a bar scene like that in the west. However things are changing on Phu Quoc and in Can Tho. The roof bar in **Holiday One Hotel** (59–65 Pham Ngoc Thach, Can Tho; tel: 0710 3 82 77 79; www.holidayonehotel.com; daily 8am–10pm) has a little pool and a wonderful view. **Rustic** (17B Nguyen Trai, corner Vo Thi Sau; tel: 09 83 36 06 27; 8pm–11pm), a bar that opened at the end of 2014, is popular among students and young foreigners who like house music, chilled beer, candles and cocktails. **Safari Restaurant & Bar** (Du Ngoan, 167 Tran Hung Dao, 4km (2.5mi) south of Duong Dong; tel: 090 5 22 46 00; daily noon–2am) attracts customers with burgers and tacos, chilled beer, island tips, billiards and TV sports.

Spirits and mythological creatures are brought to life at the 🎭 **Dao Ngo Water Puppet Show** (129 Tran Hung Dao, Duong Dong, Phu Quoc; tel: 077 62 88 77; 7:30pm, 8:45pm, Sat, Sun also 5pm; VND150,000). Vietnamese opera is an acquired taste but quite an experience. The colourful spectacle held, e.g., during the 4-day **Thuong Dien Festival** in late May/June, is performed in the extremely attractive Dinh Binh Tuy, built in 1870 (Le Hong Phong, Binh Tuy, opera 5pm–2am).

The Khmer celebrate **New Year** (Apr/May) and the **Ghe Ngo Festival** (Oct/Nov) with traditional boat races in Soc Trang.

South Coast & Highlands

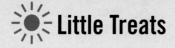 **Little Treats**

From worm to thread

In many little silk factories around **Da Lat** (➤ 107) you can find out how silk is made (e.g. in Cu Xa, 25km/15.5mi further south).

Sweet, sweeter, sweetest

Try this syrup-like strawberry jam and red strawberry wine from **Da Lat** (➤ 107) that is famous throughout the country!

Fire shows and campfires

Things get pretty lively in the clubs and bars of **Nha Trang** (➤ 110), for instance at the weekend beach parties.

Getting Your Bearings

The sea is an inviting turquoise colour, watched over by mountains with their heads in cotton-wool clouds. For anyone who can't decide between the sea and the mountains, between swimming or hiking, bodysurfing or canyoning, Vietnam's south coast is the perfect place. From here to the highlands and the villages of the ethnic minorities it is just a hop, skip and jump.

Nha Trang, a sort of Vietnamese Marbella, used to be the playground of French colonial gentlemen and the former Emperor Bao Dai, American GIs on surfboards and Russian workers in overalls. Droning basses blast out of trendy bars and clubs in the evenings and night markets and barbecue parties take over the beach.

The 3200km (2000mi)-long Vietnamese coast was totally unspoilt by tourism more of less into the 1990s; up until 1993 you would have had to look hard for a beach bungalow anywhere. The coast was firmly in the hands of fishermen. But since then the former insider tip has been spread all over the place and, on the peninsula Mui Ne alone, some 200 hotels in all price categories have popped up. The peninsula does form a beautiful and seemingly endless bay in the shade of coconut palms, a landscape with Sahara-like dunes and little canyons.

A completely different side of Vietnam can be experienced just 150km (95mi) further north on the Da Lat plateau. Surrounded by mountains up to 2100m (6900ft) high, the French found it a refreshing town 'where spring never ends' more than 100 years ago. Today, visitors can marvel at the waterfalls and cable cars, watch the cowboys and their ponies, sample the strawberry jam and strawberry wine, and enjoy the tulips and roses.

Vung Tau 8

TOP 10

⭐ Phan Thiet & Mui Ne ➤ 102

Don't Miss

At Your Leisure

Ban Don
Phuoc An
Buon Ma Thuot 35
Ban Ngam
(1A)
Buon Locai
Ninh Hoa
Dak Mil
Chu Yang Sin
2423 m
(27)
(14)
Buon Lac Dong
34 **Nha Trang**
Quang Son
Lam Vien Plateau
Gia Nghia
Bang Dung
33 **Da Lat**
CAM RANH
(28)
Nam Ban
D'Ran
(20)
Lien Nghia
Tan Son
Po Klong Garai 32
PHAN RANG/
THAP CHAM
BAO LOC
Di Linh
39
Ninh Chu Beach
rk
(20)
(1A)
Ma Da Gui
Phu
Cho Lau
Lien Huong
Phan Ri
Ham Thuan Bac
NG
9
Thuan Nam
Phan Thiet &
Mui Ne
(1A)
37
Ta Cu
oc Buu   0   20 km
0   10 mi

While kite surfers enjoy themselves on Mui Ne (right), couples and newly-weds are drawn to the Valley of Love (left)

South Coast & Highlands

Four Perfect Days

Anyone who likes swimming in the sea as well as donning a pair of hiking boots and tracing the local history of the area can expand this one day excursion into a 4-day tour of the region to the north. This can equally well be done as a package tour or with a hire car and chauffeur.

Day One

Morning
⭐**Mui Ne** (➤ 102) is the starting point for any tour away from the beach. From here you can explore the dunes which shimmer in different shades of gold and orange, as well as the peninsula's lively fishing ports. This will then leave you time to see the Champa towers.

Afternoon
Take the cable car or hike up the 700m (2,300ft)-high **37 Ta Cu** (➤ 115) a little inland where a lying Buddha greets pilgrims. There are numerous soup kitchens and eateries on the mountain catering for visitors' needs.

Evening
Back in Mui Ne finish your day with a relaxing visit to a beach bar and listen to the sound of the waves as they break on the beach.

Day Two

Morning
Take a bus or hire car and head up and up into the **33 Da Lat** (➤ 107) mountains. The French built rustic colonial villas where they spent the summer and the last emperor, Bao Dai, had his Art Deco summer palace here. This provides a short trip back to the days of the royal household – including the chance to dress up as the monarch for that souvenir photo!

Afternoon
Head off to explore the area around Da Lat, visit one of the **nine villages of the Lat ethnic minority** (➤ 108) and look over the shoulder of the silk weavers, by going to Cu Xa, for example.

Day Three

Morning/whole day
Impressive waterfalls, like Lien Khuong on the N20, several temples and a typically Vietnamese pleasure park are on today's agenda. Anyone who finds the 'Valley of Love' or the 'Lake of Sighs' too hectic and trippery can book some exciting outdoor action in Da Lat (but, as it rains a lot in this area, such plans often come to a soggy end). Whether you fancy an easy hike on **Langbiang** (➤ 109), canyoning and abseiling at a waterfall, climbing or a ropeway adventure – here you'll be spoilt for choice.

Late afternoon/evening
A stroll through the pretty old town centre in Da Lat and then around the lake round off a day full of new impressions.

Day Four

Morning
Back on the coast, take the N27 which takes you past **32 Po Klong Garai** (➤ 105), a 1,000-year-old Champa temple tower. Follow the coast road to the north until the skyline of the seaside resort of **34 Nha Trang** (right; ➤ 110) comes into view.

Afternoon
You can spend a day or two in Vietnam's 'Nice' without getting bored. After looking at the towers at Po Nagar (left), for example, it will be time to look for an inviting (seafood) eatery on the riverside.

Phan Thiet & Mui Ne

Lots of sun and optimum wind conditions attract surfers and kiters from around the world to Mui Ne, a 20km (12.5mi)-long peninsula covered with palm trees and with sheer endless sandy beaches. Nearby Phan Thiet harbour however is better known – at least by the Vietnamese, as the fish sauce Nuoc Mam comes from here.

With the beautiful Mui Ne peninsula on the doorstep and the expansive curve of the bay lined with coconut trees, this provincial capital has quickly evolved into one of the most popular seaside destinations in Vietnam since the first bungalow resort opened in 1995. A mass of other bungalow complexes, bars and restaurants, diving schools and massage parlours have sprouted up in next to no time along the 16km (10mi)-long beach road.

Vietnam's Hawaii

In the meantime some 200 hotels in all price categories vie for the custom of the (predominantly Russian) holiday-makers. Despite this, the fishermen with their cutters, baskets and nets still dominate the beach scene – in the early morning at least. However, depending on the season, wind and weather, this is sometimes just a slim strip of sand full of rubbish. This doesn't put off the surfing crowd from around the world who have declared the western part of Mui Ne beach at least to one of their top spots. Every year in February, windsurfers compete in slalom and free ride events at the **Starboard Vietnam Fun Cup** on this dry peninsula.

The sand dunes of Mui Ne seem to go on for ever

Phan Thiet & Mui Ne

THE CHAM PEOPLE
The area around Phan Thiet was ruled by the Cham, once one of the most powerful people, for several centuries. The Champa kingdom was established in the 2nd century and the Pho Shanu towers from the 8th century are among their oldest relics. From the 12th century onward, the Cham people – for a long time Hindu – had to fight off repeated attacks from Kymer and Vietnamese kings. In 1692 Nguyen Phuc Chu conquered the region although, by this time, the Cham people had already become a Vietnamese ethnic minority group. The ruined palace of the Champa king, Po Saktiraydaputih, are near what is now Phan Ri to the northeast of Phan Thiet. The remaining Cham people in Vietnam today, who number some 100,000, now profess to a very moderate form of Islam.

Excursions on Mui Ne
When lazing on the beach or surfing gets too monotonous, the peninsula is an inviting place for a short hike or a variety of other activities. The **village Mui Ne** is well worth visiting in the morning in particular when the harbour is abuzz with brightly-coloured barges, little round bamboo boats and market women, covered from head to toe, with their baskets of mussels and shrimps. At the northeastern end of the peninsula is much-photographed **Bao Trang**, a dune that varies in colour from a reddish orange to a yellowy white. It attracts lots of tourists on foot (wear shoes!) and roaring quad bikes. Once at the top, many slide down the sandy pistes again on a plastic bowl. **White Lotus Lake (Bau Tranh)**, a lakeland area surrounded by snow-white sand dunes near Hon Nghe Bay, is particularly picturesque. A one-hour hike from near the fishing village of **Ham Tien** follows a stream through the dunes and past the shimmering red, craggy cliffs of the narrow **Red Sand Canyon** and on to **Suoi Tien**, the 'fairies' fountain', a small gushing waterfall in the midst of luxuriant tropical scenery.

Insider Tip

Sitting majestically on **Ngoc Lam** hill is the southern-most Champa holy site in Vietnam – the three small **Pho Shanu towers** (➤ see box above) that were constructed in the 8th century in honour of Queen Po Shanu and restored in 1999. While they have fewer ornamental decorations than the famous Champa towers of Po Nagar (➤ 110/Nha Trang) or Po Klong Garai near Phang Rang (➤ 105), they offer a wonderful panoramic view of the coast and Phan Thiet (➤ 102).

On **Khe Ga** cape, on a small island some 25km (15.5mi) southwest of Mui Ne, is a lighthouse built in 1897 by the French. With a height of 54m (177ft) it is the tallest and oldest lighthouse in Vietnam. **Ganh Son Canyon**, a former US American military area on the mainland, should only

South Coast & Highlands

be visited with a official guide as there are dangerous areas of quicksand and landmines.

Phan Thiet

Phan Thiet, a town 20km (12.5mi) from Mui Ne, lies at the centre of one of Vietnam's largest fishing grounds. The **harbour** near Tran Hung Dao bridge is alive in the early hours of the day. A fishing fleet of around 5,000 boats lands its catch here which is then sold at the no less hectic fish market without any delay.

Fishermen in Phan Thiet harbour cleaning their nets

The **watertower** on the Ca Ty river, built in 1928–34, is another popular photo motif. Its curving three-tiered roof rises to the heavens like a little temple. Not far from here, also on the river bank, is **Duc Thanh School** where Ho Chi Minh taught Chinese, Vietnamese and martial arts in 1910/11. There is now a museum here. **Van Thuy Tu Temple**, built in 1762, in Fisherman Street further to the south, boasts the 22m (72ft)-long skeleton of a whale. Beached whales are buried in the adjacent cemetery – the most recent burial was in 2002. Vietnamese fishermen worship the huge marine mammals like guardian deities. This cult however comes from the Cham and Khmer people.

TAKING A BREAK

The tiny little family-run eatery **Bamboo Bamboo** (£/££) on the main road (81B Nguyen Dinh Chieu, Ham Tien, Mui Ne; tel: 090 3 96 63 75; daily 8am–10pm) is a good place for a bowl of soup while out and about.

Pho Shanu
➕ 215 D2 🕐 Daily about 8am–5pm 💰 VND10,000

Ho Chi Minh Museum/Duc Than School
➕ 215 D2 ✉ 39 Trung Nhi
🕐 Tue–Sun 7:30am–11:30am, 2pm–4:30pm 💰 VND10,000

Van Thuy Tu Temple (Dinh Van Thuy Tu)
➕ 215 D2
✉ Ngu Ong (Fisherman Street), Dinh Tien Hoang, Duc Thang district
🕐 Daily 7am–6pm 💰 VND10,000

INSIDER INFO

- **Information** can be found in hotels and the many tourist information offices along the main road or under www.muinebeach.net and http://muine-explorer.com.
- The **best conditions for surfing** are from September to December; kitesurfers should plan their visit between November and mid-April. Steady cross-onshore winds enable experienced sportspeople to ride waves caused by the swell for miles.

㉕ Po Klong Garai

The biggest attractions in the twin town Phan Rang-Thap Cham are slightly outside: the four distinctive Champa towers of Po Klong Garai, where virtually every tour bus stops, are landmarks in this coastal region densely clad incactii and vines. The beaches in the surrounding area, on the other hand, are as good as deserted – at least on weekdays.

The Po Klong Garai towers, without doubt a Champa cultural highlight

The towers of Po Klong Garai on Trau Hill (also known as Cho'k Hala) are among the most important remnants of the Champa culture, along with the ruins of My Son (▶ 132). They are relics of an advanced civilisation that existed here some 700 years ago as the Kingdom of Panduranga. The four towers that still exist were erected during the reign of Jaya Simhavarman III in the late 13th/14th century. Originally six towers were built to honour the revered legendary and god-like King Po Klong Garai (1151–1205), who was worshipped at the same time as Shiva and the God of Water and who reputedly died of leprosy.

The 20m (63ft)-high, three-storey **main tower (kalan)** has an entrance facing east in keeping with Champa tradition. A dancing Shiva with six arms, the Nataraja, can be seen above the entrance door. The three tiered roof is supported by lotus-shaped columns; the façade is decorated with images of gods and Champa inscriptions. Inside is the **lingam** (Mukhalingam), the phallus-like symbol for Shiva and the animal he rides on, Nandi. The former library can be recognised through it slightly vaulted roof with buffalo horn-like finials. French archaeologists have discovered other treasures such as bowls made of gold and silver and jewellery from the Champa period in digs in the region (►Insider Info).

Other Sights in the Area

On the hill Bon Acho in the village Hau Sanh (Phuoc Huu), 15km (9.5mi) south of Phan Rang in the Ninh Phuoc district, are the ruins of the three Champa towers of **Po Ro Me**. The four-storey brick buildings were the last major Cham structures erected in the early 17th century when the Champa culture (► 132) was already in decline. Only the 19m (62.5ft)-high, rather squat looking main *kalan* can still be seen today. This holy site commemorates the last Champa king, Po Ro Me (also written Po Rome, reigned 1629–51) who died as a prisoner in Vietnam. A bas-relief at the entrance shows Shiva as Po Ro Me with a moustache. Inside, there is a lingam, a statue of the king and the queen, Bia Thanh Chanh, from the Ede people. A statue of the Champa queen Bia Thanh Chih and the mount Nandi are behind.

Many symbols and depictions of Shiva – here as Nataraja – can be seen at the Po Klong Garai Champa towers

Insider Tip

Some 6km (3.75mi) east of Phan Rang is **Nih Chu beach** (► 116), a wonderful crescent-shaped beach that is generally hardly visited during the week with yellow sand and clear water. There are a few hotels and bungalows, some of which are unusually designed.

TAKING A BREAK

There are several **snack bars** serving light meals, noodle soup and drinks at the ruins (£).

➕ 215 E3

Po Klong Garai
✉ N20 direction Da Lat, 8km (5mi) west of Phan Rang
🕐 Daily 7:30am–6pm 💷 VND15,000

INSIDER INFO

- The Cham people hold **four colourful festivals** a year at their holy towers (Jan, March, Oct, Dec). The Kate New Year's festival in the seventh lunar month in the Cham calendar (i.e. in the 9th or 10th month in the Chinese lunar calendar = October) is especially opulent, with folk dancing and singing, a procession and ancient rituals in the temple towers themselves, such as 'feeding' Nandi by Cham peasants so that he will provide a good harvest.
- Anyone interested in the culture of the Cham people should visit the little Champa museum at 17 Nguyen Trai in Phan Rang (Mon–Fri 8am–11am, 2:30pm–4:30pm; VND10,000). Earthenware shards, several statues and other finds from excavations are on display.

㉝ Da Lat

Emperor Bao Dai used to swing a golf club in this once sleepy town in the Highlands. Not surprisingly really, considering the pleasant climate in the summer, surrounded by 2,300m (7,500ft)-high mountains – even if it does rain quite a lot. Before the colonial rulers and, later, tourists discovered this region for themselves, the people here made a living from fruit and vegetable farming. And to this day orchids are still grown in this area that is transformed into a sea of flowers in the spring.

The French loved Da Lat that was discovered by the doctor and explorer Alexandre Yersin at the end of the 19th century. Just a few years later Da Lat had become an exclusive climatic health resort located at an altitude of about 1,500m (5,000ft). One after another a **cathedral**, a university and the luxury **Da Lat Palace Hotel** were built. Picturesque villas in the colonial style clamber up the hill above the man-made **Xuan Huong lake**, dug in 1919. Some are elaborately ornate, castle-like villas or little gingerbread cottages in a rustic country-house style, while others are prefabricated structures. A 7km (4.5mi)-long path runs around the lake which you can explore in a paddleboat. And in **Bao Dai Palace 'Dinh 3'** (1933–38), one of the last emperor's three Da Lat villas in the southwest of the town, the private apartments can be visited including his study, assembly halls and the reception room with a piano and hunting trophies. The old wooden crate next to the main stairs is where the emperor had a steam bath!

Close by is the 🏰 **'Crazy House'** (Hang Nga Villa). The Vietnamese architect Hang Nga has designed a weird and wonderful building that also doubles as a guesthouse and gallery. 'Gaudi meets Sesame Street' is how Miss Nga describes it herself. You do however need to like the idea of being surrounded by animal and fantasy figures as well as playful (and sometimes mirrored) ornamental elements.

Insider Tip

Inspired by Art Deco: the station in Da Lat from 1930

During the day visitors can climb up to the roofs of the building that is a mixture of fairy-tale castle and grotto with concrete 'bamboo' bridges and stone spiders' webs.

There's nothing romantic about the Valley of Love at weekends; on week days things can be different

Other sights in the area

Most sights and places to visit are scattered around the forested area outside the town. A half-day outing from the old station in Da Lat is particularly popular. When at least 20 passengers have gathered, an old wooden train with a diesel engine sets off for Trai Mat, 8km (5mi) away, to **Linh Phuoc Pagoda (Chua Linh Phuoc)**. Decorated with masses and masses of pieces of ceramic, the pagoda is a popular photo motif – especially the dragon decorated with 50,000 bits of glass from beer bottles. Anyone looking for a little more peace and quiet can hike to **Tiger Cave Waterfall (Thac Hang Cop)** some 7km (4.5mi) away, reached along a (partly waymarked) trail. You will be greeted by a statue of a tiger where people stop to pose in its gaping mouth. The last tiger with flesh and bones was spotted here in the 1970s. 350 slippery steps lead down to the bottom of the waterfall with a pool for swimming. (It is advisable to hire a guide. The park has become somewhat neglected recently and the suspension bridge may be closed). There are other waterfalls worth visiting in the area.

The small, man-made **Lake of Sighs (Ho Than Tho)** is a popular, very Vietnamese destination to the east of the town where, as the legend goes, a love that lasted more than 200 years met its tragic end here. The nearby **Valley of Love (Thung Lung Tinh Yeu)** where the former emperor Bao Dai went hunting, is generally much busier. The area has always been popular by honeymoon couples but, in the meantime, families come here in their hundreds too.

ETHNIC GROUPS

Around Da Lat there are nine villages that form the **Lat community** (pronounced: *lak*) within which a variety of dialects is still spoken. Some 3000 people belong to this formerly matriarchal, largely Catholic ethnic minority group who still farm using the slash-and-burn method. Tourists should only visit these villages as part of a tour offered by one of the local travel agencies.

Insider Tip

They go for walks through the pine woods, bob about on the Lake of Sighs or the reservoir in a canoe or a swan-shaped paddleboat or dress up as cowboys and go for pony rides. Merry-go-rounds and picnics are popular and souvenirs are snapped up until the cash runs out. On week days the valley can actually be quite quiet and – when the weather is nice – you will be able to enjoy the wonderful panoramic view of **Langbiang's** twin peaks (► 197) without being disturbed.

Insider Tip

TAKING A BREAK

Stop for a cup of coffee and try the homemade joghurt in **Ca Phe Tung** (£; Hoa Binh; tel: 063 3 82 13 90; daily 7am–9pm), an oasis away from the hustle and bustle that has been a popular spot for decades. Snacks, coffee and cake are served during the day next to the old station in **Da Lat Train Café** (£/££; 1 Quang Trung; tel: 063 3 81 63 65, 090 3 34 24 42; www.dalattrainvilla.com; daily 8am–6pm).

Now and again horses and traps can still be seen on the road in and around Da Lat

➕ 215 D3

Da Lat Tourist
✉ 1 Le Dai Hanh and at No. 7 in the road 3 Thang 2
☎ 063 3 82 38 29; www.dalattourist.com.vn

Bao Dai Palace 'Dinh 3'
✉ 2 Le Hong Phong ⏰ Daily 7:30am–11:30am, 1:30pm–4:30pm 💵 VND15,000

Crazy House
✉ 3 Huynh Thuc Khang
☎ 063 3 82 20 70; www.crazyhouse.vn
⏰ Daily 8:30am–7pm 💵 VND40,000

Linh Phuoc Pagoda & Tiger Cave Waterfall
⏰ Pagoda: 8am–5pm; Tiger Cave Waterfall: 7:30am–5pm
🚆 Daily 7:45am–4pm (last train back: 5:30pm)
💵 Pagoda free; Tiger Cave Waterfall VND20,000; train ticket: VND125,000

Lake of Sighs & Vally of Love
⏰ Daily 8am–6pm 💵 VND30,000

INSIDER INFO

An experience of a different kind are tours on legendary **Easy Riders** (70 Phan Dinh Phung; www.dalat-easyrider.com, day-tour US$20–US$35, 3-day tours: US$50– US$85 a day, incl. fuel and snacks), run by a group of moped taxi-drivers from Da Lat. Anyone prepared to zoom around the area as a pillion passenger should make sure that the driver speaks English, that the bike is fit for the road and that your helmet meets western standards (there is no insurance cover...). There is virtually no top limit to prices asked – all you can do is haggle your heart out!

③④ Nha Trang

Masses of pubs, clubs and event venues vie for custom around the wide bay of this port with a skyline that seems to grow by the day. Whether fried rice, hotdogs or excellent seafood, beer gardens, barbecues, fire shows on the beach or the highest density of diving schools in Vietnam, there is no shortage of things on offer here.

The former little fishing village of Nha Trang is the oldest, liveliest and most multi-cultural seaside resort in Vietnam – and that since imperial days! Many illustrious guests have whiled away their time here. And in **Bao Dai Villa** (or Palace) in the south, now a grand hotel, one could well believe that time had stood still. Standing in the huge rooms with far-reaching views over the cliffs and the sea beyond it is not difficult to imagine the last emperor of Vietnam going for a dip off the little private beach.

Nowadays Nha Trang's flair is more a blend of Marbella, Nice and the Gold Coast. Palms and casuarinas, Flamboyant trees and sea grape bushes line the promenade down the wide beach some 6km (3.75mi) long. Swarms of boats leave every day for the **70 off-shore islands**, such as Monkey Island, the 25 diving grounds and the coral reefs. More than 100 hotels and guesthouses welcome visitors from all over the world. An armada of street hawkers ply sunbathers with drinks, snacks and massages, plait hair or file fingernails. In the evenings the beach keep-fit circuit, massage parlours, beach restaurants with campfires and 'fire dancing', street kitchens and karaoke bars are all full to bursting.

Worth a Visit

Two attractions await the culturally interested. The Champa temple of **Po Nagar** is about 1,200 years old and was former-ly Hindu. It lies in the north of the city close to the harbour full of colourful fishing boats. It is dedicated to the Champa goddess of fertility and motherhood of the same name.

Red sky in the morning can also bode well when the rising sun bathes boats off Nha Trang in a magical light

The much-visited Buddhist religious landmark comprises four brick towers that were erected between the 7th and 12th/13th centuries, destroyed and rebuilt on numerous occasions. Over the portal in the three-storey north tower (9th century) is a dancing, four-armed Shiva; inside is a statue of Po Nagar, a black sandstone figure with ten hands bearing symbolic objects representing her power and intelligence under a yellow robe. The head

Anyone wanting to share the wonderful view with the White Buddha has to climb the 150 or so steps up the hill first

is a poor copy of the original that was taken by the French. To the left of the north tower is a somewhat lower central tower (Thap Nam, 12th century) where childless couples in particular pray for success in front of the lingam, the phallus symbol associated with Shiva.

Back in the city centre you cannot fail to see the 24m (79ft)-high white **Buddha (Kim Than Phat To)** that hovers majestically on Trai Thuy Hill above **Long Son Pagoda (Chua Long Son)**. The seated figure was erected as a symbol against the Ngo Dinh Diem regime. The 7m (23ft)-high lotus flower pedestal includes the portraits of seven monks and nuns who set fire to themselves – the first in 1963 – to protest against repressions suffered during the dictatorship. Among those immortalised here is Thich Quang Duc (➤ 67).

TAKING A BREAK

On the beach there are a number of women selling refreshments and snacks, from fresh coconut milk, dragon fruit and fried noodles to chilled beer.

✚ 215 E4

Khan Hoa Tours
✉ 1 Tran Phu ☎ 058 3 52 81 00; www.nhatrangtourist.com.vn

Po Nagar
✉ Thap Ba, via Xom Bong bridge in the north of the city
🕐 Daily 6am–6pm (wear respectable clothing and take your shoes off when visiting the towers) 💵 VND22,000

Long Son Pagoda
✉ Thai Nguyen, Trai Thuy 🕐 Daily 7am–6pm 💵 Free

INSIDER INFO

That Vietnamese spa feeling can be found at **Thap Ba Hot Springs** (15 Ngoc Son, Ngoc Hiep, 10km (6.25mi) north of Nha Trang; tel: 058 3 83 53 35; www.thapbahot spring.com.vn; daily 7am–7pm, entrance fee from VND150,000, mud bath for two: VND600,000). The mud in a tub is heated up to around 38°C; the water in the spa to 40°C; massages available. Tours and shuttle buses run from Nha Trang. Or else you can try the 🏛 **100 Egg Mud Bath** nearby where children can enjoy a good mud fight!

Insider Tip

㉟ Buon Ma Thuot

The remote and magical Dak Lak Central Highlands surround the provincial capital Buon Ma Thuot and entice visitors with waterfalls, wonderful hilly scenery, coffee plantations and not least of all – elephants.

Buon Ma Thuot is Vietnam's coffee centre. **Trung Nguyen Coffee Museum** takes a close look at the cultivation and processing of the coffee bean. There are more than 10,000 items on display from the collection of the traditional coffee merchants, Jens Burg of Hamburg: coffee machines and mills, caddies from colonial goods' shops, and much more. The town however is a good base from which to explore the beautiful surrounding area.

Ban Don

For centuries now elephants have been bred, used for hunting and domesticated as working animals, for riding or for use in war, by the Ede and Mnong people in Ban Don 45km (28mi) northwest of Buon Ma Thuot. The 50 or so animals living here are still worked transporting timber although they are being increasingly used to provide rides for tourists and at festivals and folkloric shows. A large spectacle is held every year in November in Ban Don when the giants also play football!

Insider Tip

Yok Don National Park

Not far from Ban Don and the Cambodian border is **Vietnam's largest national park** – a paradise for ornithologists – which covers an area of 444mi². On any hike through the park you will see many of the 250 different species of bird living here, such as hornbills, peacocks and pheasants. Some 50 kinds of mammal, half of which are threatened with extinction, romp around the mixed forest area as well.

Bamboo leaves are a real treat for elephants and there are still a few dozen wild elephants which wander around the grassy forests in the national park. There are even a few of the last tigers and leopards have been seen by gamekeepers in an area that is not open to visitors. Boat trips on the rivers and animal expeditions on the back of an elephant are very popular.

Other Sights in the Area

Elephant rides are offered through the shallow part of **Dak Lak Lake (Ho Dak Lak)** which covers some 1,235 acres, 50km (30mi) south of Buon Ma Thuot. Visitors can also take a rowing boat out onto Vietnam's second-largest natural inland lake, go bird watching (especially cranes and storks) or try their luck fishing. 'Homestay' accommodation is available nearby, for example with the Mnog people.

In Dak Lak Central Highlands: a mahout (elephant rider) and a coffee picker

Dray Sap Waterfalls (Thac Dray Sap), 30km (18.5mi) southwest of Buon Ma Thuot, are not called the 'misty falls' for nothing. Huge volumes of water more than 100m (330ft) wide plunge from a height of 15m (50ft) and create an impressive spray.

TAKING A BREAK

The **coffee bar** at Trung Nguyen Coffee Museum (££, 7am–8pm) is in a lovely wooden longhouse.

✚ 215 D4

Trung Nguyen Coffee Museum
✉ Coffee Village, 222 Le Thanh Tong ⏰ Daily 7am–5pm 🎫 VND20,000

Ban Don
🐘 Elephant rides: VND250,000–VND500,000 per animal and hour

Yok Don National Park
☎ 050 03 78 30 28; http://yokdonnationalpark.vn
⏰ Daily 7am–5pm 🎫 VND50,000, guide VND500,000–VND750,000 (ask for Mr. Gioi, simple rooms and tents at the park centre, elephant rides possible)

Dak Lak Lake
🐘 Elephant rides: around VND300,000 per animal and hour

Dray Sap Waterfalls
⏰ Daily 6am–7pm 🎫 Free

INSIDER INFO

Don't miss the highlight in the **ethnological museum** in Buon Ma Thuot (Museum of Ethnology, 12 Le Duan; tel: 0500 3 85 04 26; daily 7:30am–11:30am, 1:30pm–4:30pm, admission: VND15,000) – the unique collection of gongs. Their music has been included on the UNESCO Intangible Cultural Heritage list since 2005. Even apart from this, the museum has beautiful, state-of-the art displays and is to be very highly recommended.

At Your Leisure

There is hardly space for another towel on the beaches of Vung Tau

36 Vung Tau

Costa del Sol in Vietnamese: families, couples and groups of colleagues on a day out turn the four (not very paradise-like) beaches into an unbelievably chaotic mass of seething bodies especially at weekends. There are certainly better beaches for swimming but surfers have staked their claim on the hilly peninsula here. The two main landmarks are **Nui Nho**

Lighthouse and the 30m (98ft)-high **Statue of Christ**, built by the Americans. You can climb the 130 steps inside – but that makes about 600 steps in all, counting those up the hill!.

Most of Vung Tau's sights can be found down the wide road along the seashore. These include **Bach Dinh Villa (White Palace)** – a beautiful colonial building that was once the governor's residence and is now home to mostly maritime objects. **Tinh Xa Pagoda (Chua Tinh Xa)** is worth seeing for its reclining Buddha. A 12m (39ft)-long Buddhist dragon boat, Thuyen Bat Nha, planted up with flowers, is on the roof terrace. It symbolises the vehicle with which humans cross and ultimately overcome the 'sea of suffering'. **Thich Ca Phat Dai Pagoda (Chua Thich Ca Phat Dai)** lies at the foot of an extensive park, Nui Lon. Large statues, such as the Sakyamuni Buddha seated on lotus flowers, trace different stations in the life of the Enlightened One. Octagonal Bao Thap Tower reputedly houses Buddha's ashes.

➕ 214 B1

Nui Nho Lighthouse
🕐 Daily 7:30am–5pm 💵 VND5,000

Statue of Christ
🕐 Daily 7:30am–11:30am, 1:30pm–5pm
💵 Free (no shorts, hot pants, tank tops, etc.)

Bach Dinh Villa
🕐 Daily 7am–5pm 💵 VND5,000

Tinh Xa Pagoda
🕐 Daily 7am–6pm 💵 Free

Thich Ca Phat Dai Pagoda
🕐 Daily 7am–6pm 💵 Free

37 Ta Cu

One place well worth visiting in the area around Phan Thiet/Mui Ne (► 102) is the 700m (2,300ft)-high Ta Cu (also spelt Takou), involving a two-hour mountain hike through the forest, in the nature reserve of the same name. One of the longest statues of Buddha in Vietnam lies stretched out on the mountain peak. The 49m (160ft)-long and 3m (10ft)-high Sakyamuni Buddha (erected 1963–66) draws pilgrims to the more than 150-year-old **Linh Son Truong Tho Monastery.** If you don't fancy the climb, the Swiss-built **cable car** will whisk you to the top in 10 minutes while you can soak in the view over the beautiful countryside.

➕ 214 C2 ✉ Ham Thuan Nam, Than Lap, 30km (18.5mi) southwest of Phan Thiet
🕐 monastery: daily 7am–11am, 1:30pm–5pm
💵 cable car: VND160,000

38 Cat Tien National Park

Covering 200,000 acres, the park stretches across the provinces of Lam Dong, Dong Nai and Binh Phuoc. The national park – one of the largest in Vietnam – is a **biosphere reserve** that enjoys special UNESCO protection. It is best visited during the dry season

A bit of luck is needed to spot the residents in Cat Tien National Park (here a rhesus monkey)

between November/December and March/April.

The area drops in a series of tiers from the Truong Son mountains southwestwards down to the plain. It comprises savannas, masses of lakes and rivers, waterfalls, lagoons and extensive swamps with a rich variety of fauna and flora. Apart from elephants, gibbons and gaurs (a species of wild cattle) the dense bush and bamboo forests are home to more than 100 species of mammal (that allegedly also include leopards and the Indochinese tiger). In winter in particular, some 350 kinds of bird congregate in the park (incl. storks, cormorants, pheasants, woodpeckers, crakes, wild geese and kingfishers), 120 species of reptile and amphibian and 460 types of butterfly. Researchers have counted some 1,600 different kinds of plants of which 170 are of

South Coast & Highlands

Insider
Tip

interest to the medical world and 52 species of orchid.

The British-run **Primate Centre** is well worth a visit, as is a project introducing Asian black bears and wild cats back into the wild and the gibbon trek very early in the morning. If you like, you can hire a bike (check it carefully first) and head off under your own steam along generally shady paths or go on a 3-hour walk to **Crocodile Lake** where, with a bit of luck, you may see some gibbons and langurs.
➕ 214 B2

National Park
✉ Office in Tan Phu at the bus stop on the N20 ☎ 061 3 66 92 28; www.namcattien.org; www.namcattien.vn 🕐 Daily 8am–5pm 💵 VND50,000, guide about VND250,000 (book several days in advance, electricity in the simple national park accommodation only until 6pm, take torches and binoculars!)

Primate Centre
☎ 061 3 66 91 59; www.wildlifeatrisk.org

39 Ninh Chu Beach
The mountains in the north shimmer a blueish colour on the horizon; the turquoise water glistens in the sun and the sand is a blinding white. Long, wide, crescent-shaped Ninh Chu Beach has turned into a popular spot away from the streams of tourists over the past few years. The Vietnamese generally descend on this 10km (6.25mi)-long beach near Phan Rang (➤ 106) at the weekends and on public holidays. And so you may well find that you have this idyllic piece of paradise completely to yourself during the week. Accommodation can be found in the handful of beach hotels and campsites under casuarina and palm trees; beach eateries cater for most people's needs.

Things are not going to stay so quiet much longer. The new 116km (72mi)-long **Coastal Highway 702** is to run parallel to Highway N1 through a wonderful and, up until now, pretty deserted stretch of coastline in Ninh Thuan province.
➕ 215 E3

Ninh Chu Beach is only this deserted on week days

Where to...
Stay

Price
of a double room per night:
£ under VND1m.   **££** VND1–VND2.4m.   **£££** over VND2.4m.

BUON MA THUOT

Dakruco £–£££
There are 119 well furnished and very spacious rooms, some with balconies and all with WiFi, in this high-rise hotel visible from miles away. In addition, there is a pool, spa, tennis court and a restaurant.
➕ 215 D4 ✉ 30 Nguyen Chi Thanh
☎ 050 03 97 08 88; www.dakrucohotels.com

CAT TIEN NATIONAL PARK

Forest Floor Lodge £££
This rustic-style lodge provides luxury accommodation in the middle of the rain forest in bungalows with four-poster beds or in deluxe tents. Good restaurant.
➕ 214 B2 ✉ Tan Phu ☎ 061 3 66 98 90;
www.vietnamforesthotel.com

DA LAT

Dream's £
This small, very successful chain of guesthouses run by the Dung family now has three sites on the same street. The consistently friendly team takes good care of its guests. Hearty breakfast, comfortable large beds, some rooms with balconies. Interesting local tours organised.
➕ 215 D3 ✉ 140/141/164 Phan Dinh Phung
☎ 063 3 83 37 48, dreams@hcm.vnn.vn

Du Parc Hotel £££
This stylish hotel opposite its small twin, the Dalat Palace Hotel, was opened in 1932 and oozes a nostalgic charm. The 140 rooms and suites with parquet floors are elegantly furnished, have WiFi but no air-conditioning (which is not necessary anyway at cooler temperatures). Breakfast is taken in the dining room at the Dalat Palace Hotel.
➕ 215 D3 ✉ 15 Tran Phu ☎ 063 3 82 57 77, 063 3 82 54 44; www.dalatresorts.com

Ngoc Lan ££
This standard category hotel was once a cinema and benefits from being right in the middle of things with a view of the lake. Guests are accommodated in 91 large, modern rooms. Those at the back are slightly smaller but also quieter. The bathrooms are more modest.
➕ 215 D3 ✉ 42 Nguyen Chi Thanh
☎ 063 3 83 88 38; www.ngoclanhotel.vn

NHA TRANG

Evason Ana Mandara Nha Trang £££
This classic hotel is the only real beach hotel right on the seafront and yet in the town at the same time. 74 luxury bungalows and villas with four-poster beds and large verandas are scattered throughout an extensive garden alongside the wide beach. The pools, PADI diving school, the range of watersports offered and the open-air restaurant and bar are big plus points. Environment-friendly considerations include organic products served and the hotel's own water treatment plant.
➕ 215 E4 ✉ 86 Tran Phu
☎ 058 3 52 22 22; www.sixsenses.com

South Coast & Highlands

RipTide £

A Canadian-Vietnamese 'homestay' a little outside the busy backpacker district in a quietish residential area. Owen and May organise day-trips and have lots of tips in store. Six simply furnished rooms/apartments with their own bathrooms and a roof terrace (min. 2 nights).

🏠 215 E4 ✉ 15/8 Thap Ba, Ngo Den
☎ 058 3 54 52 68; www.homestaynhatrang.com

Six Senses Ninh Van Bay £££

Perfect for honeymooners. This luxury hotel with 35 rustic-style, (butler) serviced, pool-side villas is hidden on a peninsula in a crescent-shaped bay. Lots of rattan, wood and bamboo, but also WiFi and hi-tech – this is still considered one of the best hotels in Vietnam.

🏠 215 E4 ✉ Ninh Van Bay, Ninh Hoa, 50km (30mi) north of Nha Trang on the Hon Heo peninsula
☎ 058 3 52 42 68; www.sixsenses.com

Some Days of Silence ££–£££

This family-run complex of nine bungalows on Doc Let Beach enjoys a secluded and idyllic location but could be a little cleaner. The prices are a bit steep but you pay for the quiet situation and the pretty garden with a small pool. Massages and meditation offered.

🏠 215 E4 ✉ Dong Hai, Ninh Hai, Ninh Hoa, 50km (30mi) north of Nha Trang
☎ 058 3 67 09 52; www.somedaysresort.com

PHAN RANG & ENVIRONS

Bau Truc ££

This somewhat dated complex comprises brick-built bungalows and rooms on lovely Ninh Chu Beach. There is a pool and an open-air restaurant-bar with sea views, barbecue and seafood. The hotel caters primarily for Vietnamese guests which means loud karaoke sessions at weekends before it falls into a deep slumber again during the week.

🏠 215 E3 ✉ Bai Ninh Chu, Van Hai, Yen Ninh
☎ 068 3 87 40 47; www.bautrucresort.com

Fusion Resort £££

Chic, chicer, 'Fusion Resort'. This spacious designer hotel which opened in 2015 combines exclusivity with deluxe service in its virtually totally glazed, pool-side villas and suites. Guests are to feel part of one big family but have their own private space with panoramic views of the sea. Everything is cool and designed down to the last detail – from imaginative open-air bathrooms with hanging tubs to hammocks with integrated sun shields.

🏠 215 E3
✉ Cam Ranh, between Nha Trang and Ninh Chu
☎ 058 3 98 97 77;
www.fusionresortnhatrang.com

PHAN THIET/MUI NE

Cat Dua Cocosand £

A real bargain, this place lies hidden off the beach road right in the middle of Mui Ne. The eight bungalows and rooms in a garden full of palm trees are looked after by a friendly host family. WiFi, TV, air-conditioning, simple but good bathrooms and hammocks. Local cafés serve breakfast.

🏠 215 D2 ✉ 119 Nguyen Dinh Chieu, Ham Tien, Mui Ne ☎ 012 73 64 34 46, cocosandcatdua@yahoo.com.vn

Cham Villas £££

A long-time favourite among European guests – and for good reason. The 18 cottages with palm-frond roofs form one of the most beautiful beach complexes in Mui Ne. Under German-Vietnamese management. Tastefully decorated, comfortable king-size beds (some with a view of the sea), wonderful tropical gardens, perfect service and a German-Vietnamese cuisine. Fruit available every day at the pool and on the beach.

🏠 215 D2 ✉ 32 Nguyen Dinh Chieu
☎ 062 3 74 12 34; www.chamvillas.com

Where to...
Eat and Drink?

Prices
Per meal (excluding drinks and service):
€ under €20   €€ €20–€40   €€€ over €40

DA LAT

Le Rabelais €€€
Fine dining in the Dalat Palace Hotel: French cuisine served by waiters dressed in livery. View over the lake; live piano music (from 7pm), high tea from 4pm–5pm.
⊞ 215 D3 ⊠ 12 Tran Phu
☎ 063 3 82 54 44 ⊕ Daily 11am–9pm

Lien Hoa Bakery €
Downstairs, there are freshly baked baguettes and croissants for breakfast and lots of tempting sweet pastries. The ever-popular eatery above is rather like a station concourse but serves tasty food.
⊞ 215 D3 ⊠ 15–17 '3 Thang 2' road
(Duong 3/2, near the market)
☎ 063 3 83 73 03 ⊕ Daily 6am–8pm

NHA TRANG

Lac Canh €
Always loud, always full, always tasty. The seafood is always fresh and the barbecued beef delicious at this simple BBQ eatery jammed packed with Vietnamese. Just follow the cloud of smoke...
⊞ 215 E4 ⊠ 44 Nguyen Binh Khiem
☎ 058 3 82 13 91 ⊕ Daily 10am–10pm

Veranda €–€€
European dishes, cocktails and breakfast are served at this pretty, air-conditioned restaurant on the promenade. Good value for money but don't be in too much of a hurry.
⊞ 215 E4 ⊠ 66 Tran Phu
☎ 058 3 52 74 92 ⊕ Daily 7am–10pm

PHAN THIET/MUI NE

Nam Tho €–€€€
There are two branches of Nam Tho run by a bustling elderly lady who greets regulars personally. Fresh fish, king prawns, scallops and crab (fair prices per kilo) are served. Menu in several languages.
⊞ 215 D2
⊠ 33/43 Nguyen Dinh Chieu, Ham Tien
☎ 016 45 81 85 61
⊕ Daily 10am–10pm

Sandals Bar & Restaurant €€€
One of the leading gourmet restaurants in Vietnam. Not just worth a visit for its excellent wines and cocktails. Imaginative 'fusion' cuisine served in the beach restaurant. Service is brisk.
⊞ 215 D2
⊠ 24 Nguyen Dinh Chieu, in the Mia Resort
☎ 062 3 84 74 40; www.miamuine.com
⊕ Daily 7am–11pm

Sunset €€
Tucked away in a modest side street, far from the madding crowd on the main drag. Idyllic garden restaurant with tables between ponds and mango trees. The friendly staff focus largely on everyday Vietnamese fare and seafood. Beer, cocktails and other nightcaps round off a pleasant evening. Lots of regulars.
⊞ 215 D2
⊠ 93/1 Nguyen Dinh Chieu, Ham Tien
☎ 097 7 26 26 76
⊕ Daily 7am–10pm

Where to…
Shop

In many places, tourists can enjoy browsing around the night markets. Haggling is not just allowed, it's a must!

Masses of clothes, beachwear and shoes, handbags, lots of glittering fakes, toys, bits and bobs in every conceivable colour and shape can be found at Nha Trang night market (Tran Phu; daily from about 5pm).

Lots of **silk farms** proffer their wares in the area around Da Lat. The art gallery **XQ Historical Village/QX Art House** (258 May Anh Dao, outside Da Lat; tel: 063 3 83 13 43; www.xqvietnam.com; daily 10am–5pm; admission: VND20,000) displays artistic, handmade items from the region, incl. beautifully hand embroidered pictures and pretty silk clothing. And of course all these things can be bought too.

Many Cham people now earn a living from crafts once again. The weavers' village **My Ngiep** east of the N1 makes woven fabrics and clothes; pottery can be bought in the village **Bau Truc** where you can watch the production process around the kilns.

Look out for local specialities around Nha Trang, such as the marvellous **sand pictures, tranh cat** (► 42). Motifs such as Chi Minh's face and Father Christmas are created by building up layers of sand behind glass. You can find such works of art for example in Nha Trang in 4B Nha Tho, at the temple ruins in Po Nagar (► 110) or in Phan Thiet City at **Phi Long Sandpainting** (Alley 4444, Thu Khoa Huan, Than Hai district).

Where to…
Go Out

Anyone who likes the night life and lots of action should head for Nha Trang. The 'happy hour' here sometimes lasts the whole day! Drinks are incredibly cheap and are served until first light.

The place to be in Nha Trang is **Sailing Club** (72 Tran Phu; tel: 058 3 82 46 28; www.sailingclubnha trang.com; daily 7:30am–11pm, until about 2am when parties are on). This is where people gather to dine and dance, watch fire shows and enjoy the Saturday night beach party. Expensive. The sound of Latino music, salsa lessons and Tex-Mex food can be found every Thursday evening from 7pm onwards at **El Latino** in Mui Ne (139 Nguyen Dinh Chieu; tel: 062 3 74 35 95; daily 8am–11pm).

The **Elephant Festival** with races, boating events and folklore shows takes place every year in March in Ban Don. The **Dalat Flower Festival** is a magnificently colourful display with music, fashion shows and a procession. It takes place in uneven years between 10 and 18 December.

Vietnam's **sailing fans** gather in Nha Trang and Mui Ne/Phan Thiet; **kitesurfers** have declared Mui Ne their eldorado. Vietnam's best **diving grounds** are off Nha Trang and there are several PADI diving schools. The leading company is Rainbow Divers (www.divevietnam.com). **Golfers** can play among some of the most beautiful scenery in the Central Highlands near Da Lat and Phan Thiet/Mui Ne (www.vietnam golfresorts.com)., Companies such as Phat Tire Ventures (www.phattire ventures.com), for example, cater for those seeking a sporting adventure in the Central Highlands.

Central Region

Little Treats

Imperial splendour

Let yourself be transported in style, in a dragon boat, to the elaborate imperial tombs in **Hue** (▶ 130).

Fulfil a wish like a true Buddhist

Experience a moment of Buddhist spirituality and light an incense stick in one of the cave temples in the Marble Mountains near **Da Nang** (▶ 135).

A calm cuppa

Whenever it starts pouring down in buckets yet again in and around **Hue** (▶ 129) and shows no sign of stopping, a cup of jasmine tea is wonderfully calming.

Central Region

Getting Your Bearings

Away from the former war zone, the history of Vietnam – that goes back thousands of years – can be explored in and around the city of Da Nang with its beach and harbour. A total of four local places have been declared UNESCO World Heritage Sites: the Imperial City of Hue, the picturesque fishing port and the

Old Town of Hoi An, the mystic and enchanting ruins at My Son and the Phong Nha caves, one of the most extensive systems in Asia that were only discovered in 2009.

Ba Don
Liem Phu
Tay Gat
Son Trach
42 Phong Nha-Ke Bang National Park
Dong Hoi
1A
Lang Mo
15
14 Tang Ky
Ban Rum
LAOS
46 DMZ (Demilitarised Zone)
Da Krong

The Champa (► 103), one of the most powerful dynasties in Asia, ruled over what is now the central region of Vietnam for some 1,000 years. They left much more than 'just' the ruins of My Son on the valley floor that has since been claimed back by the jungle. The most important collection of artefacts from the advanced culture of these people is exhibited today in the Champa Museum in Da Nang (► 134). Anyone interested in exploring the sites of Vietnam's emperors and kings will be drawn to the Citadel and the Forbidden City in Hue, the seat of the last thirteen emperors of the Nguyen dynasty. The partly very elaborate tombs of the emperors on the Perfume River are a must.

Without doubt the most popular tourist destination is the little harbour town of Hoi An. Time seems to have stood still

Fishermen along Vietnam's coast (here, near Lang Co) still use traditional coracles (round boats with no keel)

Getting Your Bearings

Nguyen emperors turned Hue into a magnificent seat from 1802 onwards

in the Old Town on the Thu Bon of this former commercial and fishing centre with markedly Chinese characteristics. The narrow streets are lined with little single-storey houses with colonnades painted all sorts of bright colours, traditional Chinese meeting houses and tiny temples.

TOP 10

Four Perfect Days

Da Nang is a good starting point for this four-day tour of the central region – best explored in a hire car. From here you can visit attractions such as the Champa ruins, Hue and Hoi An without wasting any time and then relax a little on the beach. The choice of accommodation is also better in Da Nang.

Day One

Morning

The earlier you set out for ★ **Hoi An** (right; ➤ 126) the longer you will be able to appreciate the peace and quiet in the three roads that make up the pretty Old Town, before the 'storm'. The tourist coaches generally arrive by 10am at the latest. Stroll around the narrow streets with their Chinese lanterns, old merchants' house, meeting halls, temples and museums and

don't miss out on a visit to the market and the Japanese bridge. You will always be able to find somewhere for a snack at lunchtime in one of the many places to eat, e.g. on the river promenade.

Afternoon

Back in ㊶ **Da Nang** (➤ 134) a visit to the Museum of Champa Sculpture (left) will prepare you for My Son, the valley of ruins. The museum has some 500 exhibits from the 4th–14th centuries including figures of Shiva and Uroja, the *ur*-mother of Champa kings. After returning to your hotel you may well still have time for a swim in the sea or the pool.

Day Two

Morning

Once again it is worth leaving your accommodation as early as possible as it soon gets hot and sticky in the narrow, shade-less hollow of ㊵ **My Son** (➤ 132). You will need a few hours to explore the different temple towers in what was once the religious centre of the Champa and to marvel at the reliefs on the brick-built structures that are scattered quite far apart.

Afternoon

You may fancy a shopping trip in Hoi An on the way back, for example at the lively **night market**, or perhaps you would rather head straight for the **beach in Da Nang**.

Day Three

Morning

Today's destination is ⭐**Hue** (➤ 129) with a visit to the Citadel and the Forbidden City. As a result of wars, typhoons and fires only a few buildings from the 19th century have survived on this extensive site – the Throne Room (Hall of Supreme Harmony), the Royal Theatre, the library and several smaller temples and pavilions. A trip on a dragon boat (or else in a taxi or bus) takes visitors to the **Perfume Pagoda** (➤ 131) and – depending on the agreement made with the captain – to the most important imperial tombs such as the impressive tomb of **Tu Duc** (➤ 130).

Afternoon

Back in Da Nang you could head off for the beach again to have time to digest all the impressions gained during the day.

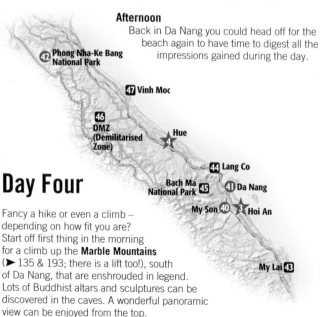

42 Phong Nha-Ke Bang National Park

47 Vinh Moc

46 DMZ (Demilitarised Zone)

Hue ⭐4

44 Lang Co

Bach Ma **45** National Park

41 Da Nang

My Son **40** ⭐3 Hoi An

My Lai **43**

Day Four

Fancy a hike or even a climb – depending on how fit you are? Start off first thing in the morning for a climb up the **Marble Mountains** (➤ 135 & 193; there is a lift too!), south of Da Nang, that are enshrouded in legend. Lots of Buddhist altars and sculptures can be discovered in the caves. A wonderful panoramic view can be enjoyed from the top.

Central Region

⭐3 Hoi An

The historical centre of Hoi An is now a protected UNESCO World Heritage Site. Some 800 atmospheric buildings line just three roads and, unlike virtually any other place in Vietnam, form an intact ensemble of houses and shops, Chinese meeting halls, private family temples and pagodas. The idyllic Old Town was left unscathed during the Vietnam War.

Once an important international port, the little town of Hoi An (formerly Faifo or Hai Pho in Chinese, 'Place on the Sea') was greatly influenced by China. It lies on the River Thu Bon, some 30km (18.5mi) southeast of Da Nang. Many Chinese, descendents of former merchant families, still live here today, some in the charming old merchants' houses.

An Old Trading Centre...

Where groups of tourists elbow past each other today was alive with merchants in the 16th–18th centuries selling silk, brocade, ivory, porcelain, tea and betel nuts. Cinnamon and sugar were exchanged for weapons, cannons and lead from Europe. As their sailing ships were dependent on the monsoon winds which only change direction every six months to get back to their home ports, the Chinese and Japanese set up trading posts here. Behind some of the dark wooden façades of the single-storey shop buildings songbirds can be seen in hanging bamboo baskets. A closer look reveals a number of architectural details such as interlocking *yin yang*, moss-covered roof tiles and the *mat cua* eyes that keep watch over the entrances to the houses (two round wooden bolts with decorated ends).

...and its Architectural Heritage

The most famous building is the Japanese bridge (**Cau Nhat Ban** or **Lai Vien Khieu**) erected in the 16th century, destroyed on several occasions and rebuilt in 1763. Painted a dusky pink, it is in a plain Japanese style with a tiled roof and extends 18m (59ft) over a side canal of the Thu Bon. It once linked the former Chinese district with that of Japanese merchants. The statues of two dogs are on the western side of the bridge; the two monkeys on the east. Building was presumably started in the Chinese year of the monkey and completed in the year of the dog.

The almost 200-year-old building **Tan Ky** in Nguyen Thai Hoc is the most visited merchant's house in Hoi An. This pretty home of a wealthy merchant is entered from the front through the shop. At the back of the property, ancestral shrines are now where there were once store

rooms with access to the river. In the middle is an open courtyard providing light and fresh air, with butts to collect rainwater. Wooden pillars have been inlaid with Chinese verses in mother-of-pearl. The house is decorated with exquisite wooden carvings such as a carp and dragon figure and a bat – both of which bring good luck. Two **mat cua** eyes watch over the entrance and the altar suspended above the kitchen doorway.

Among the 80 or so, partly still lived-in merchants' houses is **Quan Thang House**, erected in 1690, in the parallel road Than Phu to the north. It is one of the oldest buildings. Characteristic features include the tiny little inner courtyards and light-wells that lie one behind another, the high thresholds to prevent flooding, the artistically carved doors and pillars, the Chinese characters on the ceiling beams and the wall mosaics. And, of course,

Above: Hoi An's Old Town with its old shops and houses

there are shrines dedicated to ancestors, the kitchen god and the god of prosperity.

Opposite: Phuoc Kien Assembly Hall has been a UNESCO World Heritage Site since 1999

Phuoc Kien Assembly Hall (Hoi Quan Phuoc Kien) is a traditional building erected in 1692 by Fukian Chinese and is one of the most splendid of its kind. It is located a little further to the east in Tran Phu and is an oasis of peace and quiet when not besieged by groups of tourists. In the inner courtyard is the carp, *cá chép*, the promise of the transformation of good fortune, depicted in the form of an immortal dragon. The smoke from incense sticks carries the wishes and prayers of the faithful to Thien Hau, the goddess of the sea and guardian of seafarers who can be seen in a wall painting in the midst of the thundering waves. Ancestors are worshipped in the area beyond the inner courtyard as is Than Tai, the god of fortune and

Central Region

prosperity and the three Heavenly Women who ensure offspring.

The colourful **Quang Cong Pagoda (Chua Quang Cong)**, at the end of Tran Phu near the market, was dedicated by the Chinese in 1653 to General Quang Cong (198–249 CE), a legendary hero from the era of the Three Kingdoms. He is shown as a huge papier-mâché figure on the altar. The mythical carp is once again immortalised in the inner courtyard – this time as a waterspout made of ceramic.

A popular backdrop – the Japanese bridge

TAKING A BREAK

Normal tasty fare is available all day long at the **market** (£; east end of Bach Dang on the river bank) – noodle soup and the local speciality *cao lau* (a thicker type of noodle). Street saleswomen sell incredibly cheap *banh bao* – steamed pork dumplings.

✚ 217 D4

Japanese Bridge
✉ Tran Phu
🕐 Temple shrine daily 8am–6pm, otherwise open 24 hrs.
✋ Bridge: free, temple shrine: combined ticket (➤ Insider Info)

Tan Ky House
✉ 101 Nguyen Thai Hoc 🕐 Daily 8am–noon, 2pm–5:30pm ✋ ➤ Insider Info

Quan Thang House
✉ 77 Tran Phu, no tel: 🕐 Daily 8am until 5:30pm ✋ ➤ Insider Info

Phuoc Kien Assembly Hall
✉ 46 Tran Phu, no tel: 🕐 Daily 8am–6pm ✋ ➤ Insider Info

Quang Cong Pagoda
✉ 24 Tran Phu near the market 🕐 Daily 6:30am–6pm ✋ ➤ Insider Info

INSIDER INFO

Insider Tip

- Whether visiting or just on an evening stroll, everyone has to pay an entrance fee to the Old Town. The best buy is a **combined ticket** (VND120,000 for up to five sites, valid for 24 hrs), available from the tourist information office (10 Nguyen Hue, 10 Trang Hung Dao, 78 Le Loi, 47 Tran Phu; tel: 0510 3 86 27 15; www. hoianworldheritage.org.vn; daily 7am–6pm).
- **The best time to travel** is from February to April; during the rainy season from August to December the roads are not seldom under water.
- To avoid any problems when visiting the houses, temples and pagodas, please remember that **miniskirts, shorts and tank tops** are not to be worn. You should also refrain from smoking and do not give begging children either money or presents.

★4 Hue

In this former imperial city, the flair of court life has been rekindled as a folkloric attraction; dragon boats carry visitors down the Perfume River to Thien Mu Pagoda and the imperial tombs while nearby Thuan An is everything a beach should be.

Grandeur for all eternity – Khai Dinh's imperial tomb

Citadel

Hue's rapid rise to fame came after the first Nguyen emperor **Gia Long** (reigned 1802–20) made it the capital and commissioned the building of the citadel. Hoang Thanh, the Imperial City, covers 1,285 acres and was erected on the northern bank of the river to a geometric plan. Like the Forbidden City in Peking on which it was modelled it is a UNESCO World Heritage Site. Some 80 of the 300 buildings that were once on the site are on view or have been rebuilt.

Behind the massive fortified ramparts and the imposing two-storey **Noon Gate (Ngo Mon)** is the **Throne Room (Hall of Supreme Harmony, Thai Hoa Palace)**. Its huge curved roof is supported on 80 columns decorated with golden dragons. The elongated **Temple of Generations (The Mieu)** to the southwest that was also restored in 1998, has ten red-painted altars with genealogical charts of the emperor and his wives.

The **Forbidden Purple City** lies at the heart of the imperial complex. This was the preserve of the emperor, his family and servants comprising up to 300 concubines and eunuchs. The restored treasury and apartments of the emperor's mother (Dien Tho) in the northwest corner of the imperial palace complex now form a museum open to the public. The two Halls of the Mandarins (Ta Vu and Huu Vu), the pretty library (Thai Binh Lau) with a rock garden and a pond, several smaller temple shrines and

pavilions, as well as the **Royal Theatre (Duyet Thi Duong)** to the right have been carefully restored. (➤ 144).

Imperial Tombs

Three of the imperial tombs that can be found in the area have become Hue's top attractions with their enchanting landscape gardens, pavilions and temples. The **Lang Khiem** complex, that includes the tomb of Tu Duc (reigned 1847–83) who lived here during his (not very successful) sixteen-year reign, exudes a romantic but morbid charm. The restored pavilions, Xung Khiem and Luu Khiem, where the emperor wrote some 4,000 poems, meditated and played chess, are situated next to Luu Khiem pond. Steps lead up to the Hoa Khiem temple with an altar dedicated to the emperor and empress. Tu Duc once used this as a palace. His tomb lies at a slightly higher level behind a wall and courtyard (Bai Dinh) with two rows of stone sculptures of horses, elephants, guards and mandarins. The largest stele in Vietnam, on which Tu Duc inscribed his own obituary in around 5,000 characters, cannot be missed.

Lang Ung, the small, rather gloomy but equally majestic burial site of Emperor Khai Dinh (reigned 1916–25), which fuses European and Asian architectural elements, is located on the slopes of Nui Chau Chu. 160 steps lead to the courtyard with its stele pavilion and guardian figures. Beyond is the almost Baroque-like Thien Dinh palace temple, colourfully decorated with mosaics and ceiling paintings. It houses the Khai Dinh altar, a gilded bronze statue of the emperor and his tomb.

Lang Hieu, the burial site of Minh Mang (reigned 1820–41), is situated in a landscaped garden that rises up Cam Ke Hill. It demonstrates a clearly Chinese influence. The 40 buildings have a strict symmetry arranged along an east/west axis. Behind the magnificent Dai Hong Mon gate is the cour d'honneur. The two-storey Pavilion of Serenity (Minh Lau) sits at the top of Tam Tai Hill. From here, you have a view down over Tan Nguyet pond that symbolises the new moon. The crescent curves around the actual tomb. A small bridge and another 33 steps lead to Minh Mang's tomb itself.

Riding an elephant in the Citadel with the Noon Gate behind. The Perfume Pagoda is the oldest of its kind in Hue

Perfume Pagoda

Chua Thien Mu (Chua Linh Mu) rises above the northen bank of the Huong River on Ha Khe Hill. The 'Pagoda of the Celestial Lady' was built in 1601 by the Nguyen lord, Hoang, and extended and restored on several occasions. The complex is dominated by the 21m (69ft)-high, octagonal, seven-storey pagoda tower (Phuoc Duyen) that Emperor Thieu Tri had built in 1884. In one of the two pavilions to the side is a bronze bell from 1710 that weighs more than three tons; in the other there is a stele on the back of a marble turtle from 1715.

TAKING A BREAK

Soup kitchens provide visitors with the classic *bun bo hue*, a hearty noodle soup with beef.

➕ 216 C5

Vietnam Tourism
✉ 14 Nguyen Van Cu (and in all hotels) ☎ 054 3 81 83 16

Citadel
✉ Lang Khiem: near Duong Xuan Thuong village, 8km (5mi) southwest of Hue; Lang Ung: 10km (6.25mi) south of Hue; Lang Hieu: 12km (7.5mi) south of Hue
☎ 054 3 53 08 40, 054 3 52 32 37; www.hueworldheritage.org.vn
🕐 7am–5pm; summer 6:30am–5:30pm ✋ incl. palace museum: VND150,000, combined ticket with ⅔ of the imperial tombs VND280,000/VND360,000

Imperial Tombs (Royal Mausoleums)
☎ 054 3 53 08 40, 054 3 52 32 37; www.hueworldheritage.org.vn
🕐 Daily 7am–5pm, 6:30am–5:30pm (summer) ✋ Each tomb: VND100,000

Perfume Pagoda
✉ Near Huong Long village, 5km (3mi) west of Hue
🕐 Daily 7am–5pm ✋ Free

INSIDER INFO

■ An **electric shuttle bus service** is provided. A **dragon boat** for two people for 2½–5 hrs. will cost VND200,000–VND300,000; in the low season you may even manage to agree with the boat owner on a longer half-day trip with lunch on board.

■ A 🎫 **changing of the guard ceremony** takes place every day at 9am at Noon Gate.

Insider Tip

■ The area around Hue has the highest rainfall anywhere in Vietnam; between August/September and February and especially in November you must reckon with flooded roads. If you get caught in such a **rainy period** in Hue you may want to escape to Da Nang (➤ 134) on the other side of the weather divide created by the **Bach Ma mountains**.

■ A small palace, **Cung An Dinh** (Khai Tuong Lau, 150 Nguyen Hue; daily 8am–5pm, admission: VND20,000), dating from 1916–18, has been restored and opened as a museum in March 2015. It displays a mixture of Vietnamese and European Baroque items, including plasterwork and ceiling and wall paintings. Emperor Khai Dinh used the palace as a private retreat – and a place to smoke opium and play cards.

④⓪ My Son

Time seems to have stood still in the scattered ruins on the valley floor – and that for 1,400 years. Hindu gods, dancers and a few devilish faces look down on visitors as they move around over bamboo bridges and along well-worn tracks among the sparse ruins of this holy site. A lingam here (the Shiva phallus symbol), an Uroja pedestal there with erect stone breasts (the *ur*-mother); behind is a waterfall and a little pond which is actually a bomb crater.

Once a Champa religious site with a number of temples it was declared a UNESCO World Heritage Site in 1999. It lies in a narrow valley basin surrounded by hills, some 70km (45mi) southwest of Da Nang and 40km (25mi) west of Hoi An. At the end of the 19th century archaeologists from the École française d'Extrême-Orient listed more than 70 ruins from the 4th and the 7th–13th centuries. The ruins of 20 buildings can be seen today.

Luxuriant vegetation has long since taken over the Champa ruins

A Champa Religious Site

Most of the ruins were bombed by US troops in 1968. Early on, My Son had been declared a 'fire-free zone' before the Viet Cong became entrenched in the area. The largest religious structure, a 24m (79ft)-high *kalan* tower decorated with lions and elephants, was destroyed. It was reputedly the most beautiful brick building in Asia.

It is assumed that the temple complex was dedicated to a number of gods and goddesses and that temple dancers also lived here along with the priests. King Bhadravarman

Detail of an altar in My Son decorated with reliefs

(reigned 380–413) probably erected a wooden temple here in the late 4th century – he was later worshipped as the divine King Bhadresvara (the tower in the temple group 'B' may well have been dedicated to him). King Sambhuvarman had the building replaced by a structure made of more lasting materials such as bricks in the 7th century. Little by little the largest religious site of the Cham people evolved, boasting several different temple complexes which are now divided into 10 groups with different letters. The best preserved ruins are **groups B, C and D** near the entrance.

They comprise the three following characteristic brick structures: the centre is marked by a **tower (kalan)** that symbolised the (mystic) mountain of Mehru as the home of the gods. A symbol for Shiva can generally be found inside, such as a phallic lingam or the holy mount, the bull Nandi. Holy manuscripts and ritual objects were kept in the **library**. This has quite obvious Malayan-Polynesian architectural elements such as a boat-shaped roof – the Cham people had good trade links to Java, among other places. Temple dances would probably have been held in the **meditation hall (mandapa)**. Many finds excavated from this site such as frescos, lingams, Uroja pedestals and altars can now be seen in the excellent Champa Museum in Da Nang (► 134).

TAKING A BREAK

A restaurant and snack bars provide a range of food, Vietnamese dishes and cold drinks.

➕ 217 D4   🕐 Daily 6am–4:30pm   💰 VND100,000 (incl. museum)

INSIDER INFO

- The best way to get here is on a **moped, with a tour bus, by hire car or taxi** (about VND1.1m). It is less advisable to take a boat trip on the Thu Bon as this does not take you to My Son directly and involves a moped taxi trip from the pier. *Insider Tip*
- **Early risers** should head off on the 4-hour trip before breakfast is even served in hotels, leaving at around 5am. You will be rewarded by avoiding the tourist coaches that arrive between 9am and 10am at the latest and being able to explore the site before the midday heat.
- **Dancing and music performances** are held on the site (Tue–Sun 9:30am and 10:30am).
- The sun shines mercilessly at the bottom of the valley in My Son. **Sun blocker** and sufficient **drinking water** are an absolute must. *Insider Tip*

㊶ Da Nang

This modern port is the gateway to the World Heritage Sites at Hue, Hoi An and My Son, mainly thanks to its international airport. Many luxury beach hotels have opened in the past few years, especially on 'China Beach' which played a role during the Vietnam War.

Today, there are few reminders of the senseless loss of life during the Vietnam War at this spot where, on 8 March 1965 US ground forces landed, driving their tanks up the beach and where, between 1967–72 the German hospital ship 'Helgoland' lay at anchor out in the bay. The magical, top-of-the-range hotel Furama (▶ 141) that opened in 1997 was the very first of its kind anywhere in Vietnam. It is located close to the city and the mile-long **'China Beach' (Bai My Khe, Bai Bac My An)**. This golden yellow stretch of sand extends

over 30km (18.5mi) to the south as far as Hoi An. Virtually every week now a luxury hotel chain opens its Vietnamese flagship somewhere on the beach.

Da Nang itself lies beyond the beach area on the west bank of the River Han where the **Bach Dang Promenade** can be found. The most recent eye-catcher is the **Dragon Bridge** inaugurated in 2014 with 'light-spewing' dragon-like creatures which are especially spectacular at night. Otherwise the only sight really worth visiting in this aspiring city with its ever-changing skyline is the exceptional **Champa Museum**. Some 500 exhibits from the 1,000-year history of the Champa kingdom (4th–14th centuries) in South Vietnam are displayed in ten exhibition rooms – Hindu deities such as Shiva and his symbol, the lingam phallus and other figures like the mythical bird, Garuda, the elephant god, Ganesha, lions and *dvarapalas* (door guards). The most striking are perhaps the depictions of Uroja, the *ur*-mother, in the form of a breast or nipple.

Insider Tip

Da Nang's new landmark, the Dragon Bridge, is especially impressive at night

The Marble Mountains

Around 10km (6.25mi) southeast of Da Nang are the five Marble Mountains (Ngu Hanh Son, ➤ 193) which stand for five different elements – Thuy Son (water mountain), Moc Son (wood mountain), Kim Son (metal or gold mountain), Tho Son (earth mountain) and Hoa

An imposing Buddha statue greets visitors at the end of the huge cavern in Huyen Khong cave

Son (fire mountain). Emperor Minh Mang had **Tam Thai Pagoda** built in 1825 on **Thuy Son**, at 100m (328ft) the highest mountain, on a holy site where, earlier, the Cham people had worshipped Hindu gods and later Buddha. Nowadays, at weekends, many faithful come here to revere the Sakyamuni Buddha and Quan Am, the goddess of mercy.

The mountain is riddled with a labyrinth of caves. The largest, the beautiful **Huyen Khong cave** is 30m (98ft) high and was once a place of animist worship only later developing into a Buddhist pilgrimage site. During the Vietnam War the caves were used by guerillas as a hiding place and as a field hospital.

TAKING A BREAK

There is always plenty of choice at **Han market** (£; Bach Dang Promenade), ranging from fruit to rice dishes and noodle soup. There are also lots of good and cheap eateries on the river bank.

➕ 217 D4

Saigon Tourist:
✉ 357 Phan Chu Trinh ☎ 0511 3 89 72 29; www.saigon-tourist.com

Cham Museum (Bao Tang Cham)
✉ 1 Trung Nu Vuong corner 2 Thang 9
☎ 0511 3 57 48 01; http://chammuseum.danang.vn
🕐 Daily 7am–5:30pm, 2-hr guided tours at 8am and 2pm 🎫 VND40,000

Marble Mountains (Thuy Son, ➤ 193)
✉ 10km (6.25mi) southeast of Da Nang
🕐 Daily 7am–5pm 🎫 VND15,000, lift: VND15,000

INSIDER INFO

When night falls the Dragon Bridge comes alive. A 🎡 night market takes place on the Han River at weekends set against the brilliant spectacle of a dragon breathing fire and spewing water and a light show. Just join the crowd of young Vietnamese on the wide promenade, have a look at the many souvenir and street food stalls and join in the fun of the fair – and sample the noodle soup, sugar cane juice or coconut milk. Children will love the big wheel and the merry-go-rounds (Sat and Sun from 6pm, fire show: 9pm).

Insider Tip

④ Phong Nha Ke Bang National Park

A trip underground takes you into one of the most extensive and enthralling cave systems in Asia, if not in the world. It is best explored by boat or with a renowned caving adventure company.

Due to its mile-long caves full of stalactites and stalagmites the important karst region of Phong Nha was declared a UNESCO World Heritage Site in 2003. And, as recently as 2009, British explorers discovered 20 new caves with an overall length of 56km (35mi). Resistance fighters against the French literally disappeared underground here from the late 19th century onward, as did the Viet Cong in the Vietnam War. The Champa people on the other hand considered the caves holy as confirmed by inscriptions and altar finds.

Hang Phong Nha
The 15 chambers and caves which form part of the main complex of Phong Nha (Cave of Teeth) near Son Trach and **Hang Toi (Dark Cave)**, in particular, also attract a lot of local visitors. A flurry of flashlights can regularly be seen all along the 1.5km (1mi)-long main path that itself is well lit. The dripstones are sometimes bathed in coloured light. After a boat trip along the underground stream, the 'dry' Tien Son cave (also called Dong Kho) higher up can be reached via a number of steps.

Hang Thien Duong
Anyone who finds this all a little too touristy is best advised to visit the breathtaking but less commercialised Paradise Cave (Hang Thien Duong). The entrance to this system that extends some 31km (19mi) lies hidden in a narrow, jungle-like valley. 524 steps lead upwards to start with

Groups of up to 100 people are nothing unusual in the Phong Nha caves

Spotting animals is a matter of luck in the lost world of Hang Son Doong

followed by another 200 steps which take you underground. A walkway some 1km (0.6mi) long, that is also well lit, leads through spectacular caverns with countless stalactites and stalagmites.

Flora and Fauna

The surrounding Ke Bang national park is a hotspot of biodiversity. There are more than 1,000 different species of animal, including some 85 mammals, in this tropical, evergreen, primary forest. Ten endemic species of monkey, including langurs and gibbons, of which four species are threatened with extinction, are at home here, as are deer-like giant muntjaks, the Asian black bear, the serow and possibly the saola. In addition, about 2,400 species of plant (some endangered) have been recorded here (including three types of orchid, long considered extinct the world over).

TAKING A BREAK

There are all sorts of bars and food stands as well as shops selling drinks at the entrance to the Phong Nha caves.

➕ 219 D2; www.phongnhakebang.vn
🕐 Daily 6am–4pm 🖐 incl. guide: Hang Phong Nha VND150,000, Hang Tien Son VND80,000, Hang Thien Duong VND120,000; boat/kayak rental about VND100,000/person or VND350,000 per boat with a max. 14 passengers

INSIDER INFO

- Excursions to the national park can be booked as a package through **Footprint Vietnam** (30A Alley 12A, Ly Nam De, Hanoi; tel: 04 39 33 28 44; www.foot printsvietnam.com).
- A spectacular caving adventure takes a select few into **Hang Son Doong** cave which is almost 9km (6mi) long and up 200m (660ft) high. A true 'lost world' with jungle flora, beaches, rivers and clouds underground. Since 2014 this can be explored as part of a one-week long, very demanding, cave-trekking tour. Only 200 tourists who are fit and have climbing experience are allowed in every year. Cost: US$3,000; long waiting list (www.oxalis.com.vn; www.sondoongcave.org).
- Don't forget your **swimming things!**
- Avoid the main caves at **weekends** and **on public holidays**. **After rain** in November and December the caves may be closed because of flooding.
- Explore the Dark Cave in a **kayak** or cross the river on a **zip-wire**.

Insider
Tip

At Your Leisure

43 My Lai

The village of My Lai (also spelt Son My) became known the world over as a result of the massacre perpetrated on 16 March 1968. Under the command of Lieutenant William Calley, US soldiers were to root out and kill Viet Cong fighters here and in three neighbouring villages. In so doing, they abused and shot a total of 504 villagers – the elderly, women, children, infants and even pets – all killed "in a fierce fight" according to Calley's report. Calley was the only one brought to justice in the US and sentenced to life imprisonment in the first instance in 1971. He was later pardoned by President Nixon. Today, a memorial in a park-like setting commemorates those murdered with plaques and gravestones bearing the names of the victims. Several houses have been rebuilt and bullet holes and burn marks can be seen. There is also a small museum with a documentary film.

✚ 217 E3 ⏰ Museum: 8–11:30, 1:30–5
💲 VND20,000

44 Lang Co

This beautiful peninsula in a deep-blue lagoon in the South China Sea, some 40km (25mi) north of Da Nang, has nothing but typically picture-postcard scenery. Fishing boats bob about in a glistening turquoise sea and the golden sands are lined with a mass of palm trees. The best views are to be had from up high, 500m (1,650ft) above the water, from Hai Van Pass (Deo Hai Van) – providing there is a break in the clouds. This pass, reached via a number of hairpin bends on the steep N1, is the weather divide and is not called 'Cloud Pass' for nothing. The views are however sometimes rather obscured by vegetation.

Oysters, used for cultivating pearls, are farmed in the **lagoon**. The basins can be visited or you can take a **boat trip** with the fishermen and get a closer look at the huge fishing nets that are hung on poles above the water.

✚ 217 D5

45 Bach Ma National Park

Visitors can explore the area and its rich fauna – which includes the extremely rare species of antelope, the saola, and the deer-like muntjak – on several hiking trails through the national park (also referred to as Hai Van) which extends over an area of 54,500 acres. The many lakes, rivers and deep waterfalls feed pools that are ideal for swimming, such as **Do Quyen**

Water and luxuriant vegetation dominate the scenery in Bach Ma National Park

Waterfall which drops 300m (984ft) or **Thac Bac (Silver Waterfall)**. Trekking paths such as the **Five Lakes Trail** are very steep in parts with roped sections and wooden ladders – and are a challenge to experienced hikers too. A spectacular panoramic view (if the weather is fine) can be had from the 1,450m (4,757ft)-high **Bach Ma**. The park is however in the region in Vietnam with the highest rainfall, with heavy downpours between September and December in particular.

It is best to plan a visit to the park between February/March (when the rhododendrons are in bloom) and June. It gets very hot between May and August and is often very busy at weekends at this time. Facilities include a campsite, simple guesthouses, landrovers for hire and an excellent visitor centre with an orchid house.

✚ 216 C4 ☎ 054 3 87 13 30; www.bachmapark.com.vn
🕐 Daily March–Sep
7am–5pm, Oct–Feb
7:30am–4:30pm
💰 VND40,000

46 DMZ (Demilitarised Zone)

The 'demilitarised zone' (DMZ) on both sides of **Ben Hai River** is 80km (50mi) north of Hue on the 17th parallel in the province of Quang Tri that was heavily bombed in 1968/69. After the resolution passed at the Geneva Conference on Indochina in 1954, a 10km (6.25mi)-wide demarcation line separated Communist North Vietnam from the Republic of South Vietnam that was under American influence until 1975. Bullet-ridden ruins such as impressive **La Vang Basilica** near Quang Tri, not far from the N1, military cemeteries and memorials, (reconstructed) bunkers and overgrown trenches, tanks and helicopters, as well as a few remaining bits of wartime scrap are silent reminders of the war.

More than 10,000 gravestones and shrines commemorate the 'martyrs' in Truong Son National Cemetery who died while building or defending the Ho Chi Minh Trail

A visit to the **Mine Action Visitor Center**, run by the mine clearance project RENEW in Dong Ha south of the actual DMZ, is well worthwhile. Films, photos and exhibitions provide information on the very real dangers left by the war that still exist to this day, such as when children find **cluster bombs** – the size of tennis balls, orange in colour and often still intact.

The N9 leaves the coast road near Dong Ha turning inland towards Cam Lo. Just 20km (12mi) to the north is **Truong Son National Cemetery**. Many of the gravestones lined up in endless rows are purely symbolic as the bodies of many

Central Region

victims were never found. To the west of Cam Lo is the plateau camp **Khe Sanh**, the scene of the worst battle in the Vietnam War. **Hamburger Hill** lies to the south and **Dakrong Bridge**, rebuilt by the Cubans in 1975/76, near the Laos border. The legendery Ho Chi Minh Trail can be found near **Aluoi**.

➕ 219 E1

DMZ
🕐 Daily 7am–4:30pm
🎫 Free, museums VND20,000

Quang Tri Mine Action Visitor Center (RENEW)
✉ Kids First Village,
185 Ly Thuong Kiet, Dong Ha
☎ 053 3 85 84 45 (extension 114); www.landmines.org.vn
🕐 Mon–Fri 8am–5pm, Sat, Sun by prior arrangement only 🎫 Free

Insider Tip

47 Vinh Moc

North of Ben Hai, near the village of Ho Xa, a turning off the N1 leads towards the coast. After 13km (8mi) you will reach the Vinh Moc tunnels that have been preserved in their original state. Unlike the rather touristy Cu Chi Tunnels (▶ 53) these provide a very undistorted impression of life underground. They were built during the Vietnam

17 babies were born in the system of tunnels in Vinh Moc

War in 1966/67 and were initially intended as a shelter for the local population which was exposed to heavy shelling. Later, the Viet Cong took over the 3km (1.8mi)-long system of tunnels as a base. They extend over three levels and several entrances are actually on the beach. Some 1,700m (5,600ft) have now been reconstructed. The tunnels are up to 1.80m (6ft) high, lit by electricity and open up into assembly areas up to 23m (76ft) under ground level with room for about 50 people. A museum shows photos that depict everyday life in the tunnels.

➕ 219 E2
🕐 Daily 7am–4:30pm
🎫 VND25,000

THE HO CHI MINH TRAIL

This supply route some 16,000km (10,000mi) long lies hidden in the jungle and ran for a large part through the territory of the officially neutral neighbouring countries of Laos and Cambodia. It was bombed – at first secretly – by the USA between 1964 and 1973 using at least 2 million tons of explosives. Supplies were generally transported through the tunnels at night, without which the Tet Offensive would have been unthinkable. Despite heavy losses on the North Vietnamese side this was never stopped. According to estimates, 5,000 tons of materials were transported to those fighting in the south on foot, by bike or by lorry, every month.

Where to...
Stay

Price
of a double room per night:
£ under VND1m.   ££ VND1–VND2.4m.   £££ over VND2.4m.

DA NANG

Centara Sandy Beach ££–£££
A standard category hotel 5km (5mi) south of Da Nang on a quiet stretch of the beach. It comprises 61 light and bright rooms, 52 bungalows and five villas with views either over the sea or the garden, two pools, a 'kids' club', golf and tennis courses.
➕ 217 D4
✉ Bai Non Nuoc, 21 Truong, Hoa Hai
☎ 0511 3 96 17 77;
www.centarahotelsresorts.com

Furama £££
Vietnam's first luxury hotel is still very much in the top league in Da Nang to this day. The elegant villas and suites have large rooms with parquet floors, lots of high-quality woodwork and Champa elements. Set in a garden on the lagoon with swimming in the pool and the sea. A steakhouse and an Italian restaurant are just two of the places to eat. Sports and leisure activities include tai chi, a gym, fishing tours and a spa. A 'kids' club' takes care of the younger generation. Under German management.
➕ 217 D4 ✉ China Beach
☎ 0511 3 84 73 33; www.furamavietnam.com

Nemo £
This family-run hotel was opened in 2014. Very simple rooms with shower rooms on four floors with a lift. Good value for money, helpful staff, just 10 minutes on foot from Non Nuoc Beach, lots of bars and restaurants in the vicinity.

➕ 217 D4 ✉ 100/2 Nguyen Van Thoai
☎ 0511 3 95 19 51; http://danangnemohotel.com
(only in Vietnamese)

Traveller's Rest ££
Boutique guesthouse. At Phoung and Andrew's (an Australian) there are only two rooms plus a kitchen in an Art Deco style villa near the beach. But if you manage to get one of the rooms you will be enjoy the relaxed atmosphere, mini-pool in the garden, travel tips and muesli for breakfast!
➕ 217 D4
✉ 80 Ba Huyen Thanh Quan ☎ 012 29 44 44 15;
www.travellersrestdanang.com

HOI AN

Ancient House ££
A real oasis, just ten minutes on foot from the centre on the road to the beach. Lovely standard category hotel complex of little Mediterranean-style cottages around a mini-pool and lots of plants; spa. 52 cosy and comfortable rooms with large four-posters and balconies.
➕ 217 D4 ✉ 377 Cua Dai ☎ 0510 3 92 33 77;
www.ancienthouseresort.com

Green Heaven £–££
Very comfortable, reasonably priced, *Insider Tip* standard category hotel. Central and peaceful location. The lovely rooms with excellent bathrooms are arranged over two floors around a pool in the central courtyard. Friendly and professional service. Just a hop, skip and jump from the city centre. Good online connection.

Central Region

⊕ 217 D4 ✉ 21 La Hoi,
An Hoi peninsula ☎ 0511 3 96 29 69;
www.hoiangreenheavenresort.com

The Nam Hai £££

One of Vietnam's most upmarket hotels under German management. The 100 minimalistically designed beach-front pool villas, with lots of dark grey granite and exquisite dark wood, come at a price. For this, guests can expect perfect service (incl. a butler). Increase your holiday budget a little to indulge in a supreme culinary experience.
⊕ 217 D4 ✉ Dien Duong, 8km (5mi) north of Hoi An ☎ 0510 3 94 00 00; www.ghmhotels.com

HUE

Hanh Dat £

Small, modern budget hotel for the cost-conscious. Rooms have a mini-bar, some have baths and balconies. Attentive service; good views from the roof bar; lots of regulars. The centre is just 10 mins. on foot.

Insider Tip

⊕ 216 C5
✉ 15 Pham Van Dong, Vy Da district
☎ 054 3 89 84 86; www.hanhdathotel.com.vn

Saigon Morin ££–£££

Even Charlie Chaplin enjoyed the colonial flair here. This elegant hotel with 180 quaintly old-fashioned rooms is centrally located. The garden oasis in the inner courtyard with a little pool is a quiet place to have a hearty breakfast, for example.
⊕ 216 C5 ✉ 30 Le Loi
☎ 054 3 82 35 26; www.morinhotel.com.vn

PHONG NHA

Phong Nha Farm Stay £

Ideal for backpackers. Run by the Australians Ben and Bich, visitors stay in a little oasis with a pool between the paddy fields (10 rooms, no air-conditioning, 1 dormitory). Tours to nearby caves organised.
⊕ 219 D2
✉ Cu Nam, 35km (22mi) north of Dong Hoi
☎ 052 3 67 51 35; www.phong-nha-cave.com

Where to...
Eat and Drink?

Price
for a main course without drinks:
£ under VND120,000   ££ VND120,000–VND240,000   £££ over VND240,000

DA NANG

Babylon Steak Garden ££

Don't be deceived by the name. In this Vietnamese tourist restaurant with a roof terrace, vegetarians and children will find something to eat too! The extensive menu includes not just classic Vietnamese dishes such as *kim chi*, wagyu beef steaks and BBQ specialities, but also spaghetti, pasta and chips (add 15% to all the prices).

⊕ 217 D4
✉ Truong Sat corner Ho Xuan Huong
☎ 0511 3 98 79 89 ⊙ Daily 10am–10:30pm

Lam Vien ££–£££

This pretty garden restaurant lies hidden near the Pullman beach hotel in a somewhat uninspiring residential area. But it's worth seeking out. Eat outside or inside this lovely and welcoming, romantic teak building. Seafood, fried noodles, soup and all sorts of hearty grilled dishes. You pay a little more than elsewhere for the atmosphere; the portions could be a little more generous.

⊞ 217 D4 ✉ 88 Tran Van Du
☎ 0511 3 95 91 71; www.lamviendanang.com
🕐 Daily 11:30am–9:30pm

HOI AN

Ancient Faifo ££
Lovely, centrally located café in the Old Town with regional fare. After a welcome drink, guests dine in a sophisticated environment over two floors with live piano music (reserve a table on the balcony) or on a tiny patio. Classics such as *cao lau*, spring rolls or *pho* are served. The scallops are delicious as are the prawns in a ginger-tamarind sauce. Good selection of wines.

⊞ 217 D4
✉ 66 Nguyen Thai Hoc
☎ 0510 3 91 74 44; www.ancientfaifo.com.vn
🕐 Daily 7am–10pm

Bao Han £–££
Near the Palm Garden beach hotel, resolute but friendly Phi spoils her guests, many of whom are regulars, in her small, unassuming, family-run restaurant. The quality has remained consistently high since 2006. Fried rice, spring rolls, fresh seafood, fish, hot-pots – everything tastes delicious. The king prawns really are king-sized; the service is attentive; the prices okay. And the choice of wines is good too.

⊞ 217 D4 ✉ 17 Cua Dai
☎ 0510 3 50 14 40 🕐 Daily 10am–9:30pm

Little Menu £–££
This simple restaurant is hidden down a side road. Small, a bit of a squeeze and not much of a choice – but the speciality here is duck in all variations (and always without glutamate). Guests basically look over the cook's shoulder. Vietnamese cookery courses.

⊞ 217 D4 ✉ 12 Le Loi
☎ 0510 3 93 95 68; www.thelittlemenu.com
🕐 Daily 10am–10:30pm

Moon £
Pretty tourist eatery over two floors in a 200-year-old Chinese colonial building outside the Old Town. Romantic but somewhat morbid atmosphere; attentive service and excellent cook and barkeeper. Don't be in too much of a rush if you come here as it can be very full.

⊞ 217 D4 ✉ 321 Nguyen Duy Hieu
☎ 0510 3 24 13 96 🕐 Daily 11am–9:30pm

HUE

Ancient Hue £££
Near Thien Mu Pagoda. Treat yourself to a 12-course 'royal dinner' just like the Nguyen emperors of old. This stylish restaurant seats up to 250 in a wonderful ancient building; idyllic, almost bewitching replica of a temple complex with a garden, pond and the Phu Mong garden house.

⊞ 216 C5
✉ 104/47 Phu Mong Street, Kim Long
☎ 054 3 59 09 02; www.ancienthue.com.vn
🕐 Daily 11am–10pm

Banh Khoai Lac Tien £
A chance to try the local speciality **banh khoai**: crisp pancakes with prawns, pork, soya bean sprouts and a sesame-peanut dip.

⊞ 216 C5 ✉ 6 Dinh Tien Hoang,
at Thuong Tu Gate (east) at the Citadel
☎ 054 3 82 73 48 🕐 Daily 8am–10pm

Family Home Restaurant £
You'll be surprised to find that such a place still exists in this tourist centre. Simple eatery where you are like a member of the family – you eat basically in their living room while the grandmother watches television. Good Vietnamese home cooking and breakfasts. The family also organises tours.

⊞ 216 C5 ✉ 11/34 Nguyen Tri Phuong
☎ 054 3 82 06 68 🕐 Daily 7am–10pm

Where to...
Shop

In the village **Dong Hai** at the foot of the Marble Mountains, some 600 families have been involved with sculpting and other crafts since the 15th century. But how on earth do you get a life-size Buddha made of marble (or perhaps just soapstone) back home? The villages of crafts people in the area around **Hue** can look back on a long tradition. They produce bronze work, embroidery, silk paintings, lacquer work and wood carvings with inlaid mother-of-pearl as well as high-quality blue ceramics. The region is also well known for its delicate and elaborately decorated conical hats, sold for example in the village Phu Cam. Delightful excursions by boat or bike along the Thu Bon will take you to such craft village as Thanh Ha (pottery), Kim Bong (sculptured wood) and Phuoc Kieu (bronze work).

Insider Tip

Your holiday budget is in real danger in **Hoi An**, especially in the three streets in the Old Town. Tailors and dressmakers are much in demand and sewing machines are on the go all the time. But prices have shot up since word has got out and the sky is now the limit. But don't leave things to the last minute or order something the day before you leave. Have all your details ready, get estimates from several places and compare prices. You can certainly buy things with a clear conscience from **Reaching Out** (103 Nguyen Thai Hoc; www. reachingoutvietnam.com, Mon–Fri 8:30am–9pm, Sat, Sun 9:30am–8pm) – a project for the disabled producing wonderful souvenirs ranging from clothes and bags to costume jewellery.

Where to...
Go Out

Amateur actors and dance groups perform in one of the old, rather cramped merchants' houses in Hoi An: the **Traditional Art Performance Theatre** (39 Nguyen Tai Hoc; tel: 0510 3 86 11 59, several times a day up until 9pm, about VND70,000) provides a little glimpse of traditional performances with costumed dancers and tales from everyday life in Vietnam and its ancient legends. Old instruments such as the single-stringed **dan bau** are played. **Nha nhac** performances with classical court music and dance are performed to large audiences in the renowned royal theatre **Duyet Thi Duong** in Hue (Citadel, Imperial City of Hue; daily 10am–10:30am, 2:30pm–3pm, VND120,000).

Every month on the 14th day of the lunar calendar the old streets in Hoi are alight with Chinese lanterns, candles and fairy-lights during '**Hoi An by Night**'. **Hue Festival**, that lasts several days, is held in 'even' years in June and includes performances of court music, dance, water puppetry, concerts (including rock and international music), exhibitions, fashion shows, sampan and dragon boat races and firework displays (www.huefestival.com).

Many visitors attend cookery courses in Hoi An (and elsewhere). The courses given by **Vy's Cooking School** (c/o Morning Glory Restaurant, 106 Nguyen Thai Hoc; tel: 05102 24 15 55; http://msvy-tastevietnam.com) and **Red Bridge** (tel: 0510 91 04 89; www.visithoian. com), slightly further away, have always proved popular. A cycling tour and cookery course can be combined by visiting **Tra Que Vegetable Village** in Ca Ha (www. traqueherbvillage.com).

Hanoi & Environs

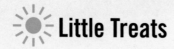 **Little Treats**

Pub crawling
The not-very-potent beer, *bia hoi*, tastes best perched on a mini plastic chair outside a corner pub in the **Old Quarter** (➤ 150).

Far from the madding crowd
Stroll from one café to the next on **Truc Bach Lake** (➤ 157). Where else in Hanoi can you hear the birds sing?

Pilgrim power
Visiting **Perfume Pagoda** (➤ 164) with thousands of Vietnamese pilgrims is an experience not to be missed.

Getting Your Bearings

French charm meets Vietnamese chaos. A tour of Vietnam's capital city is always a journey back in time over the past thousand years. Hundreds of brightly-coloured temples and pagodas are proof of a peaceful co-existence with French colonial buildings and Art Deco villas, bombastic Socialist architecture and mirrored glass-clad skyscrapers. And then there are the little streets in the Old Quarter with their charming boutiques, galleries and trendy *bia hoi* pubs...

The official founding of Hanoi was in 1010 through the Vietnamese Ly Dynasty, even though the Chinese actually erected the Dai La Citadel in the 7th century. The seat of princes and kings, administration and the military, teaching and science was established where now about 3.5 million people live within the city boundary and another 6–7 million elsewhere in the province. The 'city between the rivers' lies in the delta of the Red River, once ruled by mythical dragons and Mongols, where countless legends about the emergence of the Vietnamese people and its up to 4,000-year-old history abound.

To this day, Hanoi bears traces of the different eras and their regents – from kings and colonial rulers to Communist leaders. There are 600 temples and pagodas, many of them very ancient indeed. The neo-Classicist colonial buildings are now embassies, hotels and museums. The parks, lakes and broad avenues lined with tamarind trees give the city its nostalgic French flair despite its shift into the modern age, especially in the area around West Lake.

Vietn
51 Muse
of Eth

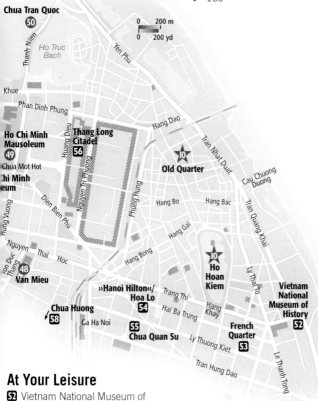

The days of the rickshaw in Hanoi are not yet numbered

Getting Your Bearings

TOP 10

Don't Miss

Chua Tran Quoc
50

Ho Truc Bach

Thanh Nien

Yen Phu

0   200 m
0   200 yd

Khue

Phan Dinh Phung

Hang Dao

Ho Chi Minh
Mausoleum
49

Huang Dieu

Thang Long
Citadel
56

Nguyen Tri Phuong

Old Quarter
⭐ 10

Tran Nhat Duat

Cau Chuong Duong

Chua Mot Hot

hi Minh
eum

Dien Bien Phu

Phung Hung

Hang Bo

Hang Bac

Tran Quang Khai

ung Vuong

Nguyen   Thai   Hoc

Hang Gai

Hang Bong

48
Van Mieu

»Hanoi Hilton«/
Hoa Lo
54

Trang Thi

Ho
Hoan
Kiem
⭐ 10

Ly Tha Tro

Vietnam
National
Museum of
History
52

Chua Huong
58

Ga Ha Noi

Hai Ba Trung

55
Chua Quan Su

Hang
Khay

Ly Thuong Kiet

French
Quarter
53

Le Thanh Tong

Tran Hung Dao

At Your Leisure

Hanoi & Environs

Two Perfect Days

Plan at least two days for a visit to the capital so that you have enough time for shopping and sampling its culinary delights, as well as exploring Hanoi's many attractions from its thousand-year-old history. Start as early in the morning as possible so as not to miss out any of the highlights listed in our recommended tour.

Day One

Morning

To soak up the mood of the city go for an hour-long walk around **Hoan Kiem Lake** (➤ 150) where the Vietnamese tirelessly perform tai chi and aerobic exercises early in the morning. The lake marks the border between the **Old Quarter** (➤ 150) and the **French district** (➤ 162). Plumb in the middle of the lake is one of the city's landmarks, the much-photographed three-storey Turtle Tower, **Thap Rua** (➤ 150). Picturesque

The Huc bridge in the northeastern corner of the lake leads to **Temple of the Jade Mountain** (➤ 150). From here it is not far to the actual heart of the Old Quarter where you should not miss a visit to the wonderfully restored traditional 'tube house' (➤ 151) and **Bach Ma Temple** (➤ 151).

Afternoon

After lunch in one of the many little eateries or soup kitchens in the Old Quarter, take a walk or a taxi some 3km (2mi) to the west, to the area south of huge West Lake. This is where you will find several unique examples of traditional architecture such as the **48 Temple of Literature** (➤ 153) from the 11th century and the **One Pillar Pagoda** (opposite page; ➤ 156). A few yards further north the road opens into large Ba Dinh Square where you can queue up to pay your respects to the embalmed first president of Vietnam in the **49 Ho Chi Minh Mausoleum** (➤ 155). The **house where he lived**

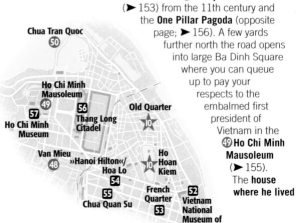

Chua Tran Quoc **50**

Ho Chi Minh Mausoleum **49**

57 Ho Chi Minh Museum

56 Thang Long Citadel

Old Quarter **10**

Van Mieu **48**

»Hanoi Hilton« / Hoa Lo **54**

55 Chua Quan Su

Ho Hoan Kiem **10**

French Quarter **53**

52 Vietnam National Museum of History

is also open to the public (HCM House, ➤ 155). And more can be found on 'Uncle Ho' in **57 Ho Chi Minh Museum** (➤ 164) nearby.

Evening
A visit to the **water puppet theatre** (left; ➤ 168) is a must on any sightseeing tour of Hanoi. Through the brightly-coloured figures and the stories they relate you will be able to understand everyday Vietnamese life and the old legends better than before.

Day Two

Morning
The **51 Ethnology Museum** (➤ 160) is well worth a visit. It is situated a little out of the way in the northeast corner of the city a few miles away. It is best reached by taxi (or take bus no. 14 from the north bank of Hoan Kiem Lake). On your way back, alight at **50 Tran Quoc Pagoda** (➤ 157). This 300-year-old pagoda on the banks of West Lake is the oldest in Hanoi.

Vietnam Museum of Ethnology
51 HANOI
58 Chua Huong

Afternoon
Battle your way through the chaos of spluttering mopeds around Hoan Kien Lake to the Old Quarter. 36 guilds were once at home here and, just like in the days of old, ancestors of those who used to work here still practice their professions in the narrow streets today and offer their products for sale (➤ 168). Anyone more interested in sightseeing than shopping can visit the infamous **54 Hanoi Hilton** prison (➤ 163) where many GIs were tortured, the **55 Ambassador's Pagoda** (➤ 163) or the **52 History Museum** (➤ 162) in the south of the Old Quarter.

Evening
Before continuing your journey tomorrow, round off your visit to the capital with dinner in one of the many restaurants before stopping off at some of the corner bars and cafés in the Old Quarter.

⭐❿ Old Quarter & Ho Hoan Kiem

Early in the morning, at first light, the banks of this lake of legends come alive. Where the first groups of people are keeping fit with tai chi or jazz dance, young couples holding hands have taken over the benches and may well stay there until late in the evening. While away the time during the midday heat or a sudden downpour in one of the countless cafés, soup kitchens and bars in the Old Quarter – and simply watch the incessant activity around you.

City Oasis

The Old Quarter, with its labyrinth of narrow streets, stretches along the north and west banks of Hoan Kiem Lake. Every evening by 5pm at the latest all hell is let loose when myriads of mopeds take over the streets, squares and pavements until everything is hopelessly jammed. The Vietnamese come to the lake at all times of day to get a breath of fresh air. And tourists are attracted by Hanoi's most important landmarks around its shore. These include the picturesque **Huc bridge** which you cross to get to the **Temple of the Jade Mountain (Den Ngoc Son)**. The temple, located on a little island, was first built in the 14th century and dedicated to a number of different saints from history – the heroic General Tran Hung Dao (1228–1300) who fended off the Mongols in 1288, the god of literature Van Xuong, the physicist La To and the war hero Quan Vu (2nd/3rd century AD).

The 300-year-old **Turtle Tower Thap Rua** situated on another island cannot be missed. According to a saga a golden turtle shrouded in legend used to live in the lake. It handed a sword to the national hero Le Loi, later King Le Thai To (c. 1384–1433), with which the Ming Chinese were finally chased out of Vietnam in 1428.

All sorts of devotional objects for a visit to a temple are available on Hang Ma

In the Labyrinth of Narrow Streets in the Old Quarter

Everyday life (still) revolves around the plastic stools in the middle of the pavements in Hanoi's Old Quarter – or on the seat of a moped which virtually none of the locals get off when shopping. Groups of elderly men squat on street corners drinking *bia hoi* (beer) and playing *co tuong* (Chinese chess). At the turn of the millennium tourists and Vietnamese returning from overseas brought a modern lifestyle to Vietnam. Designer boutiques and trendy restaurants pushed out the barbers and ear cleaners, modern pharmacies the traditional herbal apothecaries. And corner shops

The wooden Huc bridge is also known as the 'bridge of the rising sun' due to its colour

and stores have been replaced by souvenir shops, galleries and mini hotels.

The history of the Old Quarter can be traced back to the early days of Hanoi when the districts fanning out from **Thang Long Citadel** (► 163) were divided up among the **36 guilds** and the narrow streets separated into areas where all those working in one field were together and where the same goods were sold. Even today this can still be seen to a certain extent; e.g. there are streets full of bamboo and basketware (Hang Tre, Hang Bo, Hang Vai), the street of paper votive offerings (Hang Ma), where traders sell paper money to be burnt on family altars, or in Hang Quat where religious devotional objects are piled high.

Worth a Visit

Look out for the last few remaining workshops and front-room shops while exploring the area, as well as the typical, extremely narrow **tube houses** which can extend back as much as 70m (230ft). You can shuffle your way around some of these houses in the Old Quarter in felt slippers that are handed out at the entrance. A real gem is at Ma May 87 – **Ngoi Nha Di San Heritage House** that was restored using UNESCO funds. It dates from the late 19th century. Its original owners belonged to the guild of bamboo furniture makers and lived for three generations in this wooden house. The salesroom, workshop, living and sleeping areas, the kitchen, washroom and store were all linked to one another by tiny inner courtyards that brought in fresh air and daylight. The intricately carved double doors and windows depicting four mythological animals and fabulous creatures – the dragon, phoenix, quilin (a chimerical creature, part lion, dragon and stag) and a turtle – as well as antique furniture and the house altar, are all particularly noteworthy.

Ho Chi Minh drafted the declaration of independence for the Democratic Republic of Vietnam at Hang Ngang 48. The building is now home to the **Museum of Independence**. Just round the corner, in Hang Buom, is **Bach Ma Temple (Den Bach Ma)** that has a history more than 1,000 years old and, as such, the oldest temple in the Old Quarter. It was erected in 1010; the present building, however, is from the

Insider Tip

Hanoi & Environs

18th/19th centuries. Bach Ma, the white horse, is also the guardian spirit of the royal city Thang Long or Old Hanoi. From the outside the temple seems rather nondescript, but the interior is impressive – with carved and gilded wooden doors and pillars, an exquisite Bach Ma figure made of copper, a pretty historical sedan chair and an almost 200-year-old shrine to Confucius.

TAKING A BREAK

Simple **street kitchens** (£) can be found in the west corner of the Old Quarter in particular, in Tong Duy Tan and Cam Chi; generally only one dish is available: *com* are rice dishes, *pho* the omnipresent noodle soup and *bun cha* are rice noodles with grilled meat that can be sampled in Hang Manh. Everything sizzles away around the clock although things can get really full in the late evening.

➕ 211 E3

Tourist Information Center (TIC)
✉ 7 Dinh Tien Hoang ☎ 04 39 36 33 69; http://ticvietnam.com

Temple of the Jade Mountain
🕐 Daily 7am–6pm (summer), 7:30am–5:30pm (winter) 💵 VND20,000

Ngoi Nha Di San Heritage House
✉ 87 Ma May 🕐 Daily 8am–noon, 1:30pm–5pm 💵 VND10,000

Independence Museum
✉ 48 Hang Ngang, corner Hang Giay
🕐 Tue–Sun 8am–4pm 💵 VND10,000

Bach Ma Temple
✉ 76 Hang Buom 🕐 Tue–Sun 8am–11am, 2pm–5pm

The 'tube house' at Ma May 87: as property tax was based on the width of a house, homes were simply extended back a long way

INSIDER INFO

- A tip for coffee-lovers: keep your eyes open for the stronger but less bitter **ca phe chon**. Before the coffee beans used are roasted, they pass through the digestive system of cats, civets, squirrels, foxes and weasels. A cup of 'cat coffee' can cost VND650,000 in Hanoi (but beware of cheap fakes).
- Tours focussing on different themes are offered by a number of local tour guides in English, such as **Hanoi Cultural Tours** (18 Hang Huong Street, tel: 04 00 72 55 28; http://hanoiculturaltours.com).

㊽ Van Mieu
(Temple of Literature)

The well visited Temple of Literature – 1,000 years ago the seat of the first university in Vietnam and an intellectual and spiritual centre at the same time – is still the most important Confucian holy site in the country to this day.

King Ly Thanh Tong (1023–1072) had the temple built to honour Confucius in 1070. It was here that the sons of Mandarins and princes gained instruction in the philosophy of the great master (▶ 154) – even up until 1919! The king himself posed the questions at the final exams.

Tour

The outer gateway leads into the **first courtyard** where even high-ranking dignitaries had to dismount from their horses. After passing through four further gateways decorated with dragons you reach the large **inner courtyard**, laid out like a park with water basins and fountains. The third gate, called **Khue Van Cac**, is a two-storeyed pavilion from the 19th century where poetry readings are held. In the third courtyard, the so-called **Courtyard of Steles**, is the **Well of Heavenly Clarity**. The courtyard gained its name from the 82 exquisite steles that can still be seen today. These are supported by stone turtles and bear the names of 1,307 graduates – *tien sie* doctors from 1442–1779.

The 'Gate of Great Synthesis', **Dai Tanh**, provides access to the most important temple buildings. The **House of Ceremonies** in honour of the 72 wisest pupils lies in the

School children and students bring offerings to the Temple of Literature and pray for good grades

Hanoi & Environs

fourth courtyard and boasts an altar with Confucius' ancestral chart borne by two bronze cranes. The wonderful carvings with motifs such as phoenixes and dragons, yin-yang symbols and lotus flowers is especially noteworthy. The **Sanctuary of Great Success** beyond contains a statue of Confucius surrounded by his four closest disciples.

The last building you enter, the former National Academy, later the **Temple to the Parents of Confucius**, is reached through a fifth courtyard. The building is now used as a small museum. The ground floor includes a model of the Temple of Literature, exquisite robes, wooden printing plates, documents and writing instruments used by students; on the second floor there are three altars in honour of the kings Ly Nhan Tong (1066–1127, the founder of the National Academy), Ly Thanh Tong and Le Thanh Tong (1460–97).

The steles supported by turtles have been a UNESCO World Heritage Site since 2010

TAKING A BREAK

You can fill up on Vietnamese specialities in **KOTO** (££, 59 Van Mieu; tel: 04 37 47 03 37; www.koto.com.au; daily 8am–11pm) opposite. The restaurant sponsors a Vietnamese-Australian project for former street children.

✚ 210 B3
✉ Entrance: 58 Quoc Tu Giam, Dong Da district ☎ 04 35 11 48 55
🕐 Daily 7:30am–5:30pm 🎫 VND20,000

INSIDER INFO

- The many **people collecting donations** are best ignored completely as most are not genuine.
- At weekends the temple is very crowded indeed whereas on week days you can even find you are on your own.

④⑨ Ho Chi Minh Mausoleum

On Ba Dinh Square visitors become immersed in the Vietnamese hero worshipping cult surrounding Ho Chi Minh, the Communist father of their country. The former revolutionary and president read the Declaration of Independence from here on 2 September 1945, in front of 500,000 of his fellow countrymen. His house is close-by and open to the public as is the One Pillar Pagoda.

Queuing outside the mausoleum is unavoidable

Since the opening of the monumentally ostentatious marble mausoleum in 1975 people have filed passed the **glazed coffin containing the embalmed body of Ho Chi Minh** in their thousands. The revolutionary sought to prevent just this during his lifetime. In his will he decreed that he should be cremated and "my ashes divided into three parts and kept in three ceramic urns, symbolising the north, the middle and the south". Instead, peasants, school groups and Party officials, state visitors, monks and war veterans come here to pay their respects. And for tourists, the body that is removed to Moscow for two to three months a year for 'conservation reasons', has long since become one of Hanoi's greatest attractions.

Further Attractions

Behind the mausoleum there is a large park and the former **presidential palace**, built in 1900–08 as the residence of the governor general. Idyllically situated on a small lake is **Ho Chi Minh**'s house on stilts where he spent the last eleven years of his life from 1958 onwards – which is why the two-storey house also has an entrance to a bunker.

100m (330ft) to the south is the famous **One Pillar Pagoda (Chua Mot Cot ▶ 149)**, a reproduction of the original that

HO CHI MINH

Nguyen Sinh Cung was born near the city of Vinh in Central Vietnam on 19 May 1890. When he was young he toured the world as a ship's boy, living for a short time in London, New York, Moscow and in Paris where he was one of the founding members of the French Communist Party. In 1930 he set up the Vietnamese Communist Party in Hong Kong for which he was condemned to death by the French colonial powers. He did not return to his native country until 1941 – after thirty years in exile abroad – settling in North Vietnam where he spearheaded the struggle for independence as the leader of the Viet Minh coalition he had founded. From 1942 onwards he called himself Ho Chi Minh. Following the provisional division of the country after the resolution passed on Indochina at the Geneva Conference, Ho Chi Minh became the president of the Democratic Republic of Vietnam (the northern part of the country) in 1954. During the Vietnam War (1964–75; ▶ 18) he was seen as a symbolic figure by student and protest movements around the world. The president, who lived modestly right up until his death, did not live to see the reunification of his native country in 1976. 'Uncle Ho' died on 2 September 1969 aged 79.

was probably first built in 1049 but destroyed on numerous occasions, the last time by the French as they withdrew from Vietnam. The pagoda once rose above the pond perched on one single treetrunk. This has long since been replaced by a massive concrete column. Symbolising a lotus flower, it was erected by the childless King Ly Thai Tong (1028–54) and dedicated to Quan Am, the goddess of mercy, who appeared to him in a dream with a baby boy in her arims. Just a little later a male heir was indeed born to the monarch.

TAKING A BREAK

In the **Botanic Garden** that adjoins to the north (entrances: Hoang Hoa Tham and Ngoc Ha; daily 6am–10pm, admission: VND2,000) you can relax in the shade of the trees and regain your strength at one of the soup kitchens.

Ho Chi Minh Mausoleum

✚ 210 B4 ✉ ba Dinh Square, entrance: Hung Vuong 🕔 April–Sep Tue–Thu 7:30am–10am–30, Sat, Sun 7:30am–11am, Dec–March Tue–Thu 8am–11am, Sat, Sun 8am–11:30am, closed from early Sep–beginning Dec. 💵 Free

Ho Chi Minh House

✚ 210 B4 ✉ Ba Dinh Square 🕔 Daily 8am–11am, 1:30pm–4pm 💵 VND20,000

One Pillar Pagoda

✚ 210 B4 ✉ Chua Mot Cot 🕔 Daily 8am–6pm 💵 Free

INSIDER INFO

There are **strict rules** for visitors to the mausoleum. Bags and cameras must be handed in at the reception desk. You should also wear appropriate clothing – visitors in shorts, mini-skirts and tank tops will be refused entry.

50 Chua Tran Quoc
(Tran Quoc Pagoda)

This little oasis awaits visitors on a tiny island in the southeast corner of West Lake. Picturesque Tran Quoc Pagoda is one of the oldest pagodas in Vietnam and can be reached via a causeway lined with palm trees from the shore of the lake.

The beginnings of this exceptionally attractive pagoda reputedly date back to the 6th century, to the early Ly Dynasty, when King Ly Nam De first built it in a nearby village in the delta of the Red River. It was moved here in 1615 and last restored in 2011. It wood carvings, numerous figures of Buddha, monks and guards, as well as the red and gold ornamentation are impressive. The eleven-storeyed, 15m (50ft)-high, red brick **pagoda tower** is certainly quite a sight.

Despite the number of visitors you will always be able to find a quiet corner on the islet. There is a massive offshoot of the Bodhi Tree under which Buddha attained enlightenment as well as seven burial stupas with Chinese inscriptions containing the ashes of various dignitaries. Apart from lots of other statues, there is a reclining Buddha on the threshold to Nirvana – unusual for northern Vietnam – in the **main hall** as well as the many-armed goddess of mercy (Quan Am), the fat Di Lac Buddha and steles from the 17th century and old manuscripts.

A statue of Buddha looks down on visitors from each of the levels in the hexagonal pagoda tower

TAKING A BREAK

There are a number of small soup kitchens, refreshment and fruit stands on the shore of the lake as well as restaurant ships to take care of the needs of those out for a walk and visitors to the temple. Just take a seat on one of the many mini plastic chairs.

➕ 210 C5 🕐 Daily 7:30am–11:30am, 1:30pm–6:30pm 🎟 Free (both men and women must wear clothes that cover their knees and shoulders)v

INSIDER INFO

The pagoda is especially beautiful at sunset. You can then go for a stroll around the small and idyllic **Truc Bach Lake** on the far side of the causeway and the lakeside promenade with its little bars and cafés. There is another temple well worth seeing on the southern shore of Truc Bach Lake – **Den Tran Vu** (also written Quan Thanh; daily 7:30am–6pm, admission free).

Insider Tip

The Vietnamese pagoda

During the Ly and Tran Dynasties (11th–14th centuries) pagoda architecture reached its heyday but few structures from this time still exist today. Wood was used as a building material that in Vietnam's hot and humid climate weathers quickly. This meant that the holy sites had to be renovated at regular intervals. They were frequently not only rebuilt but also extended.

❶ **Gateway (tam quan):** A triple gateway leads into the temple complex. Some are magnificent structures with tiled roofs and rows of columns; others are simply made of posts with crossbeams.

❷ **Temple building (chua):** The temple comprises three parts. From the entrance to the main altar the increasing religious importance is underlined by a clear rise in levels.

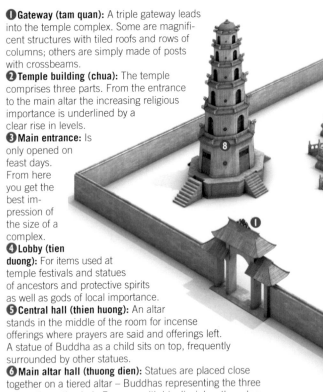

❸ **Main entrance:** Is only opened on feast days. From here you get the best impression of the size of a complex.

❹ **Lobby (tien duong):** For items used at temple festivals and statues of ancestors and protective spirits as well as gods of local importance.

❺ **Central hall (thien huong):** An altar stands in the middle of the room for incense offerings where prayers are said and offerings left. A statue of Buddha as a child sits on top, frequently surrounded by other statues.

❻ **Main altar hall (thuong dien):** Statues are placed close together on a tiered altar – Buddhas representing the three generations, the Jade Emperor with his disciples, the rulers of the underworld and sometimes statues of the benefactor.

❼ **Living area:** Monks live in the galleries or in a building behind the pagoda where pilgrims are also accommodated.

❽ **Bell tower:** Is located in the inner courtyard – either a simple wooden structure or an elaborate pavilion.

❾ **Stupa site:** Burial monuments containing the ashes of monks and abbots; their height varies according to age and rank.

The entrance gate is composed of three elements. Passing through the left-hand gate is recognition of the insignificance of being, the right-hand gate the transience of earthly existence and the central gate perpetual flux. (Photo: Gateway in Hue, 17th century; ► 129)

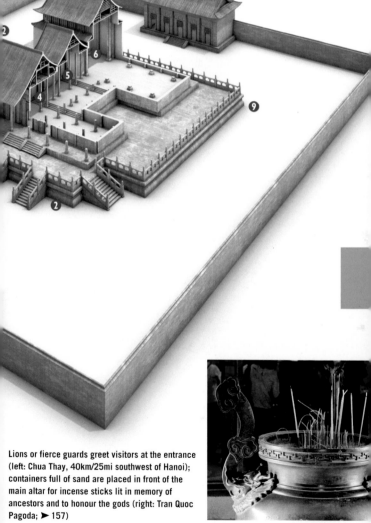

Lions or fierce guards greet visitors at the entrance (left: Chua Thay, 40km/25mi southwest of Hanoi); containers full of sand are placed in front of the main altar for incense sticks lit in memory of ancestors and to honour the gods (right: Tran Quoc Pagoda; ► 157)

🗝 Vietnam Museum of Ethnology

The ethnological museum is one of the best, state-of-the-art museums in the country. It has numerous displays of local costumes, jewellery, craft work and replicas of houses of the various ethnic groups in Vietnam which visitors are welcome to explore.

The museum, opened in 1998, is by Vietnamese standards exceptionally well presented and is not only worth visiting if you intend exploring the mountainous regions or the

Highlands around Da Lat and Dak Lak. Here you will find a lot of information on the history and traditions of all of Vietnam's 54 ethnic groups. Some 15,000 exhibits and antiques are displayed on two floors. The models, clothing, musical instruments, palm-leaf manuscripts, tools, cooking utensils and weapons, figures and puppets and the wall texts (also in English) give visitors a good overall picture. Countless photos and several videos round off the presentation.

View of the inside of the Ede longhouse; opposite page, top: figure from the water puppet theatre

Vietnam Museum of Ethnology

Tour

The **first section** is devoted to the Vietnamese themselves, the ethnic Viet and Kinh groups which make up 87% of the population. Even today, village life is centred on the community hall (*dinh*) that is dedicated to the village's protective spirit, the *thanh hoang*. The manufacture of typical Vietnamese goods and their use is shown, such as the *non* (conical hat made of palm leaves) and the cylindrical **do** (bamboo trap used by fishermen). Rituals, such as burials, are explained very clearly in other rooms on the **ground floor**, as well as the lifestyle of the Chut, Tho and Muong people from the area around Hoa Binh (► 184). The latter are well known for their unusual folkloric dancing.

Several quirky exhibits catch the eye, e.g. a lunar calendar on twelve bamboo sticks that can be unfurled rather like a fan, showing the dates best suited for the harvest, building a house or getting married. **Upstairs**, the everyday life of the mountain people, the Thai, Tay and Nung, is presented. One highlight here is the Black Thai house that visitors can go in and the explanations on the shaman cult.

The extensive 🔧 **open-air section** behind the museum building is great fun for younger visitors too. It includes a number of models of buildings that you can go in, including a 40m (140ft) Ede longhouse, Tay and Yao stilt houses, an impressive Bahnar community hall and unusual Giaray (Gia Rai) burial sites with wooden figures (not suitable for most children!). A model boat and a water puppet theatre round off the display.

TAKING A BREAK

A small open-air eatery (£) next to the outdoor area provides cheap and simple Vietnamese dishes.

➕ northwest 210 A4
✉ Nguyen Van Huyen, Cau Giay, West Lake
☎ 04 37 56 21 93; www.vme.org.vn
🕐 Tue–Sun 8:30am–5:30pm 🚌 14 💰 VND40,000

INSIDER INFO

- Allow at least two to three hours to **tour the museum**.
- Interesting souvenirs can be found in the **museum shop** that also stocks 'Craft Link' products from the ethnic groups in the mountains.
- Wheelchair users can access the upper floor via a **ramp** or the **lift**.
- A small 🔧 **playground** is located opposite..

At Your Leisure

52 Vietnam National Museum of History

The history museum, 1km (0.65mi) southeast of Hoan Kiem Lake, is housed in **two buildings**. The one on Trang Tien focuses on Vietnam's history from its beginnings up to the end of the Nguyen Dynasty in 1945. The second, the **Museum of the Revolution**, is on the other side of the road and covers events from 1858 onwards (the colonial era) and the Indochina and Vietnam Wars, up to the present day. Exhibits from the great Dong Son culture (1200–200BC) are worthy of particular note. These include big, delicately chased ceremonial drums made of bronze, stone relicts from the Champa culture, imposing Buddha statues and imperial steles, lots of ceramic items, including several from the Ly Dynasty, paintings and weapons from the colonial era and propaganda posters from the time of the struggle for independence under Ho Chi Minh.

✚ 211 F2 ✉ 1 Trang Tien and 216 Tran Quang Khai, Hoan Kiem district ☎ 04 38 24 13 84; www.baotanglichsu.vn ⏱ Daily 8am–noon, 1:30pm–5pm (closed 1st Mon. of every month) 💲 VND40,000

53 French Quarter

Insider Tip

The best way to explore the French Quarter to the south and east of Hoan Kiem Lake is either on a moped taxi or on a leisurely walk. It does however cover quite a large area, generally following the 3km (2mi)-long Trang Tien, starting in the east at the Opera House and going all the way to the Temple of Literature (► 153) in the west, following the road's continuation down Nguyen Thai Hoc. The French first settled here in 1874 and a little of the colonial flair can still be felt today. The **Old Opera House in Hanoi** (► 168), modelled on that in Paris, was officially opened in 1911; just a stone's throw further away is the former **Governor's Residence** in Ngo Quyen (built in 1918) where several scenes in the French classic **Indochine** were filmed; and the **Sofitel Legend Metropole** (► 165), one of the most beautiful hotels from colonial days anywhere in Asia. Many other sights can be found in tree-lined avenues in the French Quarter and the residential district with its many villas south of Trang Tien, such as the **Ambassadors' Pagoda** (► 163), the **History Museum** (► left) and **Hoa Lo** (► 163), as well as grand mansions, now occupied by embassies, international companies and elegant restaurants, cafés and hotels.

If you feel like extending your walk, explore the roads Phan Dinh Phung, Tran Phu and Dien Bien Phu around the **Citadel** (► 163). There are several villas from colonial days on these roads lined with tamarind trees, elegant neo-Classicist palatial residences, small fairy tale-like 'castles' and rather sober Art Deco buildings with an oriental touch.

The Old Opera House – once at the heart of society in Hanoi

Doan Mon Gate has always been the main entrance to Thang Long Citadel

54 'Hanoi Hilton'/Hoa Lo

The French called the prison they built in 1896 the 'Maison Centrale', as the lettering over the entrance still reveals today. The North Vietnamese later imprisoned and tortured US American soldiers here (including the US Senator John McCain) who sarcastically called the place the 'Hanoi Hilton'. Only a small section of the original complex still exists and has been turned into a museum. An attempt to recreate the atrocities perpetrated – of course from a Vietnamese point of view – is made with the help of photos, dummies, oppressive wall reliefs, chains, clothing and a French guillotine.

➕ 211 D2 ✉ 1 Hoa Lo, Hoan Kiem district
☎ 04 38 24 63 58
🕐 Daily 8am–11:30am, 12:30–5pm
🎟 VND30,000

55 Chua Quan Su (Ambassadors' Pagoda)

Built as a guesthouse for envoys from Buddhist countries in the 15th century, the Ambassadors's Pagoda is very popular among the Vietnamese. The present building however dates largely from 1942. The Buddhist Centre includes the research and teaching facilities of the **Vietnam Buddhist Association** as well as a library. Quan Am with her '1,000 arms' and the artistic depiction of scenes from Buddha's life are interesting.

➕ 211 D2 ✉ 73 Quan Su
🕐 5:30am–9pm (summer), 6am–9:30pm (winter)
🎟 Free

56 Thang Long Citadel

For decades the Citadel was not open to the public. Access is now possible through the imposing **main gateway, Doan Mon**, on the west side. The central section of the 'Imperial Citadel of the Rising Dragon' has been a UNESCO World Heritage Site since 2010. However, don't expect too much – only very few historical buildings in this palace complex that was originally erected in the 11th century during the Ly Dynasty have survived. The **Citadel**, constructed under Emperor Gia Long in 1802–12 was used as a barracks by French troops from 1872 onwards. Apart from the entrance gateway, the pretty **Pavilion of the Princess**, destroyed by the French and later rebuilt, and the 200-year-old flag tower **Cot Co** to the south, are worth seeing. The conquest of the South by the North Vietnamese army was planned in the unremarkable pre-fab building **'D 67'** in 1975. A sign marks the

Hanoi & Environs

place where the legendary general Vo Nguyen Giap (1911–2013) used to sit.

➕ 210 C4
✉ 19C Hoang Dieu
🕐 Tue–Sun 8:30am–11:30am, 2pm–5pm
💵 VND30,000

57 Ho Chi Minh Museum

Just a few yards to the west of the One Pillar Pagoda (➤ 156) is the huge Ho Chi Minh Museum for those interested in his life's work. It contains 120,000 exhibits, including lots of photographs, films and documents, as well as items of clothing and everyday objects used by the revolutionary. This modern building was opened in 1990 to mark the 100th anniversary of the country's father figure and sometime president. It is a cut above other, generally boring Ho Chi Minh museums in Vietnam. On the top floor there are a number of works of art and installations (some of which are surrealistically weird). The hammer and sickle and propaganda material are not lacking here either.

➕ 210 B4 ✉ 19 Ngoc Ha, Ba Dinh district
☎ 04 38 46 37 52; www.baotanghochiminh.vn

🕐 Daily 8am–4:30pm, Mon, Fri until noon
💵 VND20,000

58 Chua Huong (Perfume Pagoda)

Perfume Pagoda, a famous place of pilgrimage in northern Vietnam with several smaller holy sites, is located on Huong Tich Son, the 'mountain of scented traces' in the midst of a magnificent karst landscape, 60km (37mi) southwest of Hanoi. Perfume Pagoda was built in the 17th century in the depths of **Huong Thich cave** and is dedicated to Quan Am. It can be reached by boat on the Yen River passing through magnificent scenery. The various temples and shrines attract thousands and thousands of Vietnamese pilgrims, especially during New Year festivities in January/February, from March to April and at weekends in the summer. A modern cable car takes visitors to the temple grotto on the mountain. The alternative is a strenuous, two-hour climb (hiking boots necessary). En route you pass **Trinh Temple**, **Thien Tru Pagoda** and the cave pagodas **Tien Son** and **Giai Oan**.

➕ 221 F2
🕐 Daily 6am–4:30pm
💵 Free, cable car VND100,000

The steep path up to the cave leads past Thien Tru Pagoda

Where to...
Stay

Price
of a double room per night:
£ under VND1m.   **££** VND1–VND2.4m.   **£££** over VND2.4m.

Army ££
This quietly but centrally situated standard category hotel is especially appealing in the summer due to its huge pool. The 84 rooms with balconies are impressive partly because of their size, partly thanks to their old-fashioned but typically Vietnamese furniture that hasn't changed for decades. If you're not too particular you will feel very comfortable here, especially at the price. Foodwise you are better off looking for somewhere to eat nearby.
⊞ 211 F2
✉ 33C Pham Ngu Lao, Hoan Kiem district
☎ 04 38 25 28 96

Impressive £
Small gem under German management. This modern, family-run mini hotel is in a quiet but very central street in the Old Quarter near the cathedral and has 25 cosy rooms, some with a balcony. Several larger rooms for almost the same price are suitable for families. WiFi.
⊞ 211 D3   ✉ 54–56 Au Trieu, Old Quarter
☎ 04 39 38 15 90; www.impressivehotel.com

InterContinental Hanoi Westlake £££
An oasis with the highest of standards. This luxury hotel on West Lake accommodates its guests in 3-storey villas right on the water's edge. Or else you take an elegant suite with an original bath. An impressive breakfast buffet, three restaurants and the Sunset Bar are there to satisfy all tastes. Magical pool, comparatively cheap spa; yoga and pilates courses.

⊞ 210 C5   ✉ 1A Nghi Tam, Tay Ho district
☎ 04 62 70 88 88; www.ichotelsgroup.com

🛏 Little Hanoi Diamond £
This stylish youth-hostel is perfect for many people's needs: from an 8-bed dormitory or a somewhat cramped multi-occupancy room to classically elegant rooms with king-sized beds and even a honeymoon suite. Some of the balconies have a view of the noisy comings and goings during the day. Young guests and families feel well looked-after by the helpful staff. Fruit, coffee, tea and fruit juice are available all day long.
⊞ 211 D3   ✉ 11 Bat Dan, Old Quarter
☎ 04 39 23 17 81;
www.littlehanoihostel.com/diamond

Pullman £££
This 4-star hotel is not just for business people even if it is a little bit far from the centre. The modern, well-designed hotel has 240 luxuriously stylish rooms with every conceivable comfort, professional and extremely helpful staff and a wonderful breakfast buffet (plan a lot of time!) and of course a spa, gym and pool.
⊞ 210 A3   ✉ 40 Cat Linh
☎ 04 37 33 06 88; www.pullman-hanoi.com

Sofitel Legend Metropole £££
A hotel legend. Nowhere else can you soak up the atmosphere of the colonial age as well as within these venerable walls which have hosted such illustrious guests as Charlie Chaplin, Graham Greene, Jane Fonda and Joan Baez.

Old-fangled telephones can be seen in the lobby – although of course everything in the rooms is hi-tech. A pool, several elegant restaurants and a chocolate buffet to sweeten any stay.

🏠 211 F2 ✉ 15 Ngo Quyen, Hoan Kiem district
☎ 04 38 26 69 19; www.accorhotels.com

Tam ££

25 cosy rooms, some of which are large and have balconies, in a peaceful residential area on Truc Bach Lake. Roof-top bar on the 8th floor. Professional travel agency which is glad to give useful advice and offer its services.

🏠 210 C5
✉ 3–5 Tran Te Xuong, Ba Dinh district
☎ 04 37 15 40 69; www.tamhotel.com.vn

Win £

Central, quiet and friendly. This hotel in a peaceful street has 11 cheap rooms with wonderfully old-fashioned wooden furniture. The best rooms are to the front with balconies and modern bathrooms; some of the rooms at the back do not have windows but are quieter and cheaper. Very helpful staff.

🏠 211 E3
✉ 34 Hang Hanh, Old Quarter
☎ 04 38 26 71 50; www.winhotel.com.vn

Where to...
Eat and Drink?

Price
for a main course without drinks:
£ under VND120,000   ££ VND120,000–VND240,000   £££ over VND240,000

Bar Restaurant 96 £

It you are looking for typical and tasty fare then head for this lovely eatery in the Old Quarter. Specialities include **bun cha** rice noodles with grilled pork on a skewer or in a bamboo basket. Breakfast is also served, as are vegetarian dishes, curries and **pho** – all beautifully presented.

🏠 211 E3 ✉ 34 Gia Ngu, Old Quarter
☎ 04 39 35 23 96 🕐 Daily 9am–11pm

Cha Ca La Vong £

While the main branch in the Old Quarter is an over-priced, unfriendly tourist trap with a table-top barbecue, the restaurant on Truc Bach Lake is a world apart. Fish is cooked over glowing embers and served with vegetables, herbs and rice – delicious, even if it is the only dish.

🏠 211 E4
✉ 107 Nguyen Truong To, Ba-Dinh district
☎ 04 38 23 98 75 🕐 Daily 8am–11pm

Cong Caphe £

A film about the opium den era could have been made in this chain of vintage-style coffee shops. You sit (or lounge) on brightly-coloured cushions at low tables with ventilators whirring overhead while the Viet Cong look down from black-and-white photos and propaganda posters between 'bullet holes'. The only drug here is the first-class Vietnamese coffee.

🏠 211 E3 ✉ Branches e.g.: 35A Nguyen Huu Huan and 27 Nha Tho; www.congcaphe.com
🕐 Daily 8am–10pm

El Gaucho £££

Anyone who hankers for a tender Argentinian steak after so much rice and exotic vegetables should come here. This rustic-style steakhouse chain has two branches with well-stocked bars. But be careful: the prices could well make a mockery of your holiday budget.

➕ 211 F2 ✉ 11 Trang Tien, Hoan Kiem district ☎ 04 38 24 72 80
🕐 Daily 11am until 10:30pm
➕ 210 A5 ✉ West Lake
☎ 04 37 18 69 91; www.elgaucho.asia
🕐 Daily 4pm until 10:30pm

Foodshop 45 £

The two brothers Hue and Cuong are well known for the best Indian food in northern Vietnam. If you come here at sunset you can enjoy the lovely view from one of the several floors of this eatery (such as from the Lounge Bar) over idyllic Truc Bach Lake. Another popular branch is in the Old Quarter (32 Hang Buom; tel: 04 37 16 29 59).

➕ 210 C5 ✉ 59 Truc Bach
☎ 09 03 42 91 28; http://foodshop45.com
🕐 Daily 10am–10:30pm, Lounge 5pm–11:30pm

Green Mango ££

French and Italian-inspired dishes are mostly served in this elegant hotel restaurant as well as a few western and Thai-Vietnamese classics (steaks, pasta, pizza, curries). You can choose between the pleasant, imaginatively designed restaurant inside or the leafy courtyard. Unobtrusive music and good selection of (expensive) wines. The 'happy hour' is a bonus (daily 1pm–7pm).

➕ 211 E3 ✉ 18 Hang Quat, Old Quarter
☎ 04 39 28 99 16; www.greenmango.vn
🕐 Daily 11am–10pm

Hanoi Fusion £–££

In this simple, elongated, skinny eatery over three floors Vietnamese classics are served (**bun cha** meatballs, **chaca** grilled fish, hot-pots, etc.). Friendly and speedy service. Any number of cocktails or nightcaps available in the lounge bar at the top.

➕ 211 D5
✉ 87 Nguyen Truong To, Ba Dinh district
☎ 04 37 15 30 04
🕐 Daily 10:30am–2:30pm, 4:30pm–10pm

La Verticale £££

Go on, treat yourself! 5-star chef Didier Corlou conjures up his trendy 'West meets Asia' creations here. This fusion food is of course impeccably presented; the prices correspondingly exorbitant. The same goes for Madame Hien (15 Chan Cam; tel: 04 39 38 15 88), an offshoot of La Verticale, where prominent heads of state have dined too.

➕ 211 E1 ✉ 19 Ngo Van Sun
☎ 04 39 44 63 17; www.verticale-hanoi.com
🕐 Daily 11:30am–2pm, 6pm–10pm, closed Sun lunchtime.

Nola £

Unconventional little café-bar; a somewhat tucked-away meeting place for artists under brightly-coloured umbrellas, spread over three floors in a luxuriant green courtyard. Just follow the small, inconspicuous sign and arrows down a narrow passageway. Recharge your batteries over an (iced) coffee or fruit juice, wine or a cocktail and enjoy one of the snack meals such as omelettes or spring rolls. WiFi. Posters and artworks for sale too.

➕ 211 E3 ✉ 89 Ma May
☎ 09 34 68 84 11 🕐 Daily 9am–midnight

Song Thu ££

This pretty villa is home to a training project run by the well-known Hoa Sua School for disadvantaged youths. Vietnamese and French dishes are served either inside between pillars or on the little garden terrace – generally everything is very professional, the food delicious and the staff friendly and quick.

➕ 210 C5 ✉ 34 Chau Long, Truch Bach Lake, Ba Dinh district ☎ 04 39 42 44 48
🕐 Daily 11:30am–2pm, 6pm–9:30pm

Where to…
Shop

The best place to browse is in the Old Quarter. Silk weavers and dressmakers/tailors can be found in Hang Gai and Hang Trong, crafts and T-shirts with a picture of Ho Chi Minh in Bao Hung, Hai Van and Hang Bong, galleries and poster shops in Hang Bac. Na Tho is trendy and expensive.

There's nothing you won't be able to find in the **Dong Xuan Center** (corner Hang Khoai/Dong Xuan, Old Quarter; daily 6am–midnight), a huge indoor market – from lacquerware to textiles or even a karaoke system. Everything is here. The same applies to the **Hang Da** (Cua Dong) indoor market.

If money is no object, real (!) luxury items à la Louis Vuitton, Christian Dior, Cartier & Co. can be found in up-market **Trang Tien Plaza** (corner Hang Bai/Hang Khay; www.trang tienplaza.vn, Mon–Fri 9:30am–9:30pm, Sat, Sun 9:30am–10pm).

Hand-crafted items produced in villages in the delta of the Red River have been famous for centuries. In some of the villages you can watch the craftspeople work and buy souvenirs from them directly, e.g. ceramics in the traditional pottery village of **Bat Trang** (Gia Lam district, on the N 5), silk goods in Van Phuc (10km/6.25mi southwest of Hanoi on the N6), or typical **non** hats made of palm leaves on a bamboo frame in **Chuong** (Phuong Trung, 30km (18.5mi) southwest of Hanoi on Ha Dong Road on the way to Huong Tich Pagoda).

Nowadays tourist coaches stop at service areas with gigantic shopping centres, e.g. **Hong Ngoc Humanity Center** on the way to Ha Long Bay – but you must haggle for a good price!

Where to…
Go Out

No visit to Hanoi is complete without seeing a performance at the 🎭 **Thang Long Water Puppet Theatre** (Nha hat mua roi Thang Long, 57B Dinh Tien Hoang, Hoan Kiem Lake, Old Quarter; tel: 04 39 36 43 34; www.thanglongwater puppet.org; daily 3pm, 4:10pm, 5:20pm, 6:30pm and 8pm, Sun also 9:30am, tickets VND60,000–VND100,000). Vietnam's sagas and heroic tales of old are brought to life in this thousand-year-old form of art; a speaker gives a running commentary.

The folklore ensemble **Ca Tru Thang Long** (28 Hang Buom, Old Quarter; tel: 012 23 26 68 97; www. catruthanglong.com, Tue, Thu, Fri, Sat, Sun 8pm, tickets VND210,000) give fascinating one-hour **ca tru** performances in an old 'tube house' – this classic form of chamber music played on old traditional instruments accompanied by powerful singing may however seem a little discordant to western ears…

The **Hanoi Opera House** can only be visited when attending a performance, be it ballet, a violin concert, a play, Vietnamese or modern music (1 Trang Tien corner Ly Thai To; tel: 04 39 33 01 13; http:// hanoioperahouse.org.vn, tickets from VND200,000).

The no-frills-attached 'pub lane' **Funky Buddha** (2 Ta Hien, Old Quarter; tel: 04 32 92 76 14; daily from 11pm) has turned into a hot-spot for young Vietnamese and tourists alike. Swing a leg at the weekend in **Hanoi Rock City** (27/52 To Ngoc Van, Tay Ho district; tel: 09 43 57 19 84; www.hanoirock city.com; daily from 10pm, entrance fee: VND50,000); jazz fans can look forward to Tuesdays.

Insider Tip

The North

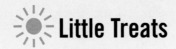 **Little Treats**

Culinary adventure
In **Bac Ha** (► 185) sour noodle soup and *thang co*, horse goulash, are all the rage – just give them a try!

Zigzagging back and forth…
…through fascinating mountainous scenery, e.g. crossing Pha Din Pass with wonderful panoramic views towards **Dien Bien Phu** (► 185).

Paddling in the South China Sea
Explore the caves and lagoons in **Ha Long Bay** (► 174) from a completely different perspective in a kayak.

Getting Your Bearings

Vietnam reveals its most beautiful side in the north – or at least its greenest! Around Sa Pa hikers can explore the craggy mountain scenery of the Tonkin region, passing lime-green coloured paddy field terraces on their way to visit the mountain people. And in fabulous and fabled Ha Long Bay junks glide around the unbelievably beautiful emerald-green UNESCO World Heritage Site.

The mountain town of Sa Pa is one of the coldest and foggiest places in Vietnam – and it can even snow here. And that was the very reason why the French came here in the 1920s. The pretty country houses and villas that the colonial rulers built for the summer months are now popular among tourists. And this is not surprising as the climatic health resort lies in breathtaking mountain scenery surrounded by terraced paddy fields. Just as in the past, you can still see stilt houses in this region and members of the ethnic mountain tribes in their brightly coloured costumes. The Hmong and Dao peoples in particular still uphold their old animist traditions.

One, if not *the* highlight of any trip to Vietnam must surely be Ha Long Bay – a magical, primeval backdrop to countless dripstone caves. This bizarre landscape with some 2,000 mountain-like islets is best explored in a

junk – even if most are now modern copies. For the more sporty, hire a kayak and paddle into the heart of this giant limestone formation that is only accessible by high tide and visit the floating fishing villages.

Countless conical mountains, some small, some large, covered with vegetation, rise straight out of Ha Long Bay

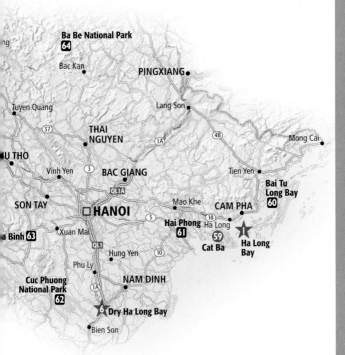

Planting rice is a tedious task that is usually done by women, as seen here near Lao Cai

Six Perfect Days

You should plan six days for this suggested tour which involves a lot of additional activities. It includes excursions into the mountains, on foot or by bike, and by kayak through the South China Sea. If you have more time to spare, it is easy to extend your stay and explore things more closely.

Day One

Morning

The best way to travel from Hanoi to ⭐**Sa Pa** (➤ 177) is to book a sleeping compartment on the night train to save time. You will arrive after a good night's sleep and can spend some time exploring the town. Wander around the lively streets with their brightly coloured souvenir stalls, markets and pretty colonial villas, country houses and cafés.

Afternoon & Evening

A walk through beautiful mountain scenery leads you to **Cat Cat** or **Thac Bac Waterfall** (➤ 178, 195). You can spend the night in villages around about in B&Bs. The Red Dao villages of **Ta Phin** and **Ta Van** (➤ 179) are particularly popular, for example.

Day Two

Morning

Set off early in the morning to continue your trek through the mountains, past rice terraces, tea plantations and over suspension bridges with a visit to some more colourful markets where the Dao, Hmong and others of the 27 different mountain tribes sell their wares. The 'Flower Hmong' in 65 **Bac Ha** (➤ 185), for instance, is especially pretty.

Afternoon/Evening

End the day in Sa Pa in front of a fire or even a camp fire (e.g. at the **Hill Station Café**, ➤ 188) before taking the night train back to Hanoi.

Day Three

Morning

The delta of the Red River can be reached by public bus, in a hire care with chauffeur or on an organised coach trip. Depending on how much time you have and your interests, a visit to the region around 63 **Hoa Binh** (➤ 184), where you can explore a number of pretty places on foot through the wonderful conical mountain scenery, is well worth while.

Afternoon & Evening
Carry on to Ninh Binh to visit ⭐ **Dry Ha Long Bay** (➤ 180). Head for the provincial capital Tam Coc, 10km (6.25mi) to the west and look for somewhere to stay here and unwind, ready for the tour the next day.

Day Four

Morning
Take a rowing boat and explore the lovely scenery around **Tam Coc** (➤ 180). Around the 'Three Grottos', the velvety-green karst mountains, home to macaques and mountain goats, are an area of timeless beauty.

Afternoon
Several noteworthy pagodas can be found in this fascinating river area, such as **Chua Bich Dong** and **Hoa Lu Temple** (➤ 181) which you can plan to visit by bike or in a horse and cart.

Day Five & Six

After four days on the road you can now put your feet up and enjoy a relaxing and romantic two-day boat trip around ⭐ **Ha Long Bay** (➤ 174). After sailing around the legendary, picture-postcard bay you can eat and stay the night on board while the boatsman takes you to one of the colourfully lit caves full of stalactites and stalagmites (e.g. **Hang Sung Sot,** ➤ 174) and a floating village (e.g. **Van Gia**, ➤ 176). If you don't want to sit still so long, you can of course hire a kayak and explore the mysterious lagoons that open up behind overhanging cliffs for yourself, e.g. spectacular **Hang Luon** (➤ 174). And there are several beaches on the island such as **Ti Tov** (➤ 176) that are an open invitation to swim or sunbathe.

Anyone who cannot get enough of this breathtaking scenery can extend their trip to the wild and mountainous island of **59 Cat Ba** (➤ 182) with its floating villages (left) – a destination that is not just interesting for active climbers.

★Ha Long Bay

Just imagine a thousand giants lying in the emerald-green water of the South China Sea, some have hunched backs and others are stretching out their limbs. Covered with vegetation, around 2,000 island mountains have been poking their limestone heads out of the sea for millions of years now. Since 1994 they have become protected UNESCO sites.

The island mountains have captured the imagination of visitors for thousands of years. About half of the 1969 islands officially have names. Most are called after animals or parts of the body – such as turtles or watchdogs, fighting cockerels, noses, breasts and even praying monks. Kings such as Le Thanh Tong in the mid 15th century extolled the beauty of the countryside in Ha Long Bay (Vinh Ha Long) in poems where 'the mountains stand like pieces on a chessboard'. The film **L'Indochine** of 1992 starring Catherine Deneuve was made in part in this natural arena.

Where dragons of old once roamed is where cruise liners and junks, passengers and canoeists from all over the world now congregate. Anyone simply interested in exploring the spectacular World Heritage Site should ignore busy **Ha Long City** – an ever-growing conglomeration of shipyards, industrial port and the whole mumble-jumble for the masses of Chinese tourists and day-trippers who come here. Many western visitors stay the night on their excursion boat or on **Tuan Chau peninsula**, 8km (5mi) to the west of Ha Long City. Alternatively you can explore the bay from the island of **Cat Ba** (► 182) as well.

Insider Tip

Breathtaking Caves

The most beautiful sight in Ha Long are the caves. There are a number of deep caverns in the towering limestone mountains full of stalagmites and stalactites. Some even have lakes (e.g. **Hang Luon, Hang Dong Tien** and **Hang Dong Me Cung** near Cat Ba in the south as well as challenging **Hang Hanh** in the northeast of the bay). These can best be explored by kayak – but only with a knowledgeable local guide familiar with the tides and where it is safe to travel. Some of the 15 caves that can be visited are very trippery with concrete paths and coloured electric lights. Tourist boats arrive at some landing stages every 15 minutes! The much-visited **Hang Sung Sot** ('Cave of Surprises'), in the south of the bay – a huge

Insider Tip

...is the name of this magical bay. Dragons are the main figures in both legends that surround its creation. One tells of a dragon which defended the Vietnamese (Viet) from their enemy from the north by digging deep valleys and holes in the earth with its giant tail. After it had finished it dived under the water making the level rise and flooding the land. The other tells of a mother dragon and her children which protected a local fisherman from being attacked by pirates by spewing out fireballs at the enemy. These landed in the sea as masses of grey lumps of ash that now point heavenwards in the form of craggy islands.

cavern covering 12,000m² (3 acres) – is so big that the groups of tourists soon disappear into one of the three main cave areas. The circuit path presents a magical sight of cave formations in a shimmering haze. **Hang Dau Go** ('Cave of the Wooden Stakes') further to the north is like a cavernous cathedral. According to legend Tran Hung Dao gathered and hid wooden stakes here with which he then sank the Mongol fleet in a battle on Bach Dang River in 1288.

The neighbouring cave, **Hang Dong Thien Cung** ('Cave of the Heavenly Palace'), extends to over 10,000m² (2½ acres). It is well worth climbing the steep steps to the cave entrance, 25m (82ft) up, which contains colourfully lit dripstones. From the entrance there is a lovely panoramic view of the bay. The same goes for **Hang Bo Nau** ('Pelican Cave'), some 3km (2mi) southeast of the little island Trong May.

A junk with a typical red ribbed sail ferries tourists to islands such as Ti Tov

The North

Islands

You can land on some of the islands and swim or sunbathe at nine small (not always clean) beaches, e.g. **Ti Tov** (also written **Ti Top**), named after the Russian astronaut Gherman Titov who visited the beach together with Ho Chi Minh in

Insider Tip

1962. On **Dao Soi Sim** 400 steps, steep in part, lead to a viewpoint with fantastic views across the bay and the junks lying at anchor.

TAKING A BREAK

Don't worry, you will find most things you want on the excursion boats. And shrewd saleswomen often row from one tourist boat to the next with an assortment of souvenirs, drinking water, fruit and suntan lotion.

✚ 222 C2
✉ Tourist Service Center, Bai Chay Pier, Ha Long City (another, less overcrowded pier for luxury boats can be found in Hon Gai district, a third one further away on the Tuan Chau peninsula)
☎ 033 3 82 48 67, 033 3 84 74 81
▶ Insider Info, each cave around VND30,000

Wind and weather have eroded and moulded the karst rock over millions of years

INSIDER INFO

- **A boat trip** around Ha Long Bay is an absolute must for any tourist who is visiting northern Vietnam. That is, of course, something the locals realise too, which is why the number of different things on offer is just a huge as the price difference. Anything between £35–£700/€50–€1,000 per boat a day is possible. Due to frequent safety issues that arise, don't save money in the wrong place. Of the 400 barges and boats several are dodgy sieves but there are also some real eye-catchers with bright-red ribbed sails. The following can be recommended: *Annam Junk* (www.annamjunk.com), the passenger ship *Emeraude* with several decks (www.emeraudehalong.com) and the floating hotels *Bai Tho Junk* and *Victory Junk* from Bai tho Cruises (£££; www.victoryhalong.com) that are equipped with every conceivable comfort.

- Be prepared to have to share the bay with **thousands of other visitors**. In summer, in particular, it can get crowded and loud in the caves; in winter, fog can roll in suddenly and spoil the view.

- Ask your boatsman to make a detour – if possible – to one of the floating villages, e.g. **Van Gia** (also spelt Cua Van), where even the school is on a houseboat.

- Another 'must' is a **kayak trip** through the magical world of Ha Long Bay. Many boat tours include a one-hour paddle excursion in the price; trips lasting several days are also on offer (2 days cost around £140/€200, incl. food and accommodation in tents or on boats). One recommended agency is Seacanoe (www.johngray-seacanoe.com). Always wear a lifejacket when out in a kayak.

★5 Sa Pa

Picturesque terraced paddy fields, delightful waterfalls, stilt houses and ethnic mountain people in brightly-coloured local costume – in and around the former French climatic health resort of Sa Pa, at the foot of Fan Si Pan, Vietnam's highest peak, one of the world's most beautiful spots waits to be discovererd. Trekking tours with 'home-stays' in the houses of the local people are more than worthwhile.

The 27 ethnic groups of northern Vietnam today number some 5 million people. They stand out in the streets and busy markets in and around Sa Pa where you may well be confronted with, for us, bizarre and sometimes archaic traditions such as the belief in nature spirits and shamanism and the enthusiasm for cockfighting. You may notice certain features that they consider beautiful such as teeth blackened using a tincture made of bamboo leaves, moths' wings and honey (especially among the Muong and Lu people) or shaved eyebrows (Dao). Although traditional stilt houses are increasingly being replaced by single-storey stone houses, they can still be found in the villages of the Tay and Thai people. The leaves of some 3,000 palm trees are needed, for instance, just for the roof.

Street scene in Sa Pa – women from ethnic mountain groups can easily be identified by their conspicuous headdresses or hairstyles

Clothes Maketh Man

The area around Sa Pa is largely the home of the **Dao** (pronounced *Dzao*, Red and Black Dao) and the **Hmong** (as well as the Mong or Meo; Black, White, Red and the 'Flower' Hmong, the Hmong Hoa, ▶ 185). Women from both ethnic groups still wear their brightly-coloured, embroidered local costume and heavy silver jewellery. Dark-blue skirts and a turban-like, sometimes chequered headpiece are characteristic of the Hmong; Red and Black Dao stand out due to their cushion-like turbans or headscarves in the respective colours. These local costumes, however, are being replaced by jeans and shirts of man-made fabrics and are often only seen nowadays on feast days and at weekly markets.

Colonial Inheritance

Sa Pa lies at an altitude of 1,560m (16,791ft) around a lake. The **overall appearance** of this former market town that, on some mornings, seems to hover above the clouds, is its main attraction – a colourful mixture of villas, rustic castle-like country houses and an old church. All date from colonial days when the French founded a military sanatorium here at the beginning of the 20th century. The railway arrived in 1922, connecting it to Lao Cai 37km (23mi) away.

Some 15 years ago, tourism woke this mountain town from its deep slumber. Guesthouses, (luxury) hotels and massage parlours shot out of the ground like mushrooms, some of them squeezed in, one next to another. Critics scathingly refer to this upheaval in and around Sa Pa as 'ethno-hype'. The legendary **love markets** of the Hmong and Dao, where locals kept a lookout and 'kidnapped' their future bride, are now only part of folkloric shows today. And even the sometimes overcrowded, traditional **weekly market** itself has had to find a new location – but then, realistically speaking, markets are held here all over the place every day. Women and young girls of the Black Hmong minority ply their hand-embroidered goods to tourists from dawn 'til dusk in the narrow streets in the Old Town – even in several languages.

Other Sights in the Area

In the much-visited village of **Cat Cat** in the Muong Hoa valley, just 3km (2mi) to the southwest of Sa Pa, you can watch women from the Hmong minority weaving and embroidering, wander around the souvenir stands and chat to the hawkers or watch a folklore show. **Cat Cat Waterfall** that drops some 20m (66ft) is located before reaching the village via a flight of steps and across a small suspension bridge. The **Silver Waterfall (Thac Bac)**, however, is more interesting. It is located some 12km (7.5mi)

The countryside around Sa Pa is characterised by the many terraced paddy fields to the west of Sa Pa and can be reached by moped or after a lovely hike. This can be combined with the **Love Waterfall** (**Thac Tinh Yeu;** 2.5km (1.5mi) to the west of Sa Pa) where you can also swim in the pool at the bottom in the summer.

The area around Sa Pa in general is a paradise for hikers (➤ 195). One of the many places to head for is **Ta Phin** (11km/7mi northeast of Sa Pa) where hand-made items such as hats and bags are produced by a cooperative, or **Ta Van** that is reached along a lovely river valley of the same name (9km/5.5mi southwest of Sa Pa). An unusual variety of flora and fauna can be seen en route. Some 2,000 plant species alone and almost 350 bird species have been sighted in **Hoang Lien Son Nature Reserve** in the Fan Si Pan area (➤ Insider Info).

A dressmaker from the Red Hmong minority carrying on with her work at Sa Pa market

TAKING A BREAK

In **Sa Pa** soup kitchens can be found on Xuan Vien near the lake. In **Cat Cat** snacks and drinks are sold at small stands; Mountain View Café is on the main road before reaching the village.

✛ 220 C4

Sapa Tourism (with the Sapa Culture Museum)
✉ 2 Fan Si Pan Rd., Sa Pa
☎ 020 3 87 19 75; www.sapa-tourism.com
🕐 Daily 7:30am–11am, 1:30pm–5pm 💷 Free

Cat Cat (village & waterfall)
✉ Cat Cat 🕐 Daily 8am–6pm 💷 VND40,000

Silver Waterfall
🕐 Daily 8am–6pm 💷 VND10,000

Love Waterfall
🕐 Daily 8am–6pm 💷 VND45,000

INSIDER INFO

- The **best time to travel** to Sa Pa is from September to November. But even then you should take **warm clothing** with you.

  Insider Tip

- 3,143m (10,311ft)-high **Fan Si Phan** is often hidden in thick fog that hangs over the Hoang Lien Son mountain range. The top of Vietnam's highest mountain can be reached by experienced climbers in two to three days. It is a strenuous tour along partly very steep paths and up fixed ladders (best time: mid-Oct to mid-Nov and Feb/March–April/May, guide and bearer essential, tent, sleeping bag, head torch and additional drinks must be brought with you, 2 days US$60).

- As an alternative try **Ham Rong** that is 'only' 1,800m (5,900ft); the climb starts up stone steps just outside Sa Pa. A pretty stone garden (Thach Lam) and wonderful views from a platform over the town are the reward (via the entrance gate in Ham Rong Street; daily 7am–5pm, admission: VND70,000).

- Good to know: The **indigo** used in souvenir clothes and bags stains slightly.

⭐6 Dry Ha Long Bay

Anyone coming to the industrial town Ninh Binh, 90km (55mi) south of Hanoi, is very probably heading for another place as the surrounding area is just as magical as Ha Long Bay. Here, it is not the emerald-green sea that glistens between the striking island mountains but gleaming paddy fields, as far as the eye can see. In so-called Dry Ha Long Bay you can row through caves or cycle along damns surrounded by karst rock formations millions of years old.

The charm of the particularly impressive scenery around the little centre **Tam Coc**, 10km (6.25mi) west of Ninh Binh, is no secret any more. Crowds of people come to the 'Three Caves' at weekends and on pubic holidays in particular, as do hawkers, caravans of rowing boats on the river and jams outside the caves. If you hire a bike, you can explore things on your own, cycling along the damns through karst scenery to floating villages, hot springs and settlements where the locals live from craftwork and embroidery (e.g. Van Lan/Minh Hai).

Pagodas and Caves

Insider Tip

Picturesque **Bich Dong Pagoda (Chua Bich Dong)** can also be reached on foot from the pier in Tam Coc. Visitors to this evocative cave temple are greeted by three Buddha statues – the Past, the Present and the Future as well as Quan Am. If you climb to the summit you will be rewarded with a breathtaking panoramic view from the **Green Cave**.

To reach **Hang Mua Cave** nearby, on Nui Ngoa Long, the 'Mountain of the Reclining Dragon', you have to climb 500 steps lined by dragons to reach the top from where there is a simply stunning view (1–2 hrs.).

This karst landscape gained its name from the fact that the mountains rise out of paddy fields rather than the South China Sea

Dry Ha Long Bay

Detour to Hoa Lu

When Vietnamese kings sought shelter from the constant attacks of the Chinese 1,000 years ago, they moved their capital into the protective karst mountains. They built Hoa Lu, the **capital of the Dai Co Viet Kingdom** (968–1009), the ruins of which can be seen today 12km (7.5mi) northwest of Ninh Binh. Two temples with wood carvings and several tombs on Nui Ma Yen, including the two oldest known tombs in Vietnam, are reminders of the brief period under their rule.

On the path to Bich Dong Cave – like passing through the fog into another world

TAKING A BREAK

Those on a tour of the 'Three Caves' can buy drinks and snacks from **floating refreshment stalls**.

➕ 221 F1

Ninh Binh Tourist
✉ Dinh Tien Hoang, Ninh Binh
☎ 030 3 84 41 01; www.dulichninhbinh.com.vn/en

Tam Coc Pier
🕐 Daily 7am–4pm 💰 VND80,000, rowing boat for 1½–3 hrs. and up to 4 people around VND400,000

Chua Bich Dong
🕐 Daily 6am–6pm 💰 Free

Hang Mua
🕐 Daily 8am–4pm 💰 VND50,000
ℹ water and sturdy shoes essential

Hoa Lu
🕐 Daily 8am–4pm 💰 VND10,000

INSIDER INFO

■ If Tam Coc is too crowded for your taste, head for **Trang An** (caves and temple, 10km (6.25mi) northwest of Ninh Binh; daily 7am–4pm, boat fare VND50,000–VND150,000, depending on number of passengers and duration). Another worthwhile detour is to **Van Long Nature Reserve** with its exquisite kingfishers, macaques, Delacour langurs and lizards (23km/14mi northwest of Ninh Binh; daily 7am–4pm, admission incl. 1–1½-hr. boat ride: VND100,000).

■ Famous **Phat Diem Cathedral**, built in 1891 (tel: 030 3 86 20 58; www.phatdiem. org; daily 8am–5pm, free) in Luu Phuong, 28km (17.5mi) southeast of Ninh Binh, is an architectural mixture between a church and a pagoda with both Christian and Buddhist symbols. During the Indochina War against the French, the area around the church saw fierce fighting as immortalised by Graham Greene in his novel *The Quiet American*.

Insider Tip

59 Cat Ba

This predominantly wild, mountainous island is a UNESCO biosphere reserve protecting valuable ecosystems such as swamps, mangrove forests, freshwater lakes, waterfalls, caves and offshore coral reefs as well as karst mountains.

Covering an area of around 350km² (135mi²), Cat Ba, 20km (12mi) to the west of Ha Long City, is the largest island in Ha Long Bay. Some 30,000 people live here from fishing and prawn farming, rice growing and tourism which means that in the rainy summer season and at weekends in particular Cat Ba City is firmly given over to crowds of karaoke

Insider Tip

fans and traffic gridlocks. The cooler autumn and winter season (Sep–Feb), when the little island is virtually deserted, is a much more pleasant time for excursions.

About half the island is taken up by **Cat Ba National Park** that extends over some 69,200 acres and protects the mangrove forests and limestone formations. 745 different species of plant grow on Cat Ba, including many types of tree, orchid and more than 350 plants of pharmaceutical value. Up until 1893 pirates hid in the caves. They are now home to macaques and the endemic

View from the summit of Ngu Lam over the dense greenery of Cat Ba National Park

Golden-Headed or Cat Ba langur that is threatened with extinction. Hikes, many of them very demanding, lead up **Ngu Lam** and to the 'frog lake' **Ao Ech** (18km/11mi).

Boats for day trips leave from the harbour in Cat Ba to **Lan Ha Bay** and its floating fishing villages, to remote island, caves and lagoons framed by sheer cliff faces.

TAKING A BREAK

Incredibly cheap food is served in a flash in the tiny soup kitchen run by the **Tu Thoa family** on the promenade (£; 190 Road ¼; daily 8am–10pm).

✚ 222 B2

Cat Ba National Park
☎ 098 4 91 90 26 🕐 Daily 7am–4:30pm 💷 VND40,000

INSIDER INFO

Lan Ha Bay near Cat Ba is a **paradise for climbers:** the views are amazing and the climbs challenging for those who like swinging from cliff faces. Trained guides and equipment available at Asia Outdoors (222 Street ¼, Cat Ba City; tel: 031 3 68 84 50 or 016 54 96 86 22; www.asiaoutdoors.com.vn).

At Your Leisure

60 Bai Tu Long Bay

A smaller bay, Bai Tu Long (Vinh Bai Tu Long), starts 30km (18.5mi) northeast of Ha Long Bay. It may have less spectacular caves but the crowds of other tourists are also smaller on these partly uninhabited semi-islands that form part of a nature reserve.

Nevertheless change is underway as the region is now focussing on seaside tourism for mostly Chinese tourists. This can be felt on the island **Van Don** (Cai Bau) that covers 450km² (174mi²) and is reached over a bridge or by hydrofoil from Ha Long City. The first hotels, set against a marvellous backdrop of rocky hunchbacked giants, have already opened. **Quan Lan** (Canh Cuoc), on the other hand, that is only 11km² (4.25mi²) in size

and lies to the southeast of the industrial town of Cam Pha, is still a sleepy little island with long, empty beaches and just eight villages whose inhabitants live largely from fishing and prawn farming.
✚ 222 C2

61 Hai Phong

The old buildings in the town centre, the **Quarter Français**, still exude a colonial flair from the days when the Europeans started to drain the swampy area in 1874 and had the harbour built in 1876. Of special note are the villas around Dien Bien Phu, the restored neo-Baroque theatre from 1904 and the cathedral (both on Hoang Van Thu), as well as the municipal museum (in Dien Bien Phu), the observatory (1902), the octagonal post-office and the station.

Den Nghe, a temple dating from the 18th/19th centuries located in the south of the town, is well known for its wonderful woodcarvings, stone statues and richly decorated stone altar. The community hall **Dinh Hang Kenh** (Nhan Tho) from

Empty beaches can still be found on Bai Tu Long Bay

The rice harvest in Cuc Phuong National Park

1717 has impressive 200-year-old woodcarvings and sculptues, including some 300 dragons in all shapes and sizes.
✚ 222 B2

Den Nghe
✉ Le Chan corner Me Linh
🕐 8am–11:30am, 1:30pm–5pm 💳 Free

Dinh Hang Kenh (Nhan Tho)
✉ Nguyen Cong Tru
🕐 9am–5pm 💳 VND10,000

62 Cuc Phuong National Park

Impressive, craggy conical mountains rising up to a height of 600m (2,000ft) characterise this, the oldest national park in Vietnam (established in 1962) which covers 61,800 acres. Tropical giant trees with buttress roots the height of an adult man and trunks with a circumference of up to 25m (82ft) are under preservation; their dense foliage keeps sunlight away from the floor that is covered with climbing plants and mosses. The national park is home to some 2,000 subtropical plants and 120 mammals, including the extremely rare Delacour langur which was re-discovered 20 years ago. Vietnamese sika deer that were almost driven to extinction as well, are now bred here. On the fringes

and in the many caves Asian black bears still roam the wild as do clouded leopards, serows and muntjaks. In April/May in particular countless beautiful butterflies can be spotted. Imposing hornbills, pheasants and mountain eagles are among the more than 300 species of feathered inhabitant.

Inside Tip

63 Hoa Binh

The partly mountainous province of Hoa Binh, 75km (47mi) southwest of Hanoi, is the home of several ethnic minority groups. There are a number of lovely places to visit among the conical mountains. The Tay, Hmong, White and Black Thai live in the picturesque **May Chau valley** in the southwest, the Muong still live in stilt houses and offer 'homestays' to tourists in **Ban Dam, Ban Giang** and **Giang Mo**. **Moc Chau**, a plateau at an altitude of 800m–1,000m (2,600ft–3,300ft), is popular among the Vietnamese. This area is largely the home of the White Thai but also the Dao, Thai and Muong who live from the cultivation of wild rice, vegetables and tea, pig and poultry farming and increasingly from tourism.
✚ 221 E2

64 Ba Be National Park

Attractions in the national park around **Ho Ba Be** include rivers, streams, and caves as well as waterfalls. Covering 740–1,235 acres, the largest lake in Vietnam and the one at the highest altitude is called 'Three Seas' (Slam Pe) in the language of the Tay people and stretches more than 8km (5mi) over three valleys.

HANOI

There are many little islands in this lake enshrouded in legend. Huge limestone formations covered in vegetation stretch far out of the water. For this reason the area is also known as the 'Ha Long Bay of Mountains' that reach a height of 1,980m (6,500ft) here. Thanks to its enormous variety of species, the 24,700-acre national park is on the list of contenders to become a UNESCO biosphere reserve. Black langurs that also live here are threatened with extinction.

🔢 221 F4 ☎ 0281 3 89 41 26
🕐 Daily 7am–6pm 💵 VND20,000

65 Bac Ha

The **Sunday market** of the **Flower Hmong** people has made this village famous. Located some 100km (62mi) northeast of Sa Pa it still presents a colourful picture. This settlement of just 3,000 inhabitants lies at an altitude of 900m (2,950ft). Since time immemorial members of the mountain Hmong and Hoa people have carried out their business with any amount of maize or rice wine to conclude a transaction. Anyone visiting the market must reckon with crowds of people. Some complain that there are more tourists now that Flower Hmong. You can wander around among the horses, cows, chickens and water buffalo, farming equipment, traditional clothes and textiles, baskets full of chillies and mountains of vegetables. Souvenirs and bits and bobs, cheap watches and clothes of man-made fibres have long been part of the scene too.

66 Dien Bien Phu

The town Dien Bien Phu was founded in 1841, under Nguyen rule, on the site of a centuries-old caravan station. During the Indochina War against the French it was the scene of much fighting.

In May 1954 a decisive battle was fought here that ultimately sealed the fate of the colonial era. From 1953 onwards the valley was turned into a fortress with tunnels and two runways. A total of 16,000 soldiers were stationed here. In the 55 days that it was besieged by the Vietnamese under General Vo Nguyen Giap, until capitulation on 7 May 1954, around 3,000–10,000 French soldiers fell as well as 8,000–20,000 Vietnamese. Many French tourists, including mercenaries and veterans now come to visit the **museum** with its life-like figures, military equipment and the reconstructed bunker of the French general Christian de Castrie, as well as the strategically important **hill A1** opposite the museum. A **memorial**, a **Viet Minh cemetery** and several old French tanks and guns can also be inspected.

Getting to Dien Bien Phu itself is an experience (unless you come by air). The N6 and Route 279 zigzag their way through magnificent mountain scenery taking in the **Pha Din Pass** which offers wonderful panoramic views.

🔢 220 B3

Dien Bien Phu Museum
🕐 Daily 7am–11am, 1:30pm–5pm
💵 VND5,000

Even the children of the Flower Hmong people are surrounded by bright colours

Where to…
Stay

Price
of a double room per night:
£ under VND1m.　　　　　**££** VND1–VND2.4m.　　　　　**£££** over VND2.4m.

CAT BA

Sea Pearl ££
85 cosy rooms on the waterfront with the best view of the bay. The roof-top restaurant is good; loud disco on the first floor (book a room at the top if you are a light sleeper). Ask for special offers in the low season. WiFi.
✚ 222 B2
✉ 219 Road ¼, Cat Ba　☎ 031 3 69 61 28; www.seapearlcatbahotel.com.vn

HAI PHONG

Avani Hai Phong Harbour View £££
This luxury hotel exudes colonial charm not just because of trips round the town in a classic car but also because of the 127 elegant rooms. Social barbecue evenings around the pool. WiFi.
✚ 222 B2　✉ 4 Tran Phu
☎ 031 3 82 78 27; www.avanihotels.com

Insider Tip

NINH BINH/TAM COC

Emeralda £££
This luxury complex in a magical location among paddy fields has 172 rooms, some with a private pool. First-class organic food served in the three restaurants; wine bar. Correspondingly high prices.
✚ 222 A1　✉ Van Long Reserve, Gia Van
☎ 030 3 65 82 33; www.emeraldaresort.com

Nguyen Shack £
They don't come much more idyllic than this! Guests stay in the lakeside village of Khe Ha in an enchanting valley. The five huts are cosily furnished with hammocks and an open-air bathroom.
✚ 222 A1　✉ Khe Ha, Tam Coc
☎ 030 3 61 86 78; www.nguyenshack.com

SA PA

Chaulong Sapa £–££
This quietly situated, standard category hotel has a magnificent view of the mountains (when not foggy); 65 spacious and cosy rooms, some with open fireplaces (in the castle-like old building) or in the new building with a small heated pool. Good discounts if booked online.
✚ 220 C4　✉ 24 Dong Loi
☎ 020 3 87 12 45; www.chaulonghotel.com

H'Mong Sapa ££
This hotel with 30 rooms is located high up above the town. The view of the mountains makes up for the climb. Heater available on request. Hmong guide organises tours. Transfer to/from Lao Cai included in the price.
✚ 220 C4　✉ 10 Thac Bac
☎ 020 3 77 22 28; www.hmongsapahotel.com

Sapa House £
Picture windows with views of the mountains, heated beds, electric fires and modern bathrooms guarantee a cosy stay in this family-run hotel with 15 large rooms. Quiet location on the uppermost edge of town; town centre 10 minutes on foot.
✚ 220 C4　✉ 3A Thac Bac
☎ 020 3 77 22 88, booking@sapahouse.com

Sapa Paradise View £–££

Centrally located, warm and friendly. The 18 rooms are extremely well equipped with heating, TV, safe, some with a balcony and a PC. The corner suite has magnificent picture windows and a balcony. Own tour agency with reliable guides.

🚩 220 C4 ✉ 18 Pham Xuan Huan ☎ 020 3 87 26 83; www.sapaparadiseviewhotel.com

Victoria Sapa £££

The most luxurious hotel in the area with a spa, tennis court and heated indoor pool is situated slightly outside Sa Pa. The 77 rooms, arranged around a garden, have charming country-house furnishings and views of the mountains.

🚩 220 C4 ✉ Xuan Vien
☎ 020 3 87 15 22; www.victoriahotels-asia.com

Where to...
Eat and Drink?

Price
for a main course without drinks:
£ under VND120,000   ££ VND120,000–VND240,000   £££ over VND240,000

CAT BA

Green Mango ££

One of the best restaurants in the town catering for tourists but also one of the most expensive. Beautifully presented food is served here in chic surroundings – Thai, Vietnamese, lots of seafood, such as fish in soya sauce or tuna steaks. There are also pizzas and pasta, tapas and salads as well as wines and delicious cocktails ('happy hour' daily 1pm–7pm). Live music on Fridays.

🚩 222 B2 ✉ ¼ Road, eastern end of promenade next to Holiday View
☎ 031 3 88 71 51; www.greenmango.vn
🕑 Daily 11am–10:30pm

Nghia £

Good Vietnamese coffee in all its variations (e.g. with yoghurt or sweetened with condensed milk) is served in this cosy café. Drop in to Nghia's for breakfast or at other times of the day to sample some of her snacks, pastries or other small dishes.

🚩 222 B2 ✉ 208 Road ¼ (promenade)
🕑 Daily 7am–9pm

Quang Anh £–££

This huge floating restaurant serves fresh fish from its own ponds – guests can choose the one they want from the tank. Lots of Vietnamese come here to eat; good value for money. Kayaks can also be hired from here and 'homestays' organised.

Insider Tip

🚩 222 B2 ✉ Ben Beo Pier
☎ 09 82 59 51 59; www.quanganhcatba.com.vn
🕑 Daily 10am–10:30pm

SA PA

Le Gecko £–££

A classic. French and Vietnamese dishes are available here not far from the post-office. There are also burgers, pizzas, pasta and cakes. Cocktails, beer and wine are served well into the night – which is unusual in Sa Pa. Cookery courses, trekking tours and five rooms to rent complete the range of services on offer.

🚩 220 C4 ✉ 4 Ham Rong
☎ 020 3 87 15 04; www.legeckosapa.com
🕑 Daily 24hrs

Street Food £

Nomen est omen. Good, honest plain home cooking at a very

reasonable price. From this cosy mini-restaurant right on the main road you can watch the cooks preparing classic Vietnamese fare. And they even have pizzas here too.

🏠 220 C4 ✉ 33 Muong Hoa
☎ 09 74 83 98 73 🕐 Daily 10am–10pm

The Hill Station Signature Restaurant £££

This small but elegant restaurant serves imaginative 'ethnic' food such as water buffalo with chillies or fried bamboo. Lots of vegetarian dishes with tofu. You can eat seated on cushions (or more comfortably at a table) by candlelight and with wonderful views. High prices. Not to be confused with the Hill Station Café (££; Muong Hoa) which offers western-style steaks, French cheese and good wines in front of a roaring fire.

🏠 220 C4 ✉ 37 Phan Si Phan
☎ 020 3 88 71 11 🕐 Daily 11am–10pm

Where to...
Shop

Anyone staying for a few days in Ha Long City should pay a visit to the 🎪 **night market at Bai Chay** (daily 6pm until 11pm). Haggling is a must at the many stands selling souvenirs, jewellery and swimwear. A children's fair will keep the young ones occupied. Inside and in front of the huge **indoor market at Sa Pa** (Dien Bien Phu, above Sa Pa Lake; daily 7am–6pm) crafts, vegetables and fruit are available. One or other speciality such as **thit cho,** dog meat, will not be to Europeans' taste.

The much-photographed Flower Hmong Sunday market in **Bac Ha** (► 185) or the Saturday market in **Can Cau** near the Chinese border

get very crowded. Less touristy but no less colourful are many of the weekday markets in the area, such as in **Bin Lu, Coc Ly** and **Tam Duong.**

Where to...
Go Out

Every year on the ninth day of the eighth lunar month (Sep) the **Buffalo Fighting Festival** in Do Son, 20km (12.5mi) southeast of Hai Phong, is held in honour of Dieu Tuoc Ton Than, the water goddess and guardian of fishermen. After a number of rituals a generally non-bloody buffalo fight follows. But even the victorious buffalo has nothing from his success as both are sacrificed to honour the gods and eaten.

Cat Ba and Lan Ha Bay have turned into an eldorado for rock **climbers** (► 182); anyone venturing here on their own should take all necessary equipment with them. If you go out into the bay or the lagoons make sure the captain is an experienced sailor who knows the tides.

The same applies to kayak trips – which is the best way to explore the water and the hidden lagoons in Ha Long and Bai Tu Long Bay. But never set off without a guide. Even in Dry Ha Long Bay you don't need to be taken everywhere but can row or paddle yourself.

The **best areas to hike** in Vietnam are in the north, around Sa Pa, for example, and in **Ba Be National Park**. Even if there is masses of quality trekking equipment on sale in Sa Pa (as well as fakes of famous brands 'made in Vietnam') it is always better taking your own worn-in hiking boots with you.

Walks

1 SAIGON'S CHINATOWN
Walk

DISTANCE: 2.5km (1.5mi)   **TIME:** 3–5 hours (incl. visiting pagoda and a break)   **START:** Hau Giang near Binh Tay Market (🚌 1) ✚ 208 B1
FINISH: Tran Hung Dao, Tan Da (soup kitchens) ✚ 209 D1

On a walk through Cholon, Saigon's Chinatown, look out for traces of the goddess of the sea. Trade has always moved with the times in the Chinese district that was founded some 300 years ago, as can be seen wherever you go – in the booming markets, in the streets and in the thick of the myriad of mopeds. Admittedly smartphones have long since replaced the abacus and exhaust fumes the opium vapours. The Chinese pagodas, temples and assembly halls however are still oases in the midst of this madness. Start as early in the morning as possible as the market, the starting point of our tour, is at its best at 7am. From 10am onwards the sun often burns down mercilessly and there is little shade.

❶–❷
Dive headfirst into the activity at **Binh Tay Market**, Cholon's central market located in the yellow ochre building. There are more than 2,300 stands inside and in the streets round about selling all sorts of everyday things. Outside at the **wet market** with all the live animals, people and mopeds, things get pretty chaotic. The Saigonese buy their hats, sweets, nuts and pots here by the kilo or the box-load and get good discounts. As a tourist you can just enjoy the sight rather than having to fill up your shopping bag. From Cho Binh Tay move on to Thap Muoi and Hai Thuong Lan Ong at the very heart of Chinatown. But not without having a look in

A market seller with betel nuts that bring good luck at weddings

Cha Tam Church (St. Francis Xavier) a few hundred yards to the left of Hoc Lac. After being overthrown in November 1963, the dictator Ngo Dinh Diem – as a Catholic – fled here with his family.

2–3

Return to Hai Thuong Lan Ong and follow the scent of the traditional apothecaries that fills the air from sacks of herbs, roots, leaves, bark and less easily definable ingredients. A powder made from dried placenta, for example, smuggled in from China, is still used as a medicine and sold here. You will pass countless Chinese lanterns, garlands and 'lucky' flags hanging in shops selling wedding accessories until you reach **Ong**

TAKING A BREAK

You could eat your way from one soup kitchen to the next every few yards along this route. Binh Tay Market has a **food court** with mountains of fruit and the market on Phan Van Khoe sells tasty vegetarian *banh mi* (baguette sandwiches), deep-fried fishcakes or fried rice with tofu and fish sauce as well as desserts made with coconut milk.

Bei Com Ga Dong Nguyen (87–91 Chau Van Liem; tel: 08 55 76 62; daily 6am–10pm) has rice dishes with chicken or ginger, lotus root soup, fried tofu, crab meat and roast pork. And for anyone who may like such things: well seasoned pig's brain.

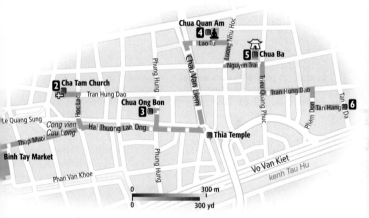

Bon Pagoda (Chua Ong Bon) – the 'Pagoda of the Bearded God' is always full as whoever makes a small donation can hope to make a little fortune.

3–4

Amongst the chaos on Hai Thuong Lan Ong take a look up at the old colonial façades here and there with their wooden panelling, some times brightly painted, other times weather-worn. Some wrought iron balconies still exist too.

Turn off at the post-office into Chau Van Liem to get to **Quan Am Pagoda (Chua Quan Am)**, dedicated to the goddess of mercy. Taoism and Buddhism are united here and the Jade Emperor, Ngoc Hoang, and a multitude of different creatures can be seen here too. The ridges of the roofs with their little figures from Chinese legends are eye-catching. The metre-long spiral incense burners hanging from the ceiling and the countless joss sticks in front of the altars

Walks

There are street food stands everywhere in Cholon

Binh Tay Market
✉ 57A Thap Muoi
☎ 08 8 57 15 12; www.chobinhtay.gov.vn
🕐 Daily 6am–7:30pm, Wet Market until about 9am 🖐 Free

Cha Tam Church
✉ Ho Lac 🕐 Daily 8am–6pm 🖐 Free

Ong Bon Pagoda
✉ Hai Thuong Lan Ong
🕐 Daily 6am–6pm 🖐 Free

Quan Am Pagoda
✉ 12 Lao Tu
🕐 Daily 6am–6pm 🖐 Free

really cannot be missed. They carry people's wishes up into the heavens. Some spirals burn for up to six months – some wish list!

4–5

Just round the corner you will come to the highlight of the tour – **Chua Ba** (▶ 66) – the most exquisite example of southern Chinese temple architecture. Located on Nguyen Trai, the goddess and guardian of the seas, Thien Hau, and the goddess of fertility, Kin Hue, are worshipped here. This is a world of scented sandalwood, Chinese characters and red and golden ornamentation. Note the little devil on the roof in the second courtyard and the pink strips of paper on the walls with the names of those who have made donations – a kind of receipt for the Taoist 'tax office'.

5–6

To finish on a delicious note, our tour takes you to the short street **Tan Da** on the corner of Pham Don, where you will find 'Cholon Best Food in Town', a street/soup kitchen behind a large gate.

Intricately carved and painted figures on the roof of Quan Am Pagoda

FOR PAGODA-LOVERS
In Cholon there are also several other interesting pagodas visited by fewer tourists, e.g. Phuoc An Hoi Quan (Hong Bang/Hung Vuong), Nghia An Hoi Quan (also known as Chua Ong, Nguyen Trai) and Tam Son (Trieu Quang Phuc). Some agencies offer this tour by rickshaw taxi which can be pleasant on a rainy day.

Insider Tip

2 CLIMBING THE MARBLE MOUNTAINS NEAR DA NANG

Walk

DISTANCE: 1.5–2km (1–1.25mi)   **TIME:** 2–3 hours (incl. 1-hr. visit to a temple)   **START/FINISH:** Dong Hai, Non Nuoc, about 10km (6.25mi) southeast of Da Nang ✚ 217 D4

'The journey is the (Buddhist) goal'. The five Marble Mountains, the 'Mountains of the Five Elements' south of Da Nang (► 135), are a popular destination for pilgrims who go from one pagoda and temple cave to the next. Steep and all the more arduous the later you set out, the path to paradise is – as one knows – difficult but worthwhile.

goddess of mercy (Quan Am), the Buddha of the Past (Sakyamuni) or the laughing, fat Buddha (Di Lac) of the Future.

1–2

Most visitors to the Marble Mountains climb **Thuy Son** (► 135), the Mountain of Water with its multitude of caves. First of all, a long, steep flight of steps near

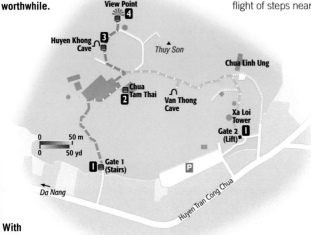

With various little detours there are four temples, six caves and at least three viewpoints to visit. The route takes you past temple towers and pavilions, burial stupas, lotus ponds and Buddhas in all sizes, poses and shapes. Almost at every step you take there are little niches in the rock face, small caverns and altars on the side of the path to the

STEPS, STEPS AND MORE STEPS!

The narrow flights of steps are only partly in the shade (leave your accommodation as early in the morning as possible!) and often slippery, there are often no railings and are not suitable for most children. Good shoes are essential especially when it is raining.

the entrance has to be conquered. Insider Tip Anyone who feels like giving up at this point should take the modern, glazed lift which saves having to climb about half the steps.

The start is from the car-park on the slope of the mountain. Two paths that cannot be missed lead to two viewpoints about 100m (330ft) further up. **Gate 1** to the south leads directly to **Chua Tam Thai** built in 1825 via 156 steps cut in the rock in the shade of tamarind trees. An alternative is **Chua Linh Ung**, reached up 108 steps through **Gate 2** in the east. To the left of the path you can reach **Van Thong Cave** with brightly painted figures guarding the site and a bewitching Quan Am.

2–3

At **Chua Tam Tai** the two paths rejoin. Head northwards and you come to a cave, entered under a weathered stone archway with an inscription in Chinese and a little Quan Am statue. The cave contains a wonderful figure of the goddess of mercy. To her left there is a lit passage through a tunnel which is sometimes quite slippery that opens up into the most impressive, if somewhat mystical **Huyen Khong Cave** with walls up to 30m (100ft) high.

TAKING A BREAK

In the road leading to the Marble Mountains there are several soup kitchens among the souvenir stands and, at the top, comparatively expensive refreshments are sold.

Once your eyes have adjusted to the light, **Thich Ca** (Buddha of the Present, fig. ➤ 135) can be seen. Carved out of the rock face, this figure of Buddha sits majestically some 10m (33ft) up. At around midday, rays of sunlight stream through the holes in the roof of the cave. Four grim-faced figures painted rather clown-like colours guard the 'Enlightened One'. Hindu, Confucian and Taoist deities are also venerated at other altars nearby. Apart from the sound of water dripping, there is an almost magical silence here on week days.

3–4

Just a little further on you come to the upper platform and can clamber up further to the right over several large rocks from where you have a fantastic **view** over the town, the other Marble Mountains nearby, the Monkey Mountain and the beaches as far as Hoi An.

Statues of Buddha, monks and Quan Am guard the path taken by pilgrims

3 FROM SA PA TO THE RED DAO OF TA VAN
Walk

DISTANCE: 5–6km (3–3.75mi) (to Cat Cat & back again) or 14km (8.7mi) plus a difference in altitude of 800m (2,625ft) (complete route)
TIME: 3–4 or 6–8 hours   **START:** Sa Pa, on the edge of the town to the west (Fansipan Road) ✚ 220 C4   **FINISH:** Ta Van ✚ 220 C4

The wonderful mountain scenery around Sa Pa can be explored on a gentle walk – albeit always pursued by brightly clad and sometimes really insistent women selling their wares. Anyone looking for a 'homestay' here will be well looked after by the Hmong and Dao who have adjusted to the needs of the 'long noses'.

Cat Cat Waterfall near Sa Pa is a big attraction in this stunning mountain area

❶–❷

The first part of the walk to the Black Hmong tourist village of **Cat Cat** is easy. A zigzagging country road that starts to the west of the market square winds its way some 3km (2mi) up to an altitude of 1,500m (4,900ft), as far as a much-photographed French villa with a tower (national park office) where, after about 30 mins., you turn down into the valley along a path with steps. You will soon see the first wooden huts between bamboo thickets and orchards. You pay an entrance fee at the barrier, stroll past the souvenir stands or turn off to the right before reaching the village itself up some steps and over a suspension bridge for the 20m (65ft)-high **Cat Cat Waterfall**, a lovely place for a rest and to take pictures.

Sa Pa ❶
Cat Cat
❷
Cat Cat
Waterfall
Y Linh Ho
San Sa Ho
Son Ta Van
0   1 km
0   0.5 mi
Lao Chai
Suspension
Bridge
❸
❹
Ta V 195

**Every conceivable shade of green –
the terraced paddy fields around Ta Van**

If you find the somewhat hard-selling ethno hype too much, just answer the repeated 'hellos' from the elderly women with a polite **chao chi** (or to younger people a more informal **xin chao**) – you will get a cheesy grin in return and they will stop trying to sell you anything.

Insider Tip

2–3

The view over the **Muong Hoa valley** of endless terraced paddy fields that glitter in the sun or shimmer a lime-green colour, are beautiful indeed. You can turn round here and head back to Sa Pa along the same route as far as where the paths fork and then take the path to the east. This will take you through picturesque countryside with green conical mountains via the villages of **Y Linh Ho, San Sat Ho** and **Lao Chai** along the valley (no sign-posts, just ask the locals). The path is clayey and leads through the paddy fields, down deep-cut mini canyons and along steeply terraced rice fields, past small rushing mountain streams which

drive clanking wooden 'rice bowl' mills. Water buffalo with young cow-hands on their backs stare from along the path. Women watch over their baskets full of indigo leaves – their hands blue from dying their fabrics – while men sit puffing bubbling hookahs (shishas). Rice is threshed by hand during the harvesting period in September. The path goes up and down and, after about 8km (5mi), you cross a narrow suspension bridge over the Song Ta Van, beyond which you will see the first houses in Sa Pa.

3–4

On arriving in **Ta Van**, a Red Dao village at an altitude of around 900m (2,953ft), you will come across more tourists who arrive on moped taxis and spend the night in one of the many 'home-stays'. And if you don't want to head back straight away, stay the night here too. Most tourists expect a relatively high 'westernised' or Vietnamese standard of comfort. However, if you ask around in Sa Pa and get a little away from the normal tourist routes, you will find accommodation with families who still live from collecting cardamom or from cultivating maize or manioc instead of from the sale of souvenirs and tourism. Rather than chips you will be given rice they have grown themselves, instead of Nescafé real Vietnamese coffee and tea. And while smoking the hookah and drinking red wine you may meet the village shaman.

TAKING A BREAK
In the mountain village San Sa Ho about half way along the path you can have a rest at the village 'shop'. In a stilt house at the entrance to the village light snacks (fried eggs with baguette), tea, lemonade and sweets are available.

FINDING THE RIGHT GUIDE
The young, English-speaking girls from the mountain people of the region (Hmong or Dao) are generally a better alternative to the official (young, male) guides from Hanoi who are often rather arrogant.

4 HIKING TO THE SUMMIT OF LANGBIANG
Walk

DISTANCE: 9km/5.5mi (4.3km/2.7mi uphill)   **TIME:** 4–5 hours
START/FINISH: Entrance to Langbiang Nationalpark (Langbiang Tourist Company), Lat village (🚌 5 from Da Lat) ✚ 215 D3

You don't need to be an experienced climber or hiker to reach the top of the 2,167m (7,109ft)-high mountain Langbiang (Nui Ba) near Da Lat. En route you will

Summit Langbiang
4 🔆 *2167 m*

Ticket Booth 3

1950 m ▲
Radar Base,
View Point »First Summit« &
Restaurant

0 ─── 500 m
0 ─── 500 yd

2 ▪ **Gravel Path**

1 ▪ **Gate & Ticket Booth**

pass red rhododendrons and wild orchids, willows, coffee plantations, palm and banana trees, glasshouses and pine forests and see butterflies, hawks and horses. A summit that nearly everyone can reach.

But avoid the rainy season if you can! The earth between the steps becomes mud, the paths are mostly overgrown and a sudden drop in temperature commonplace. Even in the dry season good hiking shoes are recommended for the last section. And inexperienced hikers should only set off with a guide.

Nui Ba National Park
✚ 214 B3   ✉ Lat village, Lac Duong
☎ 063 3 83 90 88   💲 VND20,000–VND40,000 (incl. summit)

1–2
You cannot miss the **entrance and ticket office**. Part of this not very strenuous and only partly sign-posted hike leads along a tarmac road – the first 45 mins. or 2.2km

Walks

(1.4mi) – and is also used by people on excursions and tourist jeeps which only go as far as a **radar station** (Radar Base, 'First Summit') with a cafeteria. There is however also a **rough track** that runs parallel to this first section that starts about 200m (660ft) after the entrance gate. Turn off to the right signed 'Langbiang' in huge letters. This path – not signposted – drops to start with; it is a little difficult to follow, but with a bit of intuition you will manage; the farmers you meet on the way will point you in the right direction.

❷–❸

The route passes over a narrow bridge, then keep slightly to the left and continue through coffee bushes and a section of pine wood. You will soon come onto a small

---

TAKING A BREAK

You can buy all the drinks and snacks you need at the entrance. There is a simple barbecue/cafeteria-style eatery at the radar station at an altitude of 1,950m/6,400ft, below the summit that is visited by the many day-trippers who come here by car, jeep or bus to go riding on 'zebras' – painted ponies!

---

ridge leading upwards (keep to the left) before rejoining the road again after 2km (1.25mi). Another 100m (330ft) further on turn left to the **radar station**. Here, at an altitude of 1,850m (6,070ft) is another little ticket hut that is not always manned. Continue to the right.

❸–❹

Follow the waymarked path (blue arrows and information boards) for the next 2.2km (1.4mi) through a pine wood to the summit. From here, you have a lovely view and a good chance of seeing a variety of birds such as crossbills, black bazas and the colourful, endemic collared laughing-thrush. The final 200m (660ft) is a climb through the intensely green rain forest, partly over steep and slippery steps and stones.

On the **plateau at the summit** at an altitude of 2,167m (7,109ft) there is a biological research centre. Hikers are rewarded with a wonderful 360° panorama. The view stretches across the hill scenery around Da Lat with its rich green forests, a mosaic of gleaming, moist paddy fields and fields of vegetables as well as deep-blue lakes.

Far-reaching views from Langbiang over the mountain scenery around Da Lat

Practicalities

Practicalities

WHAT YOU NEED

		UK	USA	Canada	Australia	Ireland	Netherlands
● Required							
○ Suggested							
▲ Not required							
Passport/National Identity Card (► 34)		●	●	●	●	●	●
Visa (regulations can change – check before booking; ► 34)		●	●	●	●	●	●
Onward or Return Ticket		●	●	●	●	●	●
Health Inoculations (tetanus, polio, diphtheria, hepatitis A & B, cholera; ► 204, Health)		○	○	○	○	○	○
Health Documentation (► 204, Health)		○	○	○	○	○	○
Travel Insurance		○	○	○	○	○	○
Driving Licence (international) for car hire		●	●	●	●	●	●

WHEN TO GO

High season   Low season

JAN	FEB	MAR	APR	MAY	JUN	JUL	AUG	SEP	OCT	NOV	DEC
32°C	33°C	34°C	35°C	32°C	31°C	31°C	31°C	31°C	31°C	31°C	31°C
90°F	91°F	93°F	95°F	90°F	88°F	88°F	88°F	88°F	88°F	88°F	88°F

☀ Sun   ⛅ Sunshine and Showers

Vietnam has three **climate zones**. The chart shows the average daily temperature for each month in Saigon. In the south, the rainy season is from May–Nov when you have to reckon with short but heavy downpours (best time to travel: Nov–April). In central Vietnam there is the danger of being caught in a **typhoon** in Aug–Oct when coastal roads and railway tracks can be impassable and flights cancelled (best time to travel and for swimming: April–July). In the north the rainy season is during the summer in May–Oct; the winter months here are much cooler that in the south and, from Nov/Dec onwards, you must reckon with persistent drizzle, fog and sudden drops in temperature of up to 10°C (in Nov–May). In the Highlands it is much cooler all year round (20–25 °C); it can rain all day for days on end; the driest period is Dec–March.

GETTING ADVANCE INFORMATION

Websites
- http://vietnamnews.vn
- www.gov.uk/foreign-travel-advice/vietnam
- http://en.vietnam.com
- www.thanhniennews.com

GETTING THERE

By air: Many airlines fly regularly from London and other British airports to Hanoi and Ho Chi Minh City (Saigon); few are direct flights, some with lengthy stop-overs. Combined flights for inland trips or visits to Cambodia or Laos may be available. In all cases consult your travel agent or check routes and alternatives online: e.g. Vietnam Airlines (www.vietnamairlines.com), British Airways (www.britishairways.com), Singapore Airlines (via Singapore; www.singaporeairlines.com), KLM (via Amsterdam; www.klm.com), Air France (via Paris; www.airfrance.de) or Thai Airways (via Bangkok; www.thaiairways.com). The flight time from Europe is from around 11–13 hours, depending on the route and stop-overs.

By train: Some specialist tour organisers combine a visit to Vietnam with a trip to China, for example, from where you can enter Vietnam by train. You must apply for a visa for entry into Vietnam before your journey.

By sea: From Cambodia (Phnom Penh) ships sail to Vietnam, generally into the Mekong Delta; buses connect up to Saigon. Apply for a visa in good time beforehand.

TIME

Vietnam is 7 hours ahead of London (GMT) and 6 hours ahead of Central Europe (CET). As there is no Daylight Saving Time in summer, the time difference is 1 hour less in summer.

Indochina Time (ICT) is 9 hours behind of Pacific Standard Time (PST) and 12 hours ahead of Eastern Standard Time (EST)

CURRENCY AND FOREIGN EXCHANGE

Currency: Vietnam's currency is the Vietnamese dong (VND). Prices for hotels and means of transport are often given in US dollars (and can be paid for in dollars). The plastic-looking bank notes range from VND500–VND1 million. (Some of them look very similar!). Payment in pounds sterling or euros is often possible in international hotels.

Exchange: Exchanging cash is possible at banks, hotels and at licenced gold shops and bureaux de change (which generally offer the best rates). Take your passport with you.

Exchange rates: VND10,000 ≈ £0.3 ≈ €0.42; £1 ≈ VND33,800; €1 ≈ VND23,800

Credit and cash/bank cards: Credit cards are accepted in major hotels, tourist restaurants and travel agencies. There are cash dispensers (ATMs) in every town (however, they do not always work). Cash/bank cards cannot be used in Vietnam.

Cancelling credit cards: Note the number of your credit card institution that has to be rung to cancel your credit card and freeze your account in the case of theft or loss, before leaving home.

VIET NAM NATIONAL ADMINISTRATION OF TOURISM: www.vietnamtourism.com

In the UK
11 Belgrave Square, London
SW1X 8PP
☎ 020/7201-6666

In the US
590 Fifth Avenue, 4th Floor,
New York, NY 10036
☎ 1-646/723-0200

In Canada
60 Bloor Street West,
Suite 1005,
Toronto, Ontario M4W 3B8
☎ 1-416/921 7376

Practicalities

NATIONAL HOLIDAYS (a selection)

1 Jan: **International New Year**; Late Jan/early Feb **Vietnamese New Year**; 3 Feb: **Foundation Day of Communist Party (1930)**; 30 April: **Liberation Day/Reunification Day**; 1 May: **International Labour Day**; 19 May: **Ho Chi Minh Anniversary**; 2 Sept: **Independence Day** (1945); 2/3 Sept: **Death of Ho Chi Minh (1969)**
Religious festivals are generally based on the lunar calendar. The most important festival in Vietnam is the Tet (Tet Nguyen Dan; ➤ 28). Other feast days include: the Khmer New Year, celebrated in the Mekong Delta in April/May; Buddha's anniversary (Phat Dan) in May; the 'Forgiveness of the Lost Soul' festival (Tet Trung Nguyen) in July/Aug; and – in the south in particular – Christmas on 24/25 Dec.

ELECTRICITY

 Mains voltage is 220 Volt AC current in the cities and towns; in the countryside its is generally still 110V. Continental-style plugs fit the sockets in most hotels but Russian round pin and American flat pin power points are also common. Adapters and torches are essential accessories.

OPENING HOURS

○ Shops
● Offices
● Banks
● Main Post Offices
● Museums/Monuments
● Pharmacies

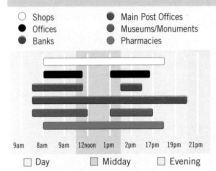

9am   8am   9am   12noon   1pm   2pm   17pm   19pm   21pm

☐ Day   ☐ Midday   ☐ Evening

Shops and chemists in tourist centres often stay open until 8pm/9pm; shopping centres from 9am–10:30pm. **Markets** open early in the morning at around 6am and close at 6pm. **Night markets** operate between 5pm/6pm–10pm/11pm. **Temples** are open from 6am/7am–6pm; **museums** have very different lunch breaks.

TIPS/GRATUITIES

Tips are given to chambermaids, waiters, bus drivers, tour guides, porters and masseurs. Taxi and cyclo taxi drivers do not expect a tip. However, if they have been ferrying you around for some time and you are happy with their service you can, of course, give them something. Small donations can be given to helpful monks and nuns at temples or put in the collection boxes. Better restaurants and hotels already add a service charge to the bill; no tip is expected in a street kitchen.

TIME DIFFERENCES

Saigon 12 noon

←
London (GMT) 5am

→
New York (EST) midnight

→
Los Angeles (PST) 9pm

→
Sydney (AEST) 4pm

STAYING IN TOUCH

Post Postage for postcards costs VND10,500; stamps are available from post offices. Letters take up to three weeks to reach Europe. Post your letters in good hotels or at the main post office).

Telephones International calls are cheapest from Internet telephone shops which also offer Skype and Yahoo! Voice services; phone calls to Europe are therefore extremely cheap (VND500–VND800/min., the connections are often bad). Self-dial calls using ground lines are possible from hotels (around VND13,000–VND26,000/min.) or, slightly cheaper, from post offices as well as with an IDD telephone card from public telephone boxes. Dialling a prefix such as 171, 177 and 178 often makes a call cheaper (does not work in all hotels).

Please note: An area code reform is in the pipeline (e.g. Hanoi wil then be 024 instead of 04). At the time of publication this had not been introduced.

International Dialling Codes Dial 00 followed by:

UK	44	Australia	61
USA/Canada	1	France	33
Irish Republic	353	Germany	49

Mobile providers and services Network operators are Viettel (www.viettelecom.com.vn, only in Vietnamese), expensive Vinaphone (www.vinaphone.com.vn) and Mobifone (www.mobifone.com.vn); the latter also has mobile phones for hire. The respective partner network will automatically be dialled up through your mobile phone's roaming function. But beware – an additional roaming fee will be charged (up to £0.7/ €1/min.)! Using a prepaid SIM card bought locally mobile phone calls in Vietnam and to Europe cost around £0.14/€0.20/min

WiFi and internet Internet access is free of charge almost everywhere (in hotels, cafés, airports, even in bus stations and on some long-distance coaches). Internet cafés, most of which also have Skype, can be found even in the most remote mountain area; social networks are sometimes blocked by the government from time to time (although this can by by-passed via a different server)

PERSONAL SAFETY

Vietnam is, basically speaking, a comparatively safe holiday destination. Nevertheless you should take the usual precautions where there are crowds of people. In addition:

■ Beward of pick-pocket at markets, airports and stations as well as on pavements where mopeds can pass.

■ In Hanoi and Saigon there are a number of bogus taxi companies and cyclo taxis have a bad reputation with regard to theft (▶ 37).

■ Reports on theft from hotel rooms is increasing, even from room safes. It is best to deposit money and other valuables at reception – and make sure you get a receipt.

■ In winter, in particular, there are sometimes strong and unpredictable sea currents, especially off Lang Co, Da Nang and Hue.

■ When out and about do not leave waymarked paths. There is still considerable danger from mines and rubbish leftover from the war.

■ Anyone who drives a car or rides a moped themselves must be particularly careful on Vietnam's roads; it is much more advisable to hire a car with a chauffeur (▶ 36).

POLICE (tourist police)	113
FIRE	114
AMBULANCE	115

Practicalities

HEALTH

 Health insurance: You are strongly recommended to take out health insurance that provides assistance and transport back home in the case of an emergency.

 Dental services: There are SOS International Clinics (www.internationalsos.com) in Saigon (167A Nam Ky Khoi Nghia St; tel: 08 38 29 85 20) and Hanoi (51 Xuan Dieu, 04 39 34 06 66). In Saigon there is also a European dental practice (Kumho Asiana Plaza, 39 Le Duan; tel: 08 62 67 66 66; www.accadent.com.vn).

 Weather: Protection from the sun and appropriate clothing (sunglasses, hat) as well as sun-blocker and enough drinking water are absolute essentials.

 Drugs: Chemists' do not meet western standards, except in Saigon and Hanoi. In the case of everyday medicines, always check the sell-by-date. Any medicine you may need should be taken with you from home.

 Drinking water: Only drink water that has been boiled or from sealed bottles. This also applies to when cleaning your teeth.

Infectious diseases: A cholera risk exists in northern Vietnam in particular (Hanoi, Ninh Binh) as well as in the Mekong Delta. For this reason do not eat ice cream, unpeeled fruit or raw vegetables. Avoid ice-cubes (*khong co da* – no ice please). **Dengue fever** is a dangerous disease transmitted by mosquitoes that are active by day and which can occur anywhere in the whole country, especially during the rainy season. To protect yourself from the mosquitoes use a spray and wear light-coloured clothing covering your whole body. This also applies in areas with a high-level risk of **malaria** – in the north (after the rainy season) and in the south (the whole year, esp. in the Mekong Delta, in Tay Ninh and around Saigon). There is a slight risk of infection during the rainy period along the coast. Make sure you take prophylactic medicine with you.

TRAVELLING WITH A DISABILITY

More and more hotels and a few museums have lifts. You will not find any easy-access buses or trains or lavatories suitable for the disabled.

CHILDREN

Nappies and baby-food in jars are available in virtually all towns and cities. Children's attractions are marked with the symbol shown above.

RESTROOMS

Lavatories in the country-side in particular are of the 'French' squat variety. Always take toilet paper with you on excursions and throw it away in the containers provided. **Nam** means 'gents', **nu** 'ladies'.

CUSTOMS

On entering the country, duty-free items include up to 1.5l alcohol (over 22%) or 2l wine, 400 cigarettes or 100 cigars or 500g tobacco, cash to the value of US$5,000. Weapons of any kind, ammunition, drugs and pornographic material are prohibited

EMBASSIES (Hanoi)

USA
☎ +84 (0)4 38 50 50 00
vietnam.usembassy.gov

UK
☎ +84 (0)4 39 36 05 00
www.gov.uk/government/
world/vietnam

Canada
☎ +84 (0)4 38 23 55 00
www.canadainter
national.gc.ca/vietnam

Ireland
☎ +84 (0)4 39 74 32 91
www.dfa.ie/irish-
embassy/vietnam

Australia
☎ +84 (0)4 37 74 01 00
vietnam.embassy.gov.au

Useful Words and Phrases

INTRODUCTION

Vietnamese is the only written language in Asia that uses the Latin alphabet. As a form of assistance all words listed in Vietnamese below are followed by a pronunciation aid in brackets. English is widely spoken in the tourist industry and many elderly people speak French.

ALWAYS USEFUL

Yes **Co, U, Da [goh/ur/dya]**
No **Khong [kong]**
Perhaps **Co le [goh lay]**
Please **Xin/Lam on [seen/lahm oin]**
Thank-you **Cam on [gam un]**
You're welcome **Khong sao [kong sao]**
Sorry! **Xin loi! [seen lai]**
Pardon? **Lap lai/Lam on [lablai/lahm oin]**
I (don't) understand **Toi (khong) hieu**
  [toy kong hju]
What is that? **Cai nay la cai gi?**
  [kai nai la kai yi]
Could you (male/female) help me please?
  (Ong/Ba) co the giup toi duoc khong?
  [ong/bä ko tä jub toy duak kong]
I would like (not like)… **…toi (khong) muon/**
  can [toy (kong) muen/gan]
I (don't) like this **Toi rat (kong) thich**
  [toy rut (kong) thik]
Have you (male/female) got …?
  Ong/Ba co …? [ong/bah ko]
How much is it? **May gio roi? [mai zhoh reu]**
Good afternoon/evening **Loi chao [lurj chow]**
Hello/Bye **Chao! [chow]**
  Talking to an older/younger man
  …Ong/Anh [ong/an]
  Talking to an older/younger woman
  …Ba/Chi/Co [bah/chi/goh]
How are you? **Ong co khoe khong?**
  [ong goh kuä kong]
My name is… **…Ten toi la [tu-en toyla]**
Good-bye **Tam biet! [tam be et]**

OUT AND ABOUT

left/right/straight on **Trai/Phai/Thang**
  [chai/pha/tang]
near/far **Gan/Xa [gan/sa]**
Where is …please? **Lam on/o dau …?**
  [lahm un/ur duh]
  …the main station? **Nha ga [nya gah]**
  …the airport? **Phi cong [fee gung]**
  …the hotel? **Khach san [chak' sahn]**
I would like to hire a **…Toi muon thue**
  [toy mu-en too-ay]
  …a bicycle **…xedap [say dap]**
  …a car /taxi **…ô-tô /tac-xi [otoh/taxi]**
How far? **May khoang cach? [my koang catch]**

ACCIDENT

Help! **Giup Do! [zyub toy]**
Watch out! **Chu Y! [chu-i]/Coi Chung!**
  [geu king]
Call…quickly! **Ong lam on goi nhanh…**
  [ong lahm oin geu najnn]
  …a doctor **Bac si [bak shee]**
  …an ambulance **Xe cuu thuong**
  [say guhturong]
  …the police **Cong an [gong ahn]**
It was my/your fault **Toi co/Ong ta loi**
  [toy goh/ong tah leu]

NUMBERS

0	**khong/linh [kong/lin]**	12	**muoi hai [moyhai]**	50	**nam muoi [namoy]**
1	**mot [moht]**	13	**muoi ba [moybah]**	60	**sau muoi [saomoy]**
2	**hai [hai]**	14	**muoi bon [moybohn]**	70	**bay muoi [beimoy]**
3	**ba [bah]**	15	**muoi nam [moynam]**	80	**tam muoi [dahmoy]**
4	**bon [bohn]**	16	**muoi sau [moysao]**	90	**chin muoi [cheenmoy]**
5	**nam [nam]**	17	**muoi bay [moybai]**	100	**mot tram [moht cham]**
6	**sau [sao]**	18	**muoi tam [moydahm]**	1,000	**mot ngan [moht nyan]**
7	**bay [bai]**	19	**muoi chin [moycheen]**	10,000	**muoi ngan [moy nyan]**
8	**tam [dahm]**	20	**hai muoi [haimoy]**	¼	**mot phan tu [moht fandur]**
9	**chin [cheen]**	21	**hai muoi mot [haimoy moht]**	½	**mot phan hai [moht fanhai]**
10	**muoi [moy]**	30	**ba muoi [bahmoy]**		
11	**muoi mot [moymoht]**	40	**bon muoi [bohnmoy]**		

Useful Words and Phrases

Please give me your name and address
Ong lam on cho toi biet ten Ong va dia chi
[ong lahm oin tscho toy bie' tehn ong wa di-e chi]

SHOPPING

Where is the…? **Toi tim o dau …?**
[toy dihm ur dao]
…chemist …**Nha thuoc tay [nya tuok dai]**
…camera shop …**Tiem ban do chup hinh**
[di-em ban doh tschub hin]
…baker's/bread shop …**Tiem banh mi**
[di-em banmi]
…shop …**Cua hang [guhang]**
…grocer's shop …**Hang thuc pham kho**
[hang durg famcho]
…market …**Cho [chur]**
What does this…cost? **Quyen…nay gia bao nhieu? [gwi-en…naija baunju]**

ACCOMMODATION

Can you recommend a…?
Ong co the tim cho toi…?
[ong goh tä tihm cho toy]
…hotel **Khach san [chak' sahn]**
…guesthouse **Phong tro [fang cho]**
Have you got…
…**Ong co con can [ong goh gon gän]**
…a single room? …**Phong rieng?**
[fang ri-eng]
…a double room? …**Phong doi?**
[fang deu]
…with a shower-room/bathroom?
…**voi Phong tam? [weu fang damm]**
…for one night? …**cho mot dem?**
[cho mohtdehm]
…for a week? …**cho mot tuan?**
[cho mohtdun]
What does a room cost with …**Gia tien bao nhieu mot phong voi [sa din bau njiu moht phong voi]**
…breakfast? …**an sang? [ansang]**
…half-board? …**an sang va an chieu?**
[ansang va an chu]

HEALTH

Can you recommend a doctor? **Omg co the tim, cho toi mot Ong bac si? [ong goh tä timh, cho toy moht ong bak shee]**

I have …**Toi co …[Toy ko]**
…a pain here …**dau o' day [dao o dai]**
…a temperature (fever) …**sot [shoht]**
…diarrhoea …**tieu chay [dee-u chai]**
…a headache …**dau dau/nhu't dau**
[daodao/njit'dao]
…toothache …**dau rang/nhu't rang**
[daorang/njit'rang]

FOOD

Where is a…here? **O dau co [ur dao goh]**
…good restaurant? …**nha hang ngon?**
[nya hang n'nong]
…a nice pub? …**tiem bia lich su?**
[di-em bia lik'sur]
Please reserve a table for four this evening
Ong/lam on, cho chung toi mot ban bon nguoi toi nay [ong/lahm oin cho coong toy moht ban bohn nyu-ay toy nai]
Cheers! **Chuc mung Ong! [chook mung ong]**
Pleased to meet you! **Han hanh duoc gap ong!**
[han hann durg'gab ong]
The food is very good **Thuc an rat ngon**
[tuk an rat'n'nong]
May I have the bill, please! **Tinh tien, lam on!**
[teen dee-en, lam oin]

VIETNAMESE SPECIALITIES

banh chung [ban cheeng] sticky rice cakes
bo bay mon [bobai mong] beef prepared in seven different ways
canh chua ca [gan chwa gah] fish soup (sweet-sour)
cha [cha] grilled pork
bun cha [bunt cha] grilled pork on a skewer
gio [jo] minced pork cooked in leaves
cha ca [chaka] grilled meat on a skewer
mam chung [mamcheeng] fermented fish with meat/vegetable filling
mien luon/ga [mi-en luun/ga] glass noodle soup with eel/chicken
heo rung [hoy rung] wild boar
cho [cho] dog (only in winter)
ech tam bot ran [ekdam bot'ram] frogs' legs in batter
oc noi [ogneu] snails (with pork)
ba ba [baba] turtle
men [men] venison
ran ho/tran [rangho/chan] cobra/python
doi [seo] bat

Road Atlas

For chapters: See inside front cover

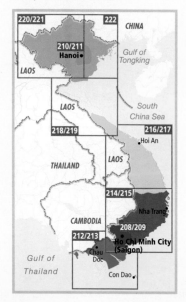

Key to Road Atlas

═══════	Main road (2 lanes plus)	✈ International airport
═══════	Main road (2 lanes)	⊕ ✦ Regional airport; airfield
══1A══	Trunk road with number	⚓ ⛴ Port; car ferry
══742══	Main road with number	🕴 ⛪ Castle; church
───────	Secondary road	★ 🕴 Place of interest; lighthouse
═══════	Road, not surfaced	🔺 ▪ Buddha temple; burial site
───────	Track	🏖 🗻 Beach; viewpoint
─ ─ ─ ─	Footpath	🌊 🌊 Waterfall; rapids
═ ═ ═ ═	Road under construction/planned	∴ ∩ Archaeological site; cave
× × × ×	Road not open to traffic	▲)(Summit; mountain pass
⇒ ⇐	Tunnel	M̂ 🕴 Museum; monument
━━━━	Railway	⭐ TOP 10
/////////	National park boundary	㉖ Don't Miss
/////////	Marine national park boundary	22 At Your Leisure

1 : 2.000.000

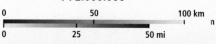

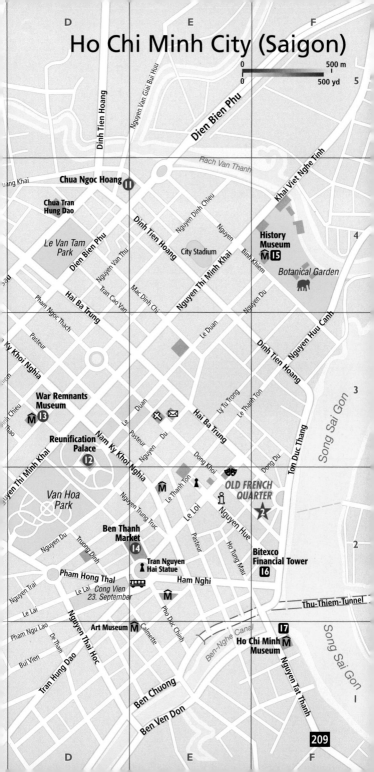

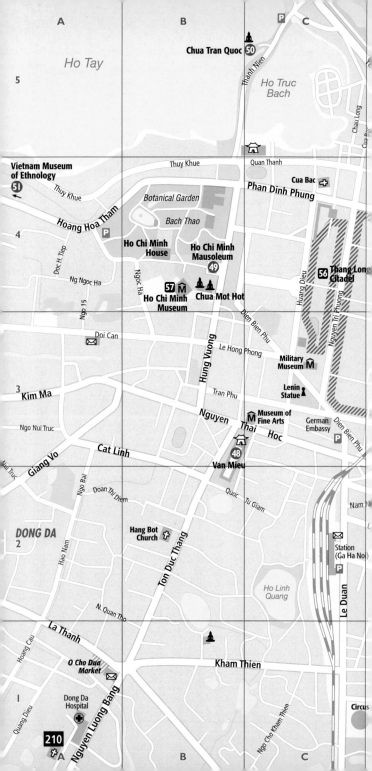

A

5
Ho Tay

Chua Tran Quoc 50

Ho Truc Bach

Thanh Nien

Chau Long

Cua Bac

4
Vietnam Museum of Ethnology 51

Thuy Khue

Thuy Khue

Quan Thanh

Cua Bac

Phan Dinh Phung

Botanical Garden

Hoang Hoa Tham

Bach Thao

Ho Chi Minh House

Ho Chi Minh Mausoleum 49

Thang Long Citadel 56

Doc H. Tiep

Ng Ngoc Ha

Ngoc Ha

57 M

Ho Chi Minh Museum

Chua Mot Hot

Dien Bien Phu

Huang Dieu

Nguyen Tri Phuong

Ngo 15

3
Doi Can

Hung Vuong

Le Hong Phong

Military Museum M

Lenin Statue

Kim Ma

Tran Phu

Ngo Nui Truc

Nguyen Thai Hoc

Museum of Fine Arts M

German Embassy

Dien Bien Phu

Nui Truc

Giang Vo

Cat Linh

48 M

Van Mieu

Ngo Bai

Doan Thi Diem

Quoc Tu Giam

Nam N

2
DONG DA

Hao Nam

Hang Bot Church

Ton Duc Thang

Station (Ga Ha Noi)

P

Le Duan

N. Quan Tho

Ho Linh Quang

La Thanh

Hoang Cau

O Cho Dua Market

Kham Thien

1
Quang Dieu

Dong Da Hospital

210

Nguyen Luong Bang

Ngo Cho Kham Thien

Circus

A   B   C

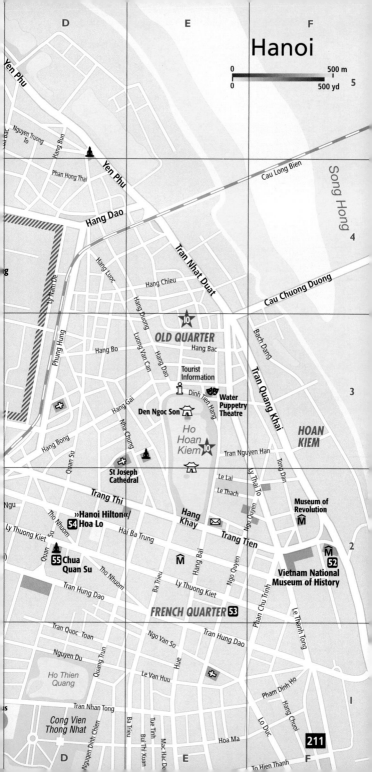

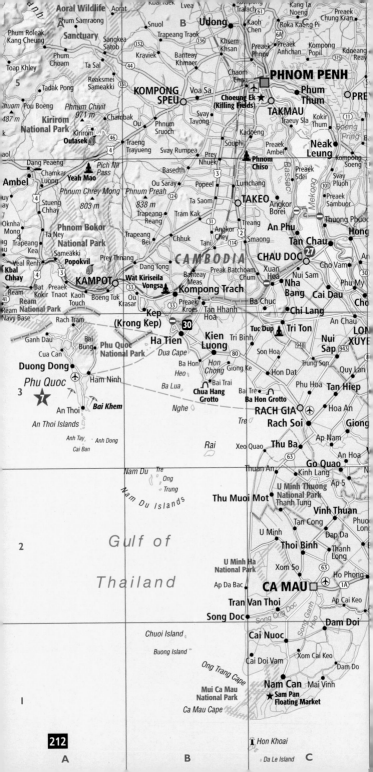

Aoral Wildlife Aorat
Phum Samraong
Snuol B Udong Kaoh Chen Kang Ta Noeng Preaek Chung Kran
Sanctuary Trapeang Traok Khsem Khsan Preaek Anhchan Kompong Popil Kdoeang Reay
Phum Roleak Kang Cheung Phum Choam Sangkea Satob Kraviek Banteay Khmaer Chaom Chau PHNOM PENH PRE
Toap Khley Ta Sal Reaksmei Sameakki KOMPONG SPEU Voa Sa TAKMAU Phum Thum
Tadak Pong Pou Boeng Phnum Chivit 971 m Chambak Ou Phnum Sruoch Svay Tavong Kadoeng Traeuy Sla Kokir Thum Neak Leung
487 m Kirirom National Park Kiriron Outasek Traeng Trayueng Svay Rumpea Prey Nhuek Preaek Ambel Souphi Boeng Pring
Ambel Dang Peaeng Pich Nil Pass Yeah Mao Basedth Ou Saray Popeel Lumchang Phnom Chiso Preaek Sdei Svay Pluoh Kompong Soeng
Chamkar Luong Phnum Chrey Mong Phnum Preah Ta Saom TAKEO Angkor Borei Preaek Sambuor Hong
Oknha Mong Stueng Chhay 803 m 838 m Trapeang Reang Tram Kak Angkor Chey An Phu Tan Chau Thuong Phuoc
Trapeang Kea Phnom Bokor National Park Trapeang Bei Chhuk Tani Treang Smaong CAMBODIA CHAU DOC 27 Cho Vam
Veal Renh Ta Ney Sameakki Prey Thnang Dang Tong Preak Batchoam Chum Xuan Hoa Nui Sam Phu My 30
Kbal Chhay Popokvil KAMPOT Wat Kiriseila Vongsa Banteay Meas Nha Bang Cai Dau Cho
Ream Ream National Park Bat Kokir Tnaot Kaoh Touch Boeng Tuk Ou Krasar Kompong Trach Preaek Kroes Tan Hhanh Hoa Ba Chuc Chi Lang An Chau
Navy Base Rach Tram Kep (Krong Kep) 30 Kien Luong Tri Binh Tuc Dup Tri Ton Nui Sap 948 LON XUYE 943
Ganh Dau Bai Bung Phu Quoc National Park Ha Tien Dua Cape Son Hoa Trung Son Quy Lan
Cua Can Ham Ninh Ba Hon Heo Hon Chong Giong Ke Hon Dat Phu Hoa Tan Hiep
Duong Dong Phu Quoc An Thoi Bai Khem Ba Lua Bai Trai Chua Hang Grotto Nghe Bai Tre Ba Hon Grotto RACH GIA Hoa An Giong
An Thoi Islands Anh Tay Anh Dong Cai Ban Rai Xeo Quao Rach Soi Ap Nam An Hoa
Thu Ba Go Quao
Nam Du Tre Ong Trung Thuan An 63 Kinh Lang Ap 5
Nam Du Islands U Minh Thuong National Park Thanh Tung Vinh Thuan Phuo
Thu Muoi Mot Tan Cong Dap Da
Gulf of U Minh Thoi Binh Thanh Long Ho Phong
Thailand U Minh Ha National Park Xom So 63 1A
Ap Da Bac CA MAU Ap Cai Keo
Tran Van Thoi Dam Doi
Chuoi Island Song Doc Cai Nuoc
Buong Island Cai Doi Vam Xom Cai Keo Dam Do
Ong Trang Cape Nam Can Mai Vinh
Mui Ca Mau National Park Sam Pan Floating Market
Ca Mau Cape
212
Hon Khoai
Da Le Island
A B C

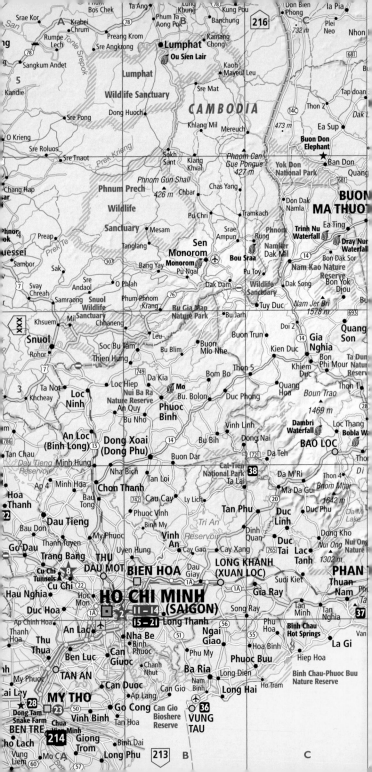

Beach
han May Dong Cape

🛥 *Lang Co*
Lang Co **44**
Ban Dao Son Tra
Nature Reserve
◦ Kim Lien
Son Tra
NG ◻ **41**
Khuong ✈ *Bai Nam*
My 2 *Bay*
Ha Quang ◦ *Cu Lao Cham*
ghia ★ **3** *Cu Lao Cham*
Son **40** Vinh **HOI AN** *Nature Reserve*
▲ Dien ◦
Nam Tra Doa 2 ◦
Phuoc
La Pass Ha Lam ◦ Vinh Giang ◦

Thon 10 ◦ **Chien Dan** ◦
An **Khuong My** **TAM KY** ◻
Cham Tower Diem Pho 1 ◦
Thon 1 ◦ Tien Ky ◦ **616** *Phu* **Site of Major US Chu Lai Military Base**
Set ◦ **Phu** *Ninh* *Nam Tram Cape*
4 m ◦ Tra My **Huong** **Hoa** *Lake* Nui ◦ **1A** *Ly Son*
◦ Lam 4 **Thanh** Binh Thuan ◦
n 3 ◦ **Tra** Chau O ◦
Tra Giap ◦ **Xuan** **Nhan Hoa** ◦ *Ba Lang An Cape*
n 1 ◦ Tra Lac ◦ **Hot Spring** **Son** ◦ An Hai
Tra Neu ◦ Xom Gioc ◦ **Tinh** **43** **My Lai Massacre Mar. 16. 1968**
◦ ★
Ngok Linh Di Lang ◦ Cho Chua ◦ **QUANG NGAI**
Nature Reserve **623** Song Ve ◦
Ngok Kring ◦ Tamao
2066 m Son Tay ◦ **Minh** Mo Duc ◦
Chum ◦ Ngoc Rik **676** ◦ **Long** Tan ◦
Vi Pron ◦ Ta Mong ◦ **Phong**
◦ Dak Pia Lang Trut ◦ **Dong** Duc Pho ◦
Chun Ba To ◦ Phuroc Dien ◦
Bu Kon ◦ Con Rieng ◦ 🛥 *Sa Huynh Beach*
Klung Go Vanh ◦ **24**
Bu Kon Chat ◦ Chau Me ◦
Ha Kon By ◦ *Nature Preserve* *N. Lang* Nuoc ◦ An ◦
Kon ◦ *Area Kon* *Ram* Giap **Tam Quan**
Ho Ram **Plong** *Cha Rang* *1085 m* Van Hoa ◦
24 **Kon Kà Kinh** Kon ◦ My Duc ◦ **Bong**
National Park Drang Ye ◦ An Tuong ◦ **Son** Lo Dieu ◦
KON TUM Krong ◦ Nghia ◦ **Phu**
lei To Ven *Chu Tomoch* Dien ◦ **My**
1250 m K' Bang ◦ **Hoi Van** Chanh Truc ◦
huoi Bu. Kon Plek ◦ Lang Dap ◦ **Hot Spring** **1A**
u Hoa An Loi ◦ Thuong ◦ An Quang ◦
Mang ✈ De Kop ◦ An Thanh ◦ **An Khe** Son **Ngo**
Yang Xom ◦ **Citadel** **May** Chanh Oai ◦
◦ Plei Dok Moi Krong ◦ **19** **Dap Da** **Thoc** Trung Luong ◦
Kong Ktu ◦ **An Khe** ★ **Loc**
Plei Pham *Kong* **Phu** **Binh**
Kla Gua *Bra Ram* Kong Chro ◦ **Phong** **Dinh** ◻ *Phuong Mai*
Plei *1006 m* *Peninsula*
Se Ho Dong ◦ Dieu Tri ◦ ✈
◦ Plei Dek Nhang Nho ◦ Lang Hong ◦ *Nui Am* **QUY NHON**
Hoa A Tang ◦ Plei Da Neo ◦ *1122 m* ▲ *Cu Mong* Tuy Phong ◦
Plei Bloum ◦ Van *Pass*
Phu Canh ◦ **Binh**
Thien **25** Lanh Van ◦ **Thanh**
uon Xam **14** A Yun Pa ◦ La Hai ◦ **Song**
◦ **687** *N. Hon Ong* **Cau**
Ban Bok ◦ **D** Buon Nu A ◦ Bon Chai ◦ Ban A *758 m* ◦ Phuroc **217**
◦ Ma Hy **215** Hoa Xuan Hoa ◦

D **E** **F**
5 **4** **3** **2** **1**

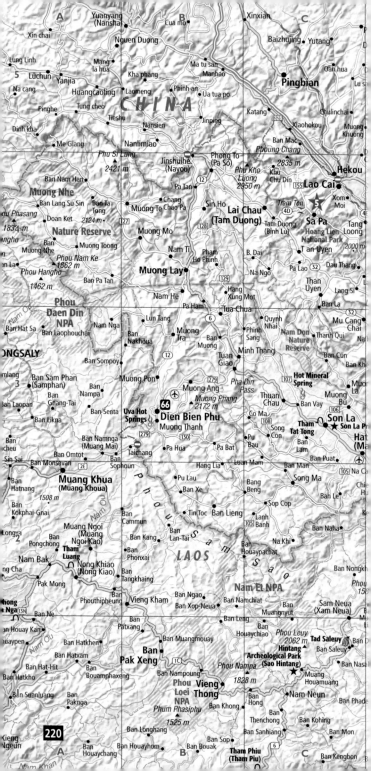

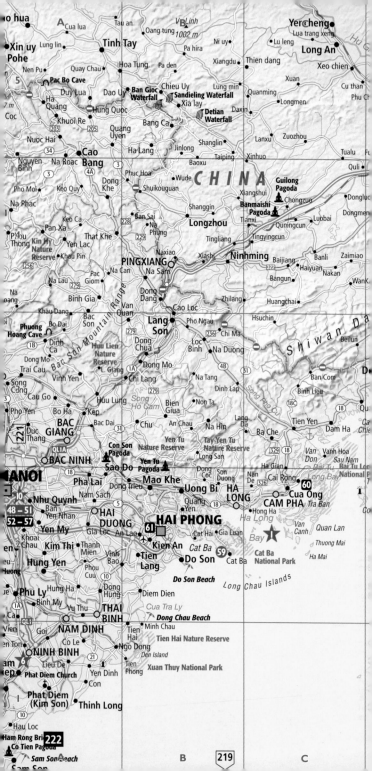

Index

Index / Picture Credits

Picture Credits

Credits

1st Edition 2016

Worldwide Distribution: Marco Polo Travel Publishing Ltd
Pinewood, Chineham Business Park
Crockford Lane, Chineham
Basingstoke, Hampshire RG24 8AL, United Kingdom.
© MAIRDUMONT GmbH & Co. KG, Ostfildern

Author: Martina Miethig
Revised editing and translation: Christopher Wynne, Bad Tölz
Program supervisor: Birgit Borowski
Chief editor: Rainer Eisenschmid

Cartography: ©MAIRDUMONT GmbH & Co. KG, Ostfildern
3D-illustrations: jangled nerves, Stuttgart

Printed in China

Despite all of our authors' thorough research, errors can creep in.
The publishers do not accept any liability for this. Whether you
want to praise us, alert us to errors or give us a personal tip –
please don't hesitate to email or post to:

MARCO POLO Travel Publishing Ltd
Pinewood, Chineham Business Park
Crockford Lane, Chineham
Basingstoke, Hampshire RG24 8AL
United Kingdom
Email: sales@marcopolouk.com

FSC
www.fsc.org
MIX
Paper from
responsible sources
FSC® C124385

10 REASONS
TO COME BACK AGAIN

1. The **scenery** is like a painted picture of terraced paddy fields and magical bays.

2. With a 3,200km (2,000mi)-long coastline there are bound to be a few **beaches** left to explore!

3. Where else can you get **mountains of fresh seafood** so cheaply every day of the year?

4. **54 ethnic minority groups** in one country – there's no other nation with such a mixture anywhere.

5. From elephants to geckos – Vietnam's fascinating **flora and fauna** is unique!

6. The **food in Vietnam** is as varied as the country is long – and it's impossible to try everything.

7. The mystical atmosphere in **incense-filled pagodas** is something you will miss.

8. A **country for all the senses** – loud, bewitching, thought-provoking and exotic.

9. There are many too many wonderful **souvenirs** for them all to fit in one case.

10. **Saigon** and **Hanoi** are changing so rapidly that there will always be something new to see.